Balancing Act

Balancing Act

*Motherhood, Marriage, and Employment
Among American Women*

DAPHNE SPAIN

AND

SUZANNE M. BIANCHI

Russell Sage Foundation • New York

The Russell Sage Foundation

The Russell Sage Foundation, one of the oldest of America's general purpose foundations, was established in 1907 by Mrs. Margaret Olivia Sage for "the improvement of social and living conditions in the United States." The Foundation seeks to fulfill this mandate by fostering the development and dissemination of knowledge about the country's political, social, and economic problems. While the Foundation endeavors to assure the accuracy and objectivity of each book it publishes, the conclusions and interpretations in Russell Sage Foundation publications are those of the authors and not of the Foundation, its Trustees, or its staff. Publication by Russell Sage, therefore, does not imply Foundation endorsement.

Library of Congress Cataloging-in-Publication Data

Spain, Daphne.
  Balancing act: motherhood, marriage, and employment among American women / by Daphne Spain and Suzanne M. Bianchi
    p. cm.
  Includes bibliographical references and index.
  ISBN 0-87154-814-3 (cloth: alk. paper)—ISBN 0-87154-815-1 (pbk.: alk. paper)
    1. Women—United States—Social conditions. 2. Women—Employment—United States.
3. Mothers—Employment—United States. I. Bianchi, Suzanne M. II. Title.
  HD1421.S675 1996
  305.4'0973—dc20   96-5087
                                                                              CIP

The paper used in this publication meets the minimum requirements of American National Standard for Information Sciences—Permanence of Paper for Printed Library Materials. ANSI Z39.48-1992.

Text design by Rozlyn Coleman.

RUSSELL SAGE FOUNDATION
112 East 64th Street, New York, New York 10021
10 9 8 7 6 5 4 3 2 1

Contents

Preface

ALTHOUGH THIS PROJECT BEGAN IN 1994 WHEN THE RUSSELL SAGE Foundation invited us to revise *American Women in Transition*, its current identity emerged only with the realization that a simple update would not suffice. Since 1986, when *American Women* was published as part of the 1980 census monograph series, cosponsored by the Russell Sage Foundation and the National Committee for Research on the 1980 Census, women have continued to experience significant changes in both their family and work lives. In particular, the movement away from marriage, a trend under way when we wrote *American Women* but much more pronounced by the 1990s, required rethinking and reorganizing the chapters on marriage and childbearing. The continued growth of nonmarital childbearing, coupled with high divorce rates, means that women continue to balance motherhood and employment, but many women now execute this balance outside marriage.

The narrowing of the gender earnings gap also necessitated a fairly dramatic revision of earlier analyses of labor force trends and the economic role of women in families. When we were writing *American Women*, the data for young college-educated women only hinted at how much women's work experience had changed and the implications that would have for earnings equality. Another part of the earnings equity story—just how austere the labor market would be in the 1980s for those with less than a college education (especially men)—was also unclear as we placed the finishing touches on *American Women* in 1984.

vii

We would like to thank the Russell Sage Foundation for the visiting summer fellowships in New York that allowed us to complete this research. Colleagues at Russell Sage who were particularly helpful include Eric Wanner, Nancy Casey, David Haproff, Madge Spitaleri, Emma Sosa, and Vivian Kaufman. Kimberly Webb Giamportone deserves special recognition for her expertise and patience in manuscript preparation. Sara Beckman and Jamie Gray provided excellent computer support, and Reynolds Farley encouraged us professionally and personally (and with many good meals) throughout the project. If the current volume is as accessible to nondemographers as we would like, the credit is due to Larry Long, whose precise prose influenced us during our formative years at the Census Bureau, and to Rozlyn Coleman, our editor at the Russell Sage Foundation.

Thanks also are due Leslie Smith and Cindy Larison for their research assistance. Three outside reviewers contributed valuable advice to the final revisions; Joan Huber's thorough, thoughtful reading was especially appreciated. Daphne Spain acknowledges the benefit of a sesquicentennial research leave from the University of Virginia to complete the project, and Suzanne Bianchi acknowledges the support of the Center on Population, Gender, and Social Inequality at the University of Maryland. Finally, as women who have experienced many of the changes documented in these chapters, we are indebted to our families for their emotional and intellectual support.

Daphne Spain
Suzanne M. Bianchi

Introduction

THE TWENTY-FIRST CENTURY PROMISES TO BE AN INTERESTING ONE FOR American women. So many of the overt barriers to women's full participation in society have been eliminated that it can be hard to remember that women have been able to vote only since 1920, legally guaranteed the same wages as men in the same jobs since the 1960s, and able to choose abortion as a way to limit their fertility since the 1970s. Yet in the 1990s, women still are not fully represented in public office, employed women still earn less than men with comparable credentials, and reproductive rights are under attack. Whether the next hundred years will see further progress toward gender equality or a possible regression to more traditional roles depends, in part, on the changes described in this book.

The 1960s and 1970s were watershed decades for women. The birth control pill went on the market, abortion was legalized, equal-pay legislation was enacted, and divorce became easier to obtain. But with those gains came additional responsibilities. Young women now must decide whether to have a child (within or outside marriage), whether to cohabit, marry, or divorce, whether to pursue a job or career, and how to construct their lives if they wish to combine one or more of these options. If women at the end of the nineteenth century felt constrained by a lack of choice, women at the end of the twentieth century sometimes express dismay at the endless array of choices they must make.

Some of the most significant changes for women have occurred in the past decade. For example, the growing incidence of motherhood outside marriage is unprecedented. In addition, more women today delay childbearing until their thirties and return to work immediately after their child's birth. As a result, women now spend longer periods of time as mothers than as spouses, and their attachment to the labor force is increasing. In the portrait of contemporary women's lives, children are in the foreground, marriage is in the background, and employment occupies an ever-expanding middle landscape. This development is a primary theme of this book.

In regard to women's work outside the home, the most important news is that the wage gap between women and men narrowed more in the past decade than in any previous period. The ratio of women's to men's earnings finally has responded to women's increased work experience and educational achievement after decades of stagnation. Women's college enrollment rates now exceed those of men, and young women and men are equally likely to have college degrees for the first time in recent history. Counterbalancing these positive developments is evidence that affirmative action and the protection of reproductive rights—policies that helped to close gender gaps in education and earnings—now seem more politically vulnerable than a decade ago. Nevertheless, we believe that women are making slow, steady progress toward equality with men.

Women as a group are more diverse than a decade ago, because of increased immigration and different rates of fertility by race and ethnicity. Census categories indicate a broad range of ethnicities and allow us to examine life patterns for Hispanic, Asian, and American Indian women as well as for black and white women. Heterogeneity also exists *within* these groups depending on immigration status and length of residence in the United States.

We intend to convey just how much the balancing act for American women has changed in the past decade. On the one side are the obligations of family life and personal relationships; on the other are the demands of market work. How these often incompatible (and sometimes overwhelming) forces are resolved is the central challenge of women's lives. The growing proportion of mothers in the labor force is no longer remarkable. What *is* remarkable is how little has been done to assist families with often conflicting responsibilities, how routinely the problems associated with juggling jobs and children are identified as a "women's issue," not a national one, and how persistent is the unequal division of labor within the home. The barriers that remain, therefore, are as important as the progress of the past decade.

*   *   *

DEMOGRAPHIC DATA ARE UNIQUELY SUITED BOTH TO CELEBRATING women's achievements and to underscoring the urgency of many families' economic and emotional needs. Demographic data also inform public discourse and policymaking. For example, what are the reasons for, and the consequences of, increased nonmarital fertility? How prevalent is cohabitation as an alternative to marriage? Why do women still earn less than men when their educational profiles are the same? Knowing how many women and their dependent children live in poverty may influence welfare reform policies; realizing that the majority of mothers with infants are in the labor force should create support for child care legislation; and understanding that almost one-third of births now occur outside marriage could lead us to new definitions of what constitutes a family. Our hope is that scholars and policy analysts will use these data to improve women's lives and those of their families.

Much of this book is about the experiences of female birth cohorts. A *cohort* refers to a group of individuals who share a unique set of experiences throughout life. Although cohorts can be defined by events other than birth, the term most commonly refers to all individuals born in a specified time period—that is, a generation. Differences between older and younger women are incorporated into the chapters using cohort analysis. Table I provides a guide to our cohort approach, showing how birth cohorts moved into various age categories during the 1980s.

Women born between 1936 and 1945, *the World War II cohort*, typically reached labor force age between the mid-1950s and mid-1960s. They entered adulthood during the ten-year period leading

TABLE I Labor Force Entry of Birth Cohorts

Birth Cohort	Generation	Labor Force Entry	Age in 1980	Age in 1990
1966–75	Baby bust	Mid-1980s through 1990s	05–14	15–24
1956–65	Late baby boom	Mid-1970s through 1980s	15–24	25–34
1946–55	Early baby boom	Mid-1960s through 1970s	25–34	35–44
1936–45	World War II	Mid-1950s through 1960s	35–44	45–54
1926–35	Parents of baby boom	Mid-1940s through 1950s	45–54	55–64
1916–25	Parents of baby boom	Mid-1930s through 1940s	55–64	65–74
1906–15	Grandparents of baby boom	Mid-1920s through 1930s	65–74	75–84

up to passage of the Civil Rights Act of 1964, which for the first time in American history barred discrimination on the basis of sex. Most of the World War II cohort of women therefore completed their education and began their families before the widespread questioning of gender and racial stereotypes that characterized the 1970s.

The next cohort of women (*the early baby boomers,* born between 1946 and 1955) reached adulthood between the mid-1960s and the mid-1970s. As a relatively large generation, it created serious dislocations as it moved through school and into the labor force. Elementary and high school classrooms bulged as administrators scrambled for space, and these early baby boomers then flooded college campuses, fueling the activism that became a defining marker of the 1960s. These women had access to the pill and to legalized abortions, a factor that radically changed sexual practices and attitudes toward marriage.

The late baby boom cohort, those born between 1956 and 1965, reached adulthood and began entering the labor force in the mid-1970s. They trailed their older brothers and sisters onto campuses and into the labor market. Following such a large cohort created disadvantages as late boomers settled into adult life: these women entered a labor market in which wage rates were stagnating rather than rising, as they had during the previous four decades. This created added financial pressure for many women, especially low-income ones whose husbands were most affected by the economic restructuring, to work outside the home.

At the same time, women continued to carry the brunt of housework and child care within their families.

Examination of the various cohorts ends with these late baby boomers—the youngest of them having reached prime working age (twenty-five and over) in 1990, the last census year. It will be several years before we can fully examine the education, employment, and earnings profile of the "baby bust" generation, born between 1966 and 1975.

This book uses data collected by the Census Bureau and other federal agencies to document postwar demographic trends. (Unpublished census data come from microdata tapes.) Two large surveys—the Current Population Survey (CPS) and Survey of Income and Program Participation (SIPP)—allow us to supplement the decennial analyses. The CPS is a monthly national survey of about sixty thousand households that has been conducted since the late 1940s. It was designed primarily to obtain information on employment and unemployment, but regular supplements to the survey address a variety of additional topics. For example, in June the survey asks questions about marital history and fertility; the October supplement asks questions about educational enrollment and attainment; and the March and April surveys ask about income and child support. The SIPP augments the CPS with questions about child care arrangements, child support payments, and income from government programs. The SIPP is a series of longitudinal panels—in which the same individuals are visited every four months over a two- to three-year period—that has been fielded by the Census Bureau since 1984, with sample sizes ranging from twelve thousand to twenty thousand households.

In addition, we use statistics collected by the National Center for Health Statistics on births, deaths, marriages, and divorces. Data on college degrees and undergraduate majors come from the National Center for Educational Statistics of the Department of Education. We also use public opinion data from the National Opinion Research Center affiliated with the University of Chicago.

The advantages of multiple sources of information must be weighed against their disadvantages. Some of the supplemental data, for example, may conflict with census data. Labor force statistics are collected in both the decennial census and the CPS, and, although the definitions are similar, their results sometimes differ. We rely on the source that is most accurate for the topic under consideration. When data from noncensus sources are clearly superior, or when information is not collected in the census but is available elsewhere, we turn to these auxiliary data sets. Because they provide sample sizes large enough to examine trends for American Indians and Asians as well as for Hispanics, blacks, and whites, the decennial censuses are the primary source for racial and ethnic comparisons.

We also draw on international indicators compiled by the United Nations, the Organisation for Economic Cooperation and Development, the International Labour Office, and the U.S. Bureau of Labor Statistics. In addition, data for several countries are available through the Luxembourg Income Study data base. Because inconsistencies in collection and reporting make international comparisons difficult, even among industrialized nations, country findings are reported according to data availability.

Statistics seldom speak for themselves. We try, in this volume, to present data on women's status in a comprehensive way, informed by demographic, sociological, and economic theory. No doubt, our interpretations will be too conservative for some and too liberal for others, but our goal is to accurately represent the changes in women's lives and the ways in which women's new balancing act is transforming society.

✳   ✳   ✳

IT IS PERHAPS WORTH MENTIONING AT THE OUTSET WHAT THIS BOOK IS *NOT* about. We do not discuss women's physical and mental health, despite their possible links to fertility, marriage, and employment. Nor do we consider sexual orientation, although it is relevant to patterns of cohabitation and marriage. Other important "gender issues" beyond the scope of this book include domestic violence, sexual harassment, adoption, and artificial insemination. Our lens is focused on basic demographic trends that can be measured with reliable and comprehensive national data.

In recognition of the change in women's lives, we begin this book with an overview of childbearing patterns among American women (chapter 1). Following that, we turn to marital status and living arrangements (chapter 2). The middle chapters (chapters

3–6) review women's socioeconomic gains of the past decade: in education (chapter 3), in labor force and occupational status (chapter 4), in earnings (chapter 5), and in economic well-being and poverty (chapter 6). Chapter 7 examines how women combine employment and family roles.

The book is organized around the central roles that women occupy throughout their lives. The dominant theme is that most women now perform a variety of paid and unpaid tasks each day, rather than specializing in motherhood at one stage of life and possibly employment at another. The strategies devised by individual women to address these simultaneous demands form the demographic patterns described in this book.

CHAPTER 1

Childbearing

As the sexual revolution caught fire during the late 1960s and early 1970s, premarital sex among young women became increasingly open. Freed from the societal constraints of the 1950s and in increasing control of their reproductive rights, women entered sexual relations with fewer inhibitions. Such sweeping changes in sexual behavior, together with other forces that will be discussed in this chapter, have contributed to a rise in out-of-wedlock births to American women. The result is that the link between motherhood and marriage has become increasingly tenuous in the late twentieth century. In recognition of the primacy of motherhood among women's varied roles, we place the chapter on childbearing first.

A woman ceases to be a wife when she divorces or is widowed, but she remains a parent as long as her child lives; or, as Alice Rossi (1968) puts it, "We can have ex-spouses and ex-jobs, but not ex-children." Although the overall fertility of American women has continued the decline characteristic of this century (with the exception of the baby boom years), three trends in childbearing over the past decade warrant special attention. The first and most significant is the increase in the proportion of births occurring to unmarried women during the 1980s. Almost one in three births took place outside marriage in 1993 compared with one in five in 1980 and one in ten in 1970. Racial differences are particularly pronounced: nearly one-quarter of births to white women and more than two-thirds of births to black women occurred outside marriage in 1993. A second trend is a rise in

1

teenage childbearing that began in about 1989, after more than a decade of decline. Because disagreement exists about just how detrimental teenage pregnancies are for women, their children, and society, considerable public debate has been devoted to this issue. A third trend is delayed childbearing. Compared with a decade ago, a larger proportion of women in their thirties are now having children.

Other trends worth noting are that birth rates rose slightly during the 1980s, then dropped again in 1991 and 1992. Even with the recent decline, however, the United States now has a fertility rate close to that necessary for natural replacement of the population (2.1 births per woman of childbearing age compared with 1.8 in 1980). Also, birth expectations among younger women have remained approximately stable despite delayed childbearing, and the proportion of women in their forties who are childless has increased slightly.

Fertility Trends and Their Explanations

Demographers look at three basic measures of fertility—the total fertility rate, the age-specific fertility rates, and the number of children ever born—all of which have registered declines over the past few decades. (The measures are described in detail in the appendix.) The total fertility rate (TFR), or the average number of children a woman has in her lifetime, reached a high of 3.6 births per woman during the baby boom and has since declined to an average of 2.1 births per woman. Age-specific fertility rates (ASFR), or the ages at which most childbearing occurs, reflect lower fertility and delayed childbearing trends. In 1960, women's birth rates peaked in their early twenties and at very high levels. Today, birth rates for women in their late twenties are as high or higher than those for women in their early twenties, and the rates decline less precipitously for women in their thirties. The third fertility measure, the number of children ever born to a woman, dropped for married women in their thirties from 3.1 in 1967 to 1.8 in 1992 (see appendix).

Two contending theories have been offered to explain U.S. fertility trends: one by Richard Easterlin (1987) and the other by William Butz and Michael Ward (1979). Easterlin proposes that fertility moves in predictable cycles that are tied to the income and employment opportunities of men. According to this theory, lifestyle aspirations are formed at an early age based on the income of one's parents. As cohorts reach adulthood and enter the labor force, they compare their own incomes—and their commensurate standards of living—with those of their parents. If their income is greater than anticipated, they will have more children; if it is less, they will have fewer children.

Coupled with this theory is Easterlin's proposition of a negative relationship between a cohort's size and its success in the labor market: small cohorts do well financially, while large cohorts suffer from increased competition for jobs. For example, the small birth cohorts of the 1930s experienced favorable labor market conditions in the 1950s and responded by increasing their fertility (thus producing the baby boom). But the large baby boom cohort entering the labor force during the 1970s faced stiffly competitive labor market conditions and responded by reducing fertility (thus the "birth dearth").

Conflicting support exists for Easterlin's model. His research implies a cohort theory of fertility (that is, preferences are formed early and do not change over the life course), yet others have shown changes in fertility to be quite sensitive to period effects (that is, the fertility rates of all age groups tend to move in the same direction at the same time). It is also true that generational cycles smooth out over time and lose their importance as determinants of fertility (Bianchi and Spain 1986, p. 54).

Some studies have found little validity in the Easterlin hypothesis, while others verify its accuracy (Bianchi and Spain 1986, p. 54; Pampel 1993). Much of the disagreement comes from applying aggregate data to an individual-behavior model and from using different definitions of "relative income." Easterlin's biggest oversight from a contemporary perspective is his emphasis on the income and employment opportunities of *men*, which tends to ignore women's role in the childbearing decision, their participation in the labor force, and the perceived opportunity costs to them of childbearing.

The Butz and Ward model perhaps overcompensates for Easterlin's exclusion of women. They argue that three factors affect the timing of fertility decisions: the proportion of women in the labor force, the earnings of women, and the earnings of men. According to this theory, while increases in a husband's income raise the demand for children, a wife's wages have the opposite effect. Increases in women's wages tend to depress fertility by amplifying the cost of the wife's forgone wages. By considering the earnings of both wives and husbands, Butz and Ward account for the postwar upswing in fertility—by linking it to the rising incomes of men—and for the decline in the 1970s—by suggesting that as more women began working outside the home their wages improved.

The Butz and Ward countercyclical theory has predicted fertility swings fairly well, but it may prove less useful in the future. Based on the assumption that the trade-offs between fertility and women's employment are made in the context of marriage, the model does not allow for the recent increases in delayed marriage, divorce, and nonmarital childbearing. Butz and Ward's hypothesized relationship between women's employment and fertility may not apply now that such a large proportion of women live outside married-couple households. Even within marriage, we may be reaching a point at which fertility is low enough and women's economic opportunities are high enough that the notion of a trade-off is outdated. Women increasingly are both parents and wage earners at the same time.

In the 1990s, it is perhaps women's and men's decisions about marriage, more so than about childbearing, that should be the subject of scrutiny. Higher earnings for women or diminished earnings for men may predict delays in marriage, just as they predicted lower fertility (Oppenheimer 1993). If so, large numbers of unmarried mothers could be taken as evidence that women are enjoying greater economic independence or that men are facing a decline in economic opportunity. If women continue to bear children, but less often within marriage, the question becomes: are marriages being delayed, or eschewed altogether, because women can afford to live independently, or are marriages being postponed, sometimes permanently, because men cannot afford to marry the mothers of their children? The answer to this question has far-reaching implications for women and men well into the next century.

FIGURE **1.1** **Fertility by Marital Status**

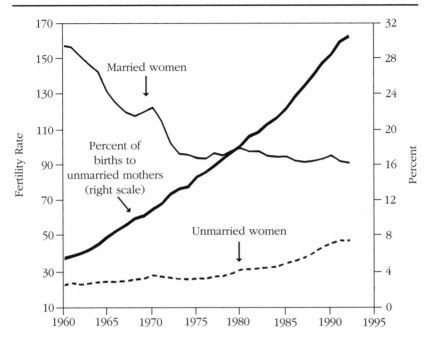

Source: Farley (1996), chapter four.
Note: Fertility rates are live births per one thousand women aged 15 to 44 by marital status.

Unmarried Fertility

Over the past three decades, the decline in marital births and the increase in out-of-wedlock births together have resulted in a higher proportion of all births occurring outside marriage (see figure 1.1). Consequently, by 1993, 31 percent of births occurred to unmarried women; 24 percent of births to white women and 69 percent of births to black women occurred outside marriage (Ventura and others 1995a).

The birth rate for all unmarried women has risen steadily since 1940, from 7.1 births per one thousand women to 45.2 births per one thousand women in 1992. This trend crosses every age category, and the largest jumps occurred during the 1980s. Women in their early twenties have the highest current nonmari-

TABLE 1.1 Fertility of Unmarried Women

Year	Total	Mother's Age at Delivery					
		15–19	20–24	25–29	30–34	35–39	40–44
All races							
1950	14.1	12.6	21.3	19.9	13.3	7.2	2.0
1960	21.6	15.3	39.7	45.1	27.8	14.1	3.6
1970	26.4	22.4	38.4	37.1	27.0	13.3	3.6
1980	29.4	27.6	40.9	34.0	21.1	9.7	2.6
1990	43.8	42.5	65.1	56.0	37.6	17.3	3.6
1992	45.2	44.6	68.5	56.5	37.9	18.8	4.1

Source: U.S. Bureau of the Census (1975), B28-35; National Center for Health Statistics (1984), table 18; *Monthly Vital Statistics Report* (1993), table 17; Ventura (1995), Table 1.
Note: Fertility rates are live births per one thousand unmarried women in a specified age group.

tal birth rate, followed by women in their late twenties, and then by teenagers (see table 1.1). The rising age at first marriage (discussed in chapter 2) has contributed to the number of women "at risk" of bearing a child out of wedlock.

Racial Differences in Nonmarital Births

Although birth rates for unmarried white women are lower than those for unmarried black women, they have risen much more rapidly, doubling since 1980. The timing of nonmarital births also varies for blacks and whites: unmarried white mothers tend to be older than unmarried black mothers. Black nonmarital births are most likely to occur to teens and women in their early twenties, while white out-of-wedlock birth rates are highest for women in their twenties (see table 1.2).

The dramatic rise in the proportion of black children born outside marriage is *not* the result of a sharp increase in childbearing among unmarried black women. Between 1970 and 1992, the birth rate to teenaged unmarried black women rose only slightly. Rather, births among *married* black women fell substantially during the 1960s and 1970s, and fewer black women (especially teenagers) are marrying (Cherlin 1992, p. 98; also see chapter 2 of this volume).

TABLE 1.2 Changes in Fertility of Unmarried White and Black Women

Race and Year	Total	Mother's Age at Delivery						
		15–19	20–24	25–29	30–34	35–39	40–44	35–44
White								
1950	6.1	5.1	10.0	8.7	5.9			2.0
1960	9.2	6.6	18.2	18.2	10.8			3.9
1970	13.8	10.9	22.5	21.1	14.2			4.4
1980	17.6	16.2	24.4	20.7	13.6	6.8	1.8	
1990	32.9	30.6	48.2	43.0	29.9	14.5	3.2	
1992	35.2	33.0	52.7	45.4	31.5	16.2	3.6	
Black								
1950	71.2	68.5	105.4	94.2	63.5			20.0
1960	98.3	76.5	166.5	171.8	104.0			35.6
1970	95.5	96.9	131.5	100.9	71.8			21.6
1980	82.8	89.2	115.1	83.9	48.2	19.6	5.6	
1990	90.5	106.0	144.8	105.3	61.5	25.5	5.1	
1992	86.5	105.9	144.3	98.2	57.7	25.8	5.4	

Source: U.S. Bureau of the Census (1975), series B28-35; National Center for Health Statistics (1984), table 18, and (1993), table 17; Ventura and others (1994), table 14.
Note: Fertility rates are live births per one thousand unmarried women in a specified age group.

The most striking difference between the current fertility patterns of blacks and whites is that a far higher proportion of black children are born to unmarried teenaged mothers than are white children. In 1988, one in five black children was born to an unmarried teenaged mother compared with one in eighteen white children; similar racial differences exist for children born to unmarried women in their early twenties (Cherlin 1992, p. 96). In 1992, when one-third of all births occurred to unmarried women, two-thirds of all black births occurred out of wedlock, compared with one-quarter of all white births (Ventura, Martin, and Taffel 1994, table 14).

Economic, social, and cultural factors lie at the heart of these divergent fertility patterns. Black women may be less likely to marry (and thus at greater risk of unmarried childbearing) than white women because black men have poorer job opportunities than white men (Wilson 1987). Additionally, black teenagers are more sexually active than white teenagers (Miller and Moore 1990, p. 1030). There is also evidence that the African heritage of American blacks emphasizes intergenerational lineage over the husband-wife family structure, giving women (especially grandmothers) a more central role in black families than in white ones (Cherlin 1992, chap. 4).

Births to Teenaged Mothers

Although they are separate issues, teenage and out-of-wedlock births often are confused in the public's mind. The reality is that nonmarital births to women in their twenties and thirties now exceed those to teenagers. It is true that births to teenagers are more likely to occur outside marriage now than in the past because contemporary teens are less likely than their predecessors to marry in response to pregnancy (see figure 1.2). But in 1990, only 30 percent of all nonmarital births occurred to teenagers compared with 50 percent in 1970 (Furstenberg 1991; Ventura 1995, table B).

Teenage pregnancies—inside or outside marriage—arouse intense public policy debates. Twenty years ago a teenage mother (but not the father) could be expelled from school; now many high schools have daycare facilities in the same buildings

FIGURE 1.2 Percent of All Nonmarital Births Occurring
to Teenagers

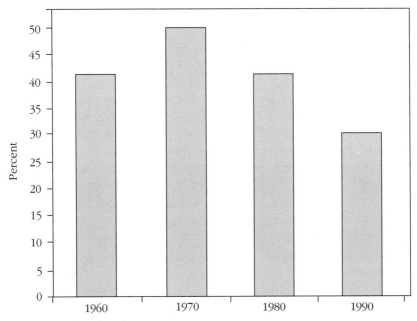

Source: Furstenberg (1991).

as classrooms and offer home tutoring to new mothers. Such
changes reflect a new public consensus that teen mothers should
not be penalized further by losing the chance for a high school
diploma.

Disagreement exists about whether teenage childbearing has
negative consequences (for mothers and their children) or
whether it is a positive adaptation to cultural and economic realities. The majority of research on this topic demonstrates that
teenaged mothers are less likely to complete high school or college, less likely to be employed or earn high wages, and more
likely to live in poverty than women who delay childbearing until
their twenties (Furstenberg 1991; Hayes 1987; Hoffman, Foster,
and Furstenberg 1993). "Revisionists," however, propose that previous research has failed to control for the disadvantaged backgrounds from which many teenaged mothers emerge, and thus

exaggerates the negative effects of teenage childbearing (Geronimus and Korenman 1992 and 1993). They also argue that early
childbearing may be an adaptive mechanism to racial discrimination and economic deprivation: neonatal mortality rates are lower
for black teens than for black women in their twenties, and
young mothers often receive child-care or financial support from
their mothers (Burton 1990; Geronimus 1987; Hamburg 1986;
Luker 1990).

Recent studies suggest that controls for economic background
reduce, but do not eliminate, the negative consequences of
teenage childbearing (Hoffman, Foster, and Furstenberg 1993).
Although relatives may be available to help with child care, intergenerational parenting can be complicated. The evidence about
mortality and the age of the mother is contradictory. Finally, it is
unlikely that individual teens operate on a rational-choice model
when deciding whether to become pregnant. In fact, when asked,
most teens believe it is better to wait until their twenties to have
children (Furstenberg 1991).

Despite what teenagers may say about the wisdom of delaying pregnancies, the majority engage in sexual intercourse and
many who are sexually active do not use effective contraception.
Data from the 1988 National Survey of Family Growth indicate
that one-quarter of females have had sexual intercourse by the
age of fifteen, and four-fifths have had sex by the age of nineteen.
("Nonvoluntary" sex—rape or incest—accounts for a large proportion of the sexual experience of girls under age fourteen.)
Only about one-half of teenagers used contraception at the time
of first intercourse. Among those using contraception, the birth
control pill has been the primary and most effective method,
although the use of condoms has been increasing. The proportion
of teen pregnancies ending in abortion increased from 29 to 42
percent between 1974 and 1985, while the proportion of teen
births occurring within marriage declined from 70 percent in 1970
to 36 percent in 1987 (Miller and Moore 1990).

Minority women under age eighteen of low socioeconomic
status are least likely to use contraceptives effectively or consistently. A misunderstanding of biology, complicated by lack of
access to confidential family planning services, also hinders successful contraceptive use. Finally, the irregular sexual activity

characteristic of teenagers may leave some girls contraceptively unprepared for sexual encounters. This list is not exhaustive, and no one factor completely determines sexual activity. A combination of demographic, social, and psychological forces affects levels of sexual activity.

Timing of Births

Despite the recent rise in teenage fertility, the majority of women still have children in their twenties or thirties. Delayed first births, fewer children, and sometimes childlessness reflect contemporary women's patterns of childbearing.

The timing of a first birth is important because it involves major changes in a woman's lifestyle and economic opportunities. Very young childbearing can conflict with the formation and achievement of educational and career goals. In contrast, those who postpone childbearing may develop interests and commitments that compete with childbearing and encourage further delay or childlessness (Rindfuss, Morgan, and Swicegood 1988). The timing of a first birth also has implications for subsequent childbearing and final family size. Long delays increase a woman's risk of disease, which rises with age, thus reducing the biological ability to bear children (Morgan 1991).

One indicator of delayed childbearing is the rise in fertility among women in their thirties. These middle-aged women have shown the most significant increases in fertility during the past decade. Among women of any marital status aged thirty to thirty-four, the birth rate in 1992 was 80.2 per one thousand women, compared with 61.9 in 1980. Among women aged thirty-five to thirty-nine, the birth rate rose from 19.8 in 1980 to 32.5 in 1992. Rates remained relatively stable for all other women aged twenty to forty-nine. (Fertility among women in their forties is still low, with rates below 6.0 for the past decade [Ventura and others 1994, table 4].)

Women who wait to have children until their thirties are more committed to market work and have higher educational attainment and wages than women who have babies in their twenties. In 1992, nearly three-quarters of first-time mothers aged thirty to forty-four were in the labor force compared with two-thirds of new mothers in their late twenties and one-half of new mothers in their early twenties. The fact that the majority of mothers are in the labor force is one of the basic changes in childbearing behavior since 1980 (Bachu 1993, table H).

Why are women delaying childbearing? One reason is that the increasing age at marriage and greater frequency of divorce remove women from the traditional context of childbearing (marriage) for longer periods of time than in the past. Another is that legalized contraception and abortion permit women to time their births, whether inside or outside marriage. Women may postpone births because they are more likely to be in the labor force and earn high wages than in the past (Ward and Butz 1979), or perhaps because poor employment opportunities for young men have influenced the timing of births (Easterlin 1987). It may also be possible that normative changes have reduced the importance of childbearing as other opportunities have made motherhood an option rather than an obligation (Bianchi and Spain 1986, p. 70).

Each of these theoretical arguments has some merit. Yet it is also necessary to examine individual characteristics to discover which women are most likely to delay childbearing or to forgo it entirely. For example, one of the clearest relationships is between educational attainment and the timing of births: more highly educated women postpone first births longer and are more likely to remain childless than less well educated ones. Education operates to delay or prevent childbearing in several ways. One is that time spent in school is typically time spent outside a reproductive union. A woman who wants a college or professional degree may prefer to complete it before starting a family. It also may be that women who pursue higher education are a self-selected group with little interest in childbearing or that traditional values and attitudes toward childbearing change while a woman is in school. One theory is that educated women respond most strongly to the prevailing socioeconomic climate and therefore are most likely to postpone fertility when economic conditions are difficult (and possibly when conditions are good, since rising opportunity costs dampen fertility). Regardless of the cause, rising educational attainment for women means that more women may become mothers later or not at all (Bianchi and Spain 1986, p. 71).

TABLE 1.3   Childlessness Among Women Aged 40 to 44
(percent)

Year	Childless Women
1976	10.2
1980	10.1
1985	11.4
1990	16.0
1992	15.7

Source: Bachu (1993), table E.

Another factor associated with delayed childbearing is labor force participation. Employed women delay family formation longer and are more likely to remain childless than women who are not employed. Women who *plan* to work also may delay a first birth because they want a smaller family. A wife in the labor force helps a family accumulate assets, and delayed childbearing eases the financial burden during the early years of marriage when couples are often trying to buy their first home. Further, highly educated women with professional careers may delay motherhood to avoid an interruption in their careers. Repeated postponement of a first birth for job-related reasons eventually may result in childlessness (Bianchi and Spain 1986, p. 71).

Table 1.3 illustrates the patterns of childlessness and indirectly of delayed childbearing. The historically low rates in 1976 1980, and 1985 reflect the effects of the high fertility of the baby boom years. By the early 1990s, the figure for all women in their early forties had risen to 16 percent, suggesting that, although motherhood declined for this group, it is still the choice for the vast majority of women, regardless of marital status. Women in their thirties (daughters of the baby boom) are nearing the completion of their childbearing years with current levels of childlessness ranging from 19 to 26 percent (slightly higher than for comparable ages in 1982). Current birth expectations and first birth patterns further indicate that younger women will complete their childbearing years with 15 to 20 percent remaining childless (Bachu 1993, pp. xi, xii).[1]

TABLE 1.4 Birth Expectations of Women Aged 18 to 34

Year	All Women	Currently Married Women
1976	2.16	2.29
1980	2.06	2.19
1985	2.06	2.20
1990	2.12	2.27
1992	2.10	2.25

Source: Bachu (1993), table 10.
Note: Lifetime births expected.

Historical research suggests that childlessness among American women rather than being a late twentieth century aberration is a "time-honored strategy for adapting to social change" (Morgan 1991, p. 803). Wives in the late nineteenth century, for instance, were childless at rates approaching 30 percent in those states where fertility control was practiced most widely—the methods included abstinence and abortion in addition to diaphragms and condoms (Degler 1980). Childlessness also was greatest among women with the highest socioeconomic status (Morgan 1991).

Thus, instead of questioning current levels of childlessness, one might ask why childlessness was so *low* during the baby boom. Morgan (1991, p. 801) believes that the answer lies in a triad of pronatalist factors: people making up for marriages and fertility that they postponed during the Depression and the war; a strong economy; and social programs such as the G.I. Bill and Social Security, which aided family formation (Modell, Furstenberg, and Strong, 1978; Rindfuss, Morgan, and Swicegood 1988). As these social and economic tides ebbed, women began bearing fewer children.

Birth Expectations

Data on birth expectations for *all* women (not just those currently married) are not available before 1976. Nonmarital childbearing has become so significant, however, that it is necessary to examine birth expectations for married and unmarried women in order to paint a complete picture. Table 1.4 shows that at least since 1976 the birth expectations for currently married women and for

TABLE 1.5 **Birth Expectations of Women Aged 18 to 34 by Selected Characteristics: 1992**

	Lifetime Births Expected	Percentage Expecting No Lifetime Births
All women, 18 to 34 years old	2.1	9.3
Educational attainment		
Not a high school graduate	2.4	7.6
High school graduate	2.0	9.0
Some college, no degree	2.1	10.0
Bachelor's degree	2.0	10.3
Graduate or professional degree	2.0	12.0
Labor force status		
In labor force	2.0	10.5
Employed	2.0	10.7
Unemployed	2.2	8.4
Not in labor force	2.4	6.0

Source: Bachu (1993), table 6.

all women have remained similar and stable, with married women's expectations slightly higher. Nor has there been much change in the proportion of young *childless* wives who expect at least one future birth; it has remained at approximately 90 percent since 1976 (Bachu 1993, table K).

The more educated a woman becomes, the lower her birth expectations and the more likely she is to anticipate remaining childless (see table 1.5). Women without a high school degree in 1992 report expecting 2.4 lifetime births compared with 2.0 for women with postgraduate degrees; 8 percent of those without a high school degree expected to remain childless compared with 12 percent of professionally educated women. Employed women have the lowest birth expectations (2.0) and women not in the labor force have the highest (2.4). Similarly, employed women are more likely to expect to remain childless than women not in the labor force (11 versus 6 percent).

Just how accurate are birth expectations in predicting future fertility? Their reliability depends on how committed the respondents feel to their expectations, as well as on the number of women who say they are uncertain about future childbearing or who fail to answer the question at all. In 1992, about 15 percent of women aged eighteen to thirty-four were uncertain about their birth expectations and another 13 percent failed to answer the question (both increases since 1976). Data are less accurate for never married women, since they are more uncertain about future fertility and less likely to answer the question than currently married women (Bachu 1993, p. xx).

Demographers disagree about the reliability of data on birth expectations. Some studies have shown them to be fairly good predictors of marital fertility, with the expectations most useful as predictors of completed cohort fertility if adjusted for proportions married within each cohort. Other studies suggest that reproductive intentions tend to overestimate short-range fertility rates. Still others argue that lowered fertility precedes lowered expectations, so that norms change in response to changes in behavior (Bianchi and Spain 1986, p. 58; Blake 1974; O'Connell 1991).

In the 1990s, the typical ideal family comprises two children, although preferences may vary depending on the sex of the children already born (Yamaguchi and Ferguson 1995). In the early 1970s, Blake (1974) attributed the decline in ideal family size that occurred over the preceding decade to Americans' greater awareness of population problems and predicted that it might be a temporary response. The two-child norm is still operative twenty years later, however, perhaps more as a practical response to the economic and time constraints characterizing contemporary family life than to concerns about overpopulation. Part of the persistence of the two-child norm may be the availability of contraception and legalized abortion, which allow women to achieve their reproductive goals more easily than in the past.

Contraception and Abortion

In 1951, birth control crusader Margaret Sanger joined forces with Katharine McCormick (heir to the McCormick reaper fortune) to propose their idea for an oral contraceptive to Gregory Pincus, a research scientist in Massachusetts. The financial backing of McCormick and the formidable will of Sanger were driving forces behind the scientific collaboration between Pincus and Harvard gynecologist John Rock, who receives the most public recognition for the work, that within a decade produced the birth control pill (Asbell 1995). That discovery became the cornerstone of the "contraceptive revolution" of the 1960s (Westoff and Ryder 1977).

The pill improved women's ability to control their fertility, and it was the first time sexual activity could be successfully separated from procreation with little forethought. Those were significant changes for women (and men), and it would have been unusual if changes in sexual mores had *not* occurred in response. The popularity of the birth control pill peaked in the 1970s and has since declined, partly because of confusion about its long-term health effects and partly because surgical sterilization (male and female) has become more accepted among couples who have completed their families.

Remarkably few nonsurgical contraceptive options have become available to women in the past decade. The "morning-after pill" can be prescribed by a doctor, but its mass production (as RU 486) has been limited because international pharmaceutical firms are hesitant to enter the U.S. market. Norplant (a timed-release capsule inserted just under the skin in an office procedure) has been stigmatized as a politically unpopular attempt to control black teenage pregnancies. The intrauterine device (IUD), with usage rates never higher than 10 percent in the 1970s, fell rapidly out of favor after one brand, the Dalkon Shield, was withdrawn from the market by its manufacturer. Only 1 percent of all women now use an IUD.

Approximately three-fifths of all American women used some form of contraception in 1990 (Peterson 1995). The most typical form of contraception among married couples is sterilization (either tubal ligation or vasectomy): 44 percent of currently married women and 42 percent of formerly married women (or their partners) were sterile in 1990. The contraceptive practices of unmarried women differ from those of married ones. In 1990, sexually active single (never married) women were almost twice as likely as married women (11 percent compared with 6 percent) to risk an unintended pregnancy by failing to use contraception. Perhaps unmarried women are less prepared for sexual activity, either because they are not in a stable relationship or because they resist defining themselves as sexually active. Among never married women using contraception, the most common choice was the birth control pill (22 percent compared with 15 percent for married women) (Peterson 1995, table 3).

Although the Catholic Church specifically forbids any contraceptive practice other than the rhythm method, reported contraceptive use differs little by religion. Both Catholic and Protestant fertility followed the same postwar decline, but there is debate about whether the Catholic–non-Catholic differential in fertility has converged. Jones and Westoff (1979) announced the "end of 'Catholic' fertility" over fifteen years ago, yet a replication of their work found a continued fertility differential by religion, especially in the higher rates of childlessness among Protestants (Mosher and Hendershot 1984). In general, most studies support convergence of fertility over time (Bianchi and Spain 1986, p. 62), with recent data showing *lower* fertility for Catholics than for Protestants because Catholics are marrying later and less frequently (Mosher, Williams, and Johnson 1992).

In addition to the reproductive freedom created by contraception, the availability of legalized abortion since the *Roe v. Wade* Supreme Court decision of 1973 has improved women's ability to time their pregnancies. Between 1980 and 1992, the number of abortions performed annually remained roughly stable at one and a half million. The ratio of abortions to live births, however, has declined significantly since the 1980s. In 1983, there were 433 abortions per 1,000 live births; by 1992, that ratio had dropped to 379 abortions per 1,000 live births. The abortion rate per 1,000 women also has declined, from 28.5 in 1983 to 25.9 in 1992 (Ventura and others 1995b).

This decline in the rate of abortions may be due to more effective contraceptive use, thus reducing the use of abortion to terminate unplanned pregnancies. Or it could be due to the reduction in federal funding that prevents Medicaid from paying for abortions. Another part may be due to the hostile climate in which doctors who perform abortions, and their patients, find themselves. The group Operation Rescue has been particularly effective in blockading clinics where abortions are performed and in harassing women seeking abortions. The murder of a doctor who performed abortions in Florida was the catalyst for a federal mandate declaring heightened security for clinics in which abortions are performed. Faludi (1991) argues that such "backlashes" against women's rights develop whenever reproductive control is at issue.

Such extremist positions as those adopted by members of Operation Rescue are not generally shared by the American public. Between 1970 and 1993, the proportions of Americans supporting abortion if the mother's or child's health is endangered have remained stable at approximately 90 and 80 percent, respectively. Proportionately fewer (in the 40 to 50 percent range) approve of abortion if a family cannot afford another child or if the mother wants no more children. There has actually been a slight increase, however, in the proportion of Americans who think abortion should be available for any reason at all (from about 35 percent in the late 1970s to 40 percent in 1993) (Farley, forthcoming, chap. 2). Despite such widespread public support for abortion under a variety of conditions (even "on demand"), the abortion issue becomes more controversial each year. In 1995, the name of Henry Foster, an African American physician from Alabama, was withdrawn from nomination for U.S. Surgeon General because his record of performing abortions became a political liability.

Racial and Ethnic Comparisons

Postwar trends in fertility have been similar for most racial and ethnic groups in the United States. Diverging trends in nonmarital births between whites and blacks, however, and the younger age structure of some recent immigrant groups have created important differences. The significant differences in nonmarital fertility between blacks and whites were discussed earlier in this chapter. The focus in this section is on other racial and ethnic groups.

Hispanic women aged fifteen to forty-four had significantly higher fertility than non-Hispanic women in 1992 (95.2 versus 59.5 births per 1,000 women). Hispanic women accounted for a disproportionately high share of all births among women aged fifteen to forty-four, partly because Hispanic mothers are significantly less likely to be in the labor force than non-Hispanic ones. The proportion of Hispanic births that occurred out of wedlock in 1992 (about one-quarter) was closer to the rate for white births than for black births (Bachu 1993, tables A, B, and

TABLE 1.6 Children Ever Born per Woman, by Race
          and Ethnicity

Group	1970	1980	1990
White	1.6	1.2	1.2
Black	1.9	1.6	1.4
American Indian	2.0	1.7	1.6
Asian	1.5	1.2	1.1
Hispanic	1.9	1.6	1.5

Source: Harrison and Bennett (1995), table 4A.1.

H). Part of the high fertility of Hispanics can be explained by recent trends in U.S. immigration. A substantial proportion of the new immigrants—who tend to be younger and to have higher fertility rates than the general population—are Hispanic (Chiswick and Sullivan 1995).

Asian women have birth rates much closer to whites than to Hispanic or black women. In 1992, the Asian birth rate was 63.5 per 1,000 women aged fifteen to forty-four (compared with 61.6 for whites, 69.2 for blacks, and 95.2 for Hispanics). Approximately one-half of Asian mothers were in the labor force in 1992, a slightly lower rate than for white or black mothers but higher than for Hispanics (Bachu 1993, tables A and H). Although recent Asian immigrants have the second highest completed family size (at 3.2 children ever born per women aged forty-five and over), they also have the highest proportion of women aged fifteen to thirty who remain childless (70 percent in 1990) (Chiswick and Sullivan 1995, p. 257).

Among all racial and ethnic groups in the United States, American Indians have had the highest fertility rate since 1970, although it has now declined. Asians have had the lowest rate historically. Each of the groups, however, has averaged two or fewer children since 1970 (see table 1.6).

International Comparisons

The current total fertility rate is near replacement level (2.1) in the United States and is among the highest of industrialized nations (see figure 1.3). Fertility in many European countries has contin-

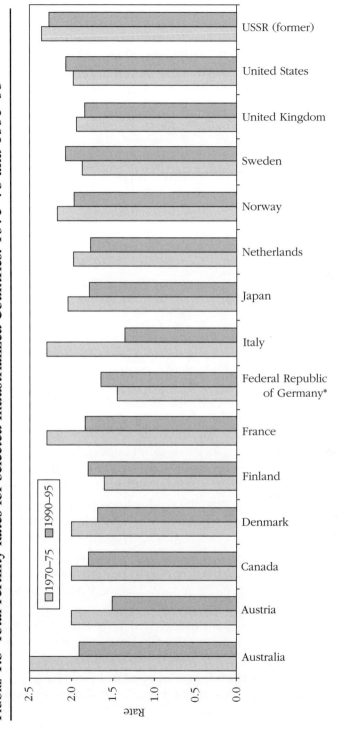

FIGURE 1.3 Total Fertility Rates for Selected Industrialized Countries: 1970–75 and 1990–95

Source: United Nations (1995), table 2; * United Nations (1994), table 14.

21

Table 1.7 Percentage of Births to Unmarried Women for Selected Industrial Countries: 1970 and 1990/92

Country	1970	1990/92
Australia	8	24
Austria	13	25
Canada	10	23
Denmark	11	47
Federal Republic of Germany	6	12
Finland	6	27
France	7	32
Italy	2	7
Japan	2	1
Netherlands	2	13
Norway	7	43
Sweden	18	50
United Kingdom	8	31
United States	11	28
USSR (former)	8	11

Source: United Nations (1995), chart 1.27A.

ued to decline despite pronatalist policies that include subsidized maternity leave (in Scandinavian countries) and family allowances for each child (in France) (Kamerman 1995). Countries with prolonged low fertility, such as the Federal Republic of Germany, are heavily reliant on guest workers to fill their labor force needs.

In its rate of births to unmarried women, the United States is intermediate among comparable industrialized nations (see table 1.7). The increase in the proportion of births occurring out of wedlock since 1970 has been significant for almost all countries. Out-of-wedlock births now typically account for one-quarter to one-half of all births in most of the developed economies. The high rates for Sweden, Norway, and Denmark reflect the greater incidence of cohabitation in these countries, while France's cohabitation pattern is intermediate between that of Scandinavia and that of the United States (Cherlin 1992; also see chapter 2 of this volume). Japan is alone among industrialized nations in having an insignificant proportion of nonmarital births.

Teenagers in the United States have higher pregnancy rates than in any other industrialized country, although there is no evidence that they have higher rates of sexual intercourse. Sex education courses in U.S. public schools tend to be ineffective in preventing pregnancies. American teenagers have been slow to adopt contraception, possibly because of the difficulty of obtaining confidential information and birth control devices and possibly because of their reluctance to think of themselves as sexually active (Miller and Moore 1990, p. 1030).

International data on contraception and abortion for the industrialized nations indicate that between 73 and 81 percent of married women of reproductive age use contraception (the figure is 74 percent for the United States) and that abortion is legal in all countries (United Nations 1995, p. 28).

Summary

The high fertility of the baby boom years is no longer news, so that the farther away we get from the baby boom the more anomalous this era of American fertility appears. Demographers no longer ask why fertility is now so low, but why it was so high for such a prolonged period after World War II. In fact, the more recent development is that the total fertility rate has returned to replacement level after having spent several decades below it.

Proportionately more births are occurring outside marriage for both whites and blacks. More than two-thirds of all births to black women and nearly one-quarter of all births to white women now occur out of wedlock. Black women tend to have children at earlier ages than white women and are less likely to marry, which means that they are more likely than whites to be unwed teenaged mothers. The issue of teenage out-of-wedlock pregnancies continues to generate an intense public debate that is often tinged with racial rhetoric.

Highly educated women and women in the labor force have the lowest birth expectations and the highest expectations for childlessness. Regardless of employment status and educational attainment, however, most women expect to have two children, a figure that has remained stable since the 1970s.

Although women expect approximately the same number of children as previous generations did, they are waiting longer to have them, with birth rates rising for married and unmarried women in their thirties. However, delayed fertility can sometimes mean forgone fertility, as illustrated by a slight rise in the proportion of women in their forties who are childless.

Reductions and delays in fertility mean that women have more opportunities to pursue alternatives to the mothering role. Later chapters on education, labor force participation, and earnings describe the changes for women that have accompanied these trends in fertility.

CHAPTER 2

Marriage and Living Arrangements

DRAMATIC CHANGES HAVE OCCURRED IN WOMEN'S MARRIAGE PATTERNS and living arrangements over the past few decades. The majority of American women still marry, but they are now older when they do so and spend a smaller proportion of their adult lives married. Women remain unmarried longer because they delay first marriage until their mid- to late twenties, they divorce at a much higher rate than in the past, even though the rate has declined slightly in recent years, they cohabit more frequently, as living together has become a more acceptable alternative to marriage, and, among the elderly, they are more likely than men to be widowed. In other words, the centrality of marriage has declined for women over time.

An important consideration when contemplating this drift away from marriage is that a woman's marital status remains a strong predictor of her economic well-being: married women have higher household incomes, are more likely to own their homes, and are less likely to live in poverty than unmarried women. Moreover, a woman's marital status continues to be linked with educational attainment, fertility, and her labor force participation. Thus, a woman's decision whether to marry often has important consequences for her and for her children's economic welfare.

TABLE 2.1 Median Age at First Marriage by Gender

Year	Women	Men
1900	21.9	25.9
1910	21.6	25.1
1920	21.2	24.6
1930	21.3	24.3
1940	21.5	24.3
1950	20.3	22.8
1960	20.3	22.8
1970	20.8	23.2
1980	22.1	24.6
1990	23.9	26.1
1992	24.4	26.5

Source: U.S. Bureau of the Census (1975), series A158-159; (1981), table A; (1992c).

Delay in First Marriage

The median age at first marriage now exceeds the high recorded at the beginning of this century. In 1900, one-half of all women married by age 22 and one-half of all men married by age 26; by 1992, the median age at first marriage for women was 24.4 and for men was 26.5. During the intervening baby boom years, women and men married much earlier. Although the difference between men's and women's age at first marriage has declined (see table 2.1), the remaining two-year difference means that men still have a slight time advantage when it comes to securing educational or occupational achievements prior to marriage.

When women marry later, they can attend school longer, enter the labor force, and live independently. In other words, their young adult years become more similar to men's. Women who marry older also are less likely to divorce but are more likely to have children out of wedlock. Another consequence of delayed marriage is an increase in young single adults. The proportion of women in their early twenties who had never married doubled between 1950 and 1990 (from about one-third to almost two-thirds), while the proportion of women in their late twenties who had never married almost tripled during the same period (from 13 percent to 32 percent). Changes for men were similarly dramatic: the proportion of men

TABLE 2.2 **Percentage of Americans Who Have Never Married**

Age Group	1950	1960	1970	1980	1990
Total women,					
15 and over	18.5	17.3	20.6	22.9	23.4
15–19	82.9	83.9	88.1	91.2	94.3
20–24	32.3	28.4	36.3	51.2	64.6
25–29	13.3	10.5	12.2	21.6	32.0
30–34	9.3	6.9	7.4	10.6	18.2
35 and over	8.2	7.2	6.5	5.7	6.7
Total men,					
15 and over	24.9	23.2	26.4	29.7	30.7
15–19	96.7	96.1	95.9	97.2	97.7
20–24	59.0	53.1	55.5	68.2	78.8
25–29	23.8	20.8	19.6	32.1	46.0
30–34	13.2	11.9	10.7	14.9	26.3
35 and over	8.8	7.8	7.1	6.3	8.4

Source: U.S. Bureau of the Census (1953), table 104; (1963), table 176; (1973), table 203; (1983a), table 264; (1992a), table 34.

in their early twenties who had never married rose by twenty percentage points between 1950 and 1990, and the proportion never married in their late twenties doubled (from 24 percent to 46 percent). Approximately one-fifth of women and one-quarter of men in their early thirties were still single in 1990 (see table 2.2).

Some unmarried young adults maintain independent households, some live at home with their parents, and some come and go several times before the transition to independent living or marriage is complete. The "empty nest" syndrome is being replaced by a "return to the nest" phenomenon as young adults remain single longer and are increasingly likely to live at home for some time during that unattached period. Reversing a pattern of previous decades, young women were *more* likely to be living at home in 1990 (41 percent) than in 1980 (36 percent) (Hogan and Lichter 1995, table 3.10). The ease with which young adults make the transition out of the parental home varies by whether they are leaving to get married or to live independently or cohabit. Marriage typically results in a more clearly demarcated move than either a decision to live alone or to cohabit (Avery, Goldscheider, and Speare 1992; Goldscheider, Thornton, and Young-DeMarco 1993).

Women delay marriage for numerous reasons. Both women and men are staying in school longer, and higher educational attainment is associated with later age at marriage and greater educational similarity between spouses (Cherlin 1992; Mare 1991; Qian and Preston 1993). Women are more likely to be employed now, and labor force participation and higher earnings also are correlated with delayed marriage (Becker 1981). These developments are consistent with Easterlin's (1978) hypothesis that the depressed economic conditions of the 1970s, combined with the labor market entry problems of the baby boom cohort, made it difficult for young people to marry and start a family at the standard of living they had come to expect from their relatively affluent post–World War II homes.

A shortage of marriage-aged men with good jobs is another explanation for women's later age at marriage, especially within the black community (Kiecolt and Fossett 1995; Lichter and others 1992; Sampson 1995; Wilson 1987). Another hypothesis is that welfare benefits discourage women from marrying (Murray 1984). However, benefits have declined during the period that age at marriage has increased, and delayed marriage is characteristic of both poorer and wealthier women (McLanahan and Casper 1995). The cultural changes of the 1960s and 1970s that produced the women's movement—easily available contraception and legalized abortion—also influenced norms about sexual behavior and non-marital options for women (McLanahan and Casper 1995). And, finally, the knowledge that divorce increasingly follows marriage may cause some young adults to hesitate before tying the knot.

The forces motivating women's marital decisions are widely debated. Cherlin (1992) believes that women's increased economic independence is the key to the movement away from marriage, as do McLanahan and Casper (1995). Oppenheimer (1994), however, argues that more attention should be paid to the market position of *men*, whose deteriorating opportunities have contributed to the postponement of marriage. Their disagreements clearly echo larger themes about the relative weights that should be assigned to women's and men's earnings, and the resulting incentives to marry.

Divorce

It is hard to remember that Nelson Rockefeller's divorce was an issue in his 1964 presidential campaign. By the time Ronald Reagan was elected president in 1980, his divorce barely made the papers. The changing mood of the electorate reflects a tolerance formed by demographic reality: it is the rare voter now who does not have at least one family member or friend who has been divorced.

Although marked by prominent upswings and downturns, the annual divorce rate (the number of divorces per one thousand married women aged fifteen and over) has risen steadily throughout the twentieth century. The rate—which spiked after both world wars—declined during the Depression and baby boom, rose swiftly after 1967, only to ebb quietly in the 1980s (Cherlin 1992, p. 21; Pavalko and Elder 1990). In 1960, there were only 35 divorced persons for every one thousand married adults, compared with 152 in 1992 (McLanahan and Casper 1995, p. 9; U.S. Bureau of the Census 1992c, table D) (see figure 2.1).

Women who married during the 1950s have experienced an unusually low likelihood of divorce by historical standards, while those who married during the 1960s and 1970s (the early baby boomers) experienced an unusually high probability of divorce. As first marriages of the baby boom endure past the most maritally disruptive years (the first seven years), however, those rates decline. Lifetime estimates of divorce are not yet available for women married during the 1980s, but they appear to be lower than those for women married in the 1960s and 1970s. Still, it is likely that one-half of *all* marriages will end in divorce or separation if current rates continue (Cherlin 1992, pp. 24, 25).

The causes of divorce are endlessly debated in the public arena. Age at first marriage appears repeatedly as one of the most powerful predictors of divorce: the younger the bride and groom, the greater the risk of divorce, even among couples with similar educational and childbearing experiences. Length of marriage is also strongly correlated with marital dissolution: the probability of divorce declines steadily the longer a couple stays married (Bianchi and Spain 1986, pp. 26, 27).

FIGURE 2.1 U.S. Divorce Rates

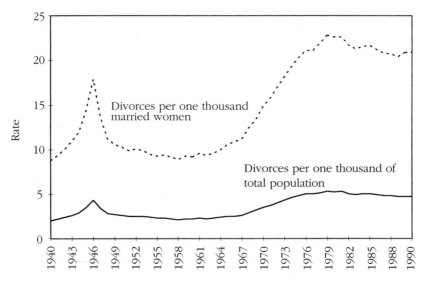

Source: Clark (1995a), table 1.

A wife's participation in the labor force also increases the likelihood of divorce. The nature of this relationship may be more complicated than it appears, however. It could be that paid work gives a woman economic assets that upset traditional gender roles within the marriage or that provide the potential for her independence. Or it may be that hours worked outside the home become a source of tension in the marriage or that women who are employed see themselves in less traditional roles (Greenstein 1995). It even may be the obvious possibility that employed wives come into contact with more "spousal alternatives" than those who stay at home (South and Lloyd 1995). For these and other reasons, wives in the labor force are more likely to divorce than wives who are not. Because after 1960 younger married women have been more likely to work, and younger wives are more likely to divorce than older wives, it is feasible that the increase in younger wives' participation in the labor force during the 1960s and 1970s contributed to the rise in the divorce rate (Cherlin 1992, p. 53;

Greenstein 1990; Johnson and Skinner 1986; Spitze and South 1985). (Disagreement persists about whether a guaranteed minimum income increases the risk of divorce [Cain and Wissokej 1990; Groeneveld, Hannan, and Tuma 1977; Hannan and Tuma 1990].)

Attitudes toward divorce have become more liberal over time, as the different political fates of Nelson Rockefeller and Ronald Reagan illustrate, making it easier for couples to contemplate divorce. National opinion polls indicate that the proportion of Americans who thought divorce should be easier to obtain peaked in the early 1970s and declined during the 1980s, although it remains high by historical standards. This trend replicates that of actual divorce rates. The recent disenchantment may indicate a growing intolerance for divorce, or it may simply reflect the fact that as divorce became easier to obtain during the 1970s, a result of no-fault divorce laws, the issue's prominence diminished.

Although the causes and correlates of divorce are complicated, its consequences for women are fairly simple: a woman's economic well-being typically falls, while a man's typically rises. It is true that family income declines for *both* women and men after divorce but the drop is much greater for women (24 percent) than for men (6 percent), and former husbands are more likely to see their income (relative to their household's needs) increase than are former wives, who usually retain custody of children from the marriage (Burkhauser 1990; Duncan and Hoffman 1988). Women's roles as primary child caretakers also limit their earnings potential, resulting in more serious economic consequences for women than men (Smock 1994). The child-support payments awarded to divorced mothers seldom are enough to bring the family's income up to the living standard typical of married couples, and only about one-half of divorced mothers receive the full amounts due them (Scoon-Rogers and Lester 1995). Even younger women, who married more recently and have greater labor force experience than older women, are not protected from the severe economic costs of divorce (Smock 1993). Twice as many women (22 percent) as men (10 percent) see their income plummet by more than 50 percent after divorce (Burkhauser and others 1990, table 2).

Cohabitation

As societal norms governing sexual behavior have loosened and divorce rates have risen, cohabitation has become an increasingly popular prelude to first marriage as well as an alternative to remarriage after divorce. Between 1980 and 1992, the proportion of all householders that were cohabiting increased from 3 percent to 6 percent. Even more striking, more than half of marriages since 1985 began as cohabitation, up from 8 percent in the late 1960s (Bumpass 1990; Bumpass and Sweet 1989). Figure 2.2 demonstrates the rising popularity of cohabitation as an alternative to marriage. Time spent cohabiting also reinforces the delays in marriage discussed earlier.[1]

We know much more about cohabitation now than we did a decade ago. For example, we know that cohabitation before marriage may increase the risk of divorce (DeMaris and Rao 1992; Schoen 1992). This result may be due to total amount of time spent in the relationship (Teachman and Polonko 1990); a selection bias arising from the fact that people who live together may be less committed to marriage (Axinn and Thornton 1992; Lillard, Brien, and Waite 1995); or the tensions arising from unsupportive or dispproving parents (Nock 1995). We also know that parents' divorce increases a child's chance of cohabiting as an adult (but not the subsequent risk of divorce) (Thornton 1991) and that, as among marriages, the presence of young children has a stabilizing effect on cohabiting couples (Waite and Lillard 1991; Wu 1995). Although couples often report that they marry in order to have families, the timing of the first birth for women who have cohabited is similar to that for married women who have *not* cohabited; in other words, the transition from cohabitation to marriage does not appear to be greatly influenced by the desire to start a family (Manning 1995).

People may choose cohabitation because it provides some of the advantages of marriage without the legal or economic restrictions. For example, cohabiting couples and married couples report equal levels of satisfaction with the division of household labor and child care and are similar in their level of agreement about most day-to-day issues. But cohabiting couples expect

FIGURE **2.2** **Number of Unmarried Couples Cohabiting**

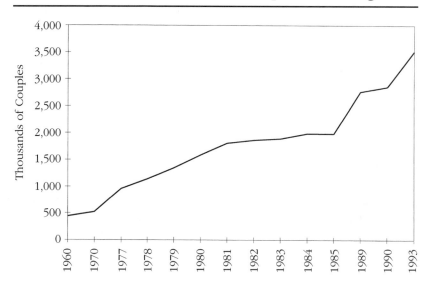

Source: U.S. Bureau of the Census (1960), table 15; (1994a), table D.

fewer "exit costs" to leaving a relationship than do married couples and perceive more positive benefits to ending the relationship than do married couples (Nock 1995). This satisfaction with daily routine, combined with lower overall commitment, suggests that cohabitation occupies an intermediate status between singlehood and marriage.

An important sidebar to the rise in cohabitation is the increasing presence of children in cohabiting households. Among the 3.3 million such households in 1992, 34 percent included children under the age of fifteen, compared with 27 percent of the 1.6 million cohabiting households in 1980 (U.S. Bureau of the Census 1992c, table K). Children in cohabiting households are increasingly likely to be from former marriages, as over two-thirds of all cohabiting couples in 1992 included at least one divorced person (an increase from one-half in 1981) (Spanier 1983; U.S. Bureau of the Census 1992c, table 8). The greater likelihood that children will live in a cohabiting household reflects the shift from cohabitation as a precursor to first marriage to cohabitation as a precursor to or substitute for remarriage. Thus, a lifestyle that not long ago was considered a young person's radical choice has become a midlife transition for many women and men (Bumpass, Sweet, and Cherlin 1991; Sweet and Bumpass 1987). Recent evidence suggests, in fact, that many officially defined "single-parent" families are actually two-parent unmarried families (Bumpass, Raley, and Sweet 1995).

Remarriage

While cohabitation after divorce is more of an option than it once was, about two-thirds of divorced women and three-fourths of divorced men eventually remarry (Cherlin 1992, p. 28). Divorced women are less likely to remarry than divorced men because women are more likely to retain custody of children, whose care may preclude the cultivation of a separate social life, and because men typically draw potential spouses from a wider age range than do women (so that older men are more likely to remarry than older women) (Cherlin 1992). Unfortunately, remarriage has generated remarkably little research in the past decade compared with that on cohabitation, perhaps because cohabitation is an increasingly important factor in the postponement of remarriage.

Divorces and remarriages rose together until the mid-1970s. As the divorce rate continued to climb, however, the remarriage rate declined as women waited longer to remarry. In the 1980s, both the divorce rate and the remarriage rate declined (see figure 2.3). The decline in the remarriage rate was confirmed in 1990, when the rate of thirty-six remarriages for every thousand divorced and widowed women was lower than it was in 1970. Figure 2.3 also illustrates the slight decline in divorce rates during the 1980s and the more dramatic reduction in the rate of first marriages (from eighty-eight women per one thousand never married women in 1960 to fifty-eight in 1990).

Cohabitation contributes to these trends. While the remarriage rate was declining during the late 1970s, the rate of union formation (the sum of marriage and cohabitation) was increasing, and the majority of persons who remarried during the 1980s had lived

FIGURE 2.3 Rates of First Marriage, Divorce, and Remarriage

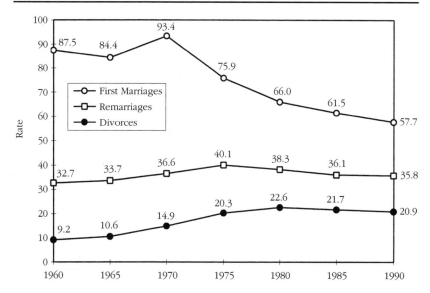

Source: National Center for Health Statistics (1964), table I-M; (1968), table 1.7; (1974), table 1.20; (1979), table 1.7; (1984), tables 4, 10; (1990), table 1; Clark (1995a), table 1; Clark (1995b), table 6.

Note: First marriages per one thousand never married women aged 14 and over (15 and over after 1987); remarriages per one thousand divorced and widowed women aged 14 and over (15 and over after 1987); divorces per one thousand married women aged 15 and over.

with someone before that marriage. Greater familiarity may breed discontent, however, as the rate of divorce during the first several years of remarriage is significantly higher than in the initial years of first marriage (Cherlin 1992, pp. 28, 29).

The complicated family structure resulting from remarriages may contribute to their early demise. Although divorce and remarriage are increasingly common at the societal level, their effects on family life still must be negotiated by individuals. The multiple demands (emotional, financial, and simple scheduling) of children from one or two former marriages (or from the remarriage) often must be coordinated with the noncustodial parent, and the sheer proliferation of quasi-kinship relationships may strain both parent-child and spousal relations (Cherlin 1992, p. 80).

FIGURE 2.4 Percentage of Women and Men Aged 65
and Over Who Are Widowed

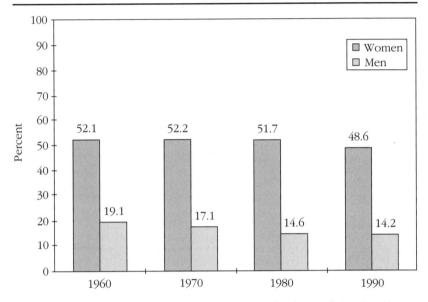

Source: U.S. Bureau of the Census (1953), table 104; (1963), table 176; (1973), table 203; (1983a), table 264; (1992a), table 34.

Widowhood

A woman is more likely to be widowed than her husband whether she is in a first or subsequent marriage. Nearly one-half of women aged sixty-five and over were widowed in 1990, a slight decline from 1960. By comparison, only 19 percent of elderly men were widowed in 1960 and that proportion had declined to 14 percent by 1990 (see figure 2.4). This stark gender contrast in the likelihood of being widowed results from women's longer life expectancy (seventy-nine years compared with seventy-two years for men), their tendency to marry men older than themselves, and the higher remarriage rate among widowed men (Treas and Torrecilha 1995).

The older the population, the more pronounced the difference in widowhood between women and men. In their late sixties, 30 percent of women and 7 percent of men were widowed in 1990; at ages ninety and above, 86 percent of women and 53 percent of men were widowed (Treas and Torrecilha 1995, p. 66).

TABLE 2.3 **Homeownership Rates by Type of Household: 1982 and 1993 (percent)**

Age of Householder	Married Couples		Female Family Householders		Females Living Alone	
	1982	1993	1982	1993	1982	1993
Total, all ages	78.5	79.1	47.1	44.5	51.2	54.8
Under 25	32.6	26.6	8.9	8.8	7.5	8.3
25–29	53.9	50.1	17.3	14.3	14.3	15.6
30–34	71.9	67.1	31.3	23.9	24.7	29.9
35–39	80.4	77.1	43.5	36.7	35.6	38.9
40–44	83.9	82.3	54.2	49.1	38.9	44.4
45–49	86.6	85.1	57.2	58.0	45.5	52.6
50–54	88.2	88.0	66.7	62.7	51.7	58.5
55–59	89.6	90.2	66.4	65.4	60.5	61.3
60–64	89.4	90.5	71.5	72.9	63.8	66.6
65 and over	86.6	90.2	75.1	78.8	62.2	64.5

Source: Hughes (1994).
Note: Data indicate proportion of households in each category that own their own home.

These differences have significant effects on women's living arrangements and quality of life. Whereas wives generally care for their husbands as they grow old, women are more likely to rely on grown children, live with other family members, or enter a nursing home, although the majority of elderly widows live alone (Kramarow 1995; Silverstein 1995; Weinick 1995). The propensity for widows to live with, or depend on, their adult children may be reduced among families with fewer children and those that experience divorce (Aquilino 1994; Cooney 1994; Lye and others 1995; Macunovich and others 1995).

Homeownership rates are highest for the elderly, the majority of whom are widows. Because the cohort now reaching old age entered the housing market during the affordable years after World War II, their ownership rates are high compared with younger cohorts (Myers and Wolch 1995; Sweet 1990). In 1993, almost two-thirds of elderly women who lived alone owned their own homes (the average for all households). This proportion was low, however, when compared with the 90 percent of elderly married couples who owned their own homes (see table 2.3).

Homeownership rates for both elderly female family house-holders and elderly women living alone have increased slightly since 1982. In contrast, homeownership rates for younger female family householders have *declined* since 1982 for every age group except those in their late forties. The absence of homeownership is especially pronounced for female householders most likely to have young children (those in their thirties).

The elderly are now better off financially than they were in the past, and widows are now less likely to live in poverty than children are. Yet, elderly widows are still more likely than elderly men to be poor because their economic security is tied more closely to Social Security benefits than to wages or pensions. Not every widow becomes poor after her husband's death, nor is she likely to lose the house she owned with her husband. Limited sources of personal income, though, leave many women vulnera-ble to poverty after their husband's death (Treas and Torrecilha 1995).

Growth of Mother-Child Families

The trend toward later marriage and postponement of remarriage has contributed to the growth of single-parent families. In 1990, 24 percent of all families had only one parent at home, compared with 8 percent in 1950. In 1994, 29 percent of all households were maintained by a woman (U.S. Bureau of the Census 1995b, table A).

To give some historical context, during the 1940s, the num-ber of mother-child families increased by 6 percent, a figure that was offset by a decline in the number of father-child families (Sweet and Bumpass 1987, pp. 362, 372). The number of one-parent households began to increase after World War II, rising from 1.5 to almost 2.2 million. Growth accelerated in the late 1960s and 1970s, and by 1980 the number of single-parent families stood at 5.9 million (see table 2.4). Mothers are more typically the single parent than fathers. Of the 7.3 million single-parent families in 1990, 82 percent consisted of women and their children.

In the 1980s, although the number of one-parent families con-tinued to increase, the *rate* of increase slowed significantly

TABLE 2.4 **Single-Parent Households with Own Children Under Age 18**

	Thousands of Households					Percent Change			
	1950	1960	1970	1980	1990	1950s	1960s	1970s	1980s
Total	19,847	25,661	27,973	30,136	30,878	29.3	9.0	7.7	2.5
Single parent	1,531	2,191	3,428	5,871	7,383	43.1	56.5	71.3	25.8
Mother-child	1,256	1,891	3,007	5,062	6,028	50.6	59.0	68.4	19.1
Father-child	275	300	421	809	1,355	9.1	40.3	92.1	67.4
Two parent	18,316	23,470	24,545	24,265	23,495	28.1	4.6	-1.1	-3.2

Source: U.S. Bureau of the Census, (1955), table 4; (1964), table 188; (1973), table 54; (1983a), table 46; (1993c), tables 38 and 40.
Note: Percent change = (Year 2–Year 1)/Year 1 * 100.

(Bianchi 1994). Whereas the increase in divorce fueled the growth in one-parent families in the 1960s and 1970s, delayed marriage and childbearing outside marriage were the more important factors in the 1980s (Bianchi 1994; Wojkkiewicz, McLanahan, and Garfinkel 1990). In the early 1990s, nearly one-third of mother-child households were headed by a never married mother, up from 4 percent in 1960 (Bianchi 1995, table 2.) Also, during the 1980s, the mix of single mothers shifted toward those least financially able to support children on their own, a topic we return to in the discussion of poverty in chapter 6.

A less well known phenomenon of the 1980s is that father-child families increased faster than mother-child families. As a result of the women's movement, many states made their custody and child support laws more gender neutral, opening the door for more fathers to seek and gain custody of children after divorce (Grief 1995). By 1990, almost one-fifth of single-parent families were maintained by a father, although only 3 percent of all children lived in this type of household. Children in father-child families were better off financially than those in mother-child families but were still less well off than those in two-parent families (Bianchi 1994, table 5).

Marital and fertility histories reveal that many women will spend some of their adult years as a single parent: about one-half of mothers of children born in the early 1980s will become single parents by age thirty-five. If cohabiting couples are included with married couples in the count of two-parent families, about one-third of women (and children) who became a single parent in the 1980s did so because they gave birth outside a union. Because cohabiting unions are less stable than marital unions, the likelihood that a mother will eventually end up as a single parent is high for those in cohabiting unions (Bumpass and Raley 1995; Bumpass and Rendall 1995).

Whether cohabiting couples are counted as two-parent or one-parent families affects estimates of how long women and their children remain in a single-parent situation. For the women who bore children in the early 1980s, the average length of time as a single parent is 6.6 years when married couples alone are considered two-parent families and a much shorter 3.6 years when cohabiting unions are included. Under the first definition, the length of time women spend as single parents has increased over time, whereas under the broader, second definition the average duration has been shrinking (Bumpass and Raley 1995).

In addition to the role of unmarried partners, grandparents are important in assisting single-parent families (Ghosh, Easterlin, and Macunovich 1993). Among single mothers, almost one-third live at some point in their parents' home and the average length of that stay is almost two years. Perhaps as much as one-third of the time that single parents spend outside a marital union is spent either living with a cohabiting partner or living in a parent's home (Bumpass and Raley 1995). Although single parents do adjust to the demands of raising children alone, perhaps by living in their parents' household, it is still true that mothers raising children without a partner face a high likelihood of poverty and their children experience educational and psychological disadvantages (Dawson 1991; Grall 1992; McLanahan and Booth 1989; McLanahan and Sandefur 1995).

Racial and Ethnic Comparisons

Differences in household structure constitute one of the most significant differences between black and white families in the United States. The growth in mother-child households, a politically controversial development, has been pronounced throughout the postwar period. In 1993, 47 percent of black families were maintained by women, compared with 14 percent of white families (U.S. Bureau of the Census 1994c, table E).

The highly combustible race issue complicates discussion of these differences between white and black families. When it was published in 1965, a report by Senator Daniel P. Moynihan generated intense controversy that is still being debated by scholars and politicians of both races (see Tucker and Mitchell-Kernan 1995). Moynihan contended that the "pathological" nature of black poverty could be traced to the deterioration of black nuclear family life, which, in turn, resulted from black male unemployment. His critics charge that immense strains arising from a racially discriminatory society caused the breakdown in the family. Still others point out that Moynihan's emphasis on the negative consequences of black family structure ignores the strengths of extended kinship networks among blacks. Also widely discussed has been whether the increased incidence of black single-mother families has been of recent origin, or a legacy of African or slave heritage: a new data set spanning the past century suggests that blacks historically have had high rates of single parenthood and that the growing racial differences in family structure between 1940 and 1980 result from a significant decline in an extended, two-generation family structure among *whites* rather than a steep increase in single parenthood among blacks (Ruggles 1994).

Postwar growth in the number of single-parent families has been dramatic for both blacks and whites. White mother-child families increased from fewer than 1 million in 1950 to 3.6 million in 1990, while black mother-child families increased from 285,000 to 1.9 million. The most rapid growth for both groups occurred during the 1960s and 1970s. During the 1980s, the rate of growth of mother-child families fell precipitously (see table 2.5).

Racial differences in women's marital status arise from a greater likelihood among black women to never have married, to be divorced, or to cohabit, although rates of widowhood are similar for white and black women. Cohabitation contributed more to the decline in marriage rates among blacks than whites. National estimates show that one-quarter of blacks cohabit, 20 percent of Hispanics, and 14 percent of whites (Bumpass, Sweet, and Cherlin 1991; Hatchett, Veroff, and Douvan 1995). In 1992, black women were the least likely group to be currently married and the most likely to never have married or to be divorced. These trends combine to make single motherhood a less transitory state for black mothers and their children than for white mother-child families (Bumpass and Sweet 1989).

Numerous explanations have been proposed for the divergent marriage rates of blacks and whites. One is a relative shortage of "suitable" black male partners (that is, those with a good education and job) (Lichter, LeClere, and McLaughlin 1991; Lichter and others 1992), thus affecting the "exchange" value of marriage for blacks (Schoen 1995). In contrast to the decline in employment opportunities for black men, job prospects for black women have improved since World War II. In 1940, 60 percent of employed black women worked as low-paid domestics; by 1980, over one-half of employed black women were white-collar workers, and

TABLE 2.5 Single-Parent Households with Own Children Under Age 18 by Race

	Thousands of Households					Percent Change			
	1950	1960	1970	1980	1990	1950s	1960s	1970s	1980s
White									
Single parent	1,200	1,638	2,382	3,760	4,579	36.5	45.4	57.9	21.8
Mother-child	971	1,394	2,058	3,166	3,608	43.6	47.6	53.8	14.0
Father-child	229	244	324	594	971	6.6	32.8	83.3	63.5
Two parents	16,990	21,625	22,268	20,997	19,777	27.3	3.0	-5.7	-5.8
Black									
Single parent	331	552	989	1,727	2,127	66.8	79.2	74.6	23.2
Mother-child	285	497	901	1,568	1,897	74.4	81.3	74.0	21.0
Father-child	46	55	88	159	230	19.6	60.0	80.7	44.7
Two parents	1,326	1,845	1,951	1,950	1,780	39.1	5.7	-0.1	-8.7

Source: U.S. Bureau of the Census (1955), table 4; (1964), table 188; (1973), table 54; (1983a), table 46; (1993c), tables 38 and 40.
Note: Percent change = (Year 2–Year 1)/Year 1 × 100.

black women earned as much as white women with the same education (Farley and Allen 1987).

Culture and history also account for part of the divergence. Extended kin, especially a grandmother, plays a much more important role in the care of black children than among whites (Cherlin and Furstenberg 1986). Greater reliance on relatives for child care reduces the pressure to get married and may simplify cohabitation or single motherhood as a marital alternative (Hogan, Hao, and Parish 1990; Loomis and Landale 1994; Manning 1995). An African heritage that stresses lineage lines (rather than the nuclear family) and marriage as a gradual process (rather than as a single event) often following the birth of a child have influenced black family formation as well (Cherlin 1992).

Although blacks are currently the single largest minority in the United States, Hispanics will overtake their numbers by the beginning of the next century and Asians will have a distinct presence. In 1990, blacks were 12 percent of the population, Hispanics were 9 percent, and Asians were approximately 4 percent; by 2020, blacks are projected to be 13 percent of the population, Hispanics 16 percent, and Asians 7 percent (Harrison and Bennett 1995, p. 142). One of the difficulties of making generalizations about Asians and Hispanics is the great amount of diversity that exists *within* these populations. Asians may be Chinese, Korean, Indian, or Vietnamese, to name only a few nationalities, and Hispanics may be from Central America, South America, Spain, or Puerto Rico. Marriage patterns and living arrangements therefore differ within categories.The timing of immigration and the region of the country in which the group settles also affect minority family structure (Burr and Mutchler 1992; Harrison and Bennett 1995; Landale 1994).

These ethnic groups have followed the same general trend in the decline of married-couple households in the United States as whites and blacks (with the exception of Asians, the only group *more* likely to be married in 1990 than in 1970). Within this overall trend, however, differences emerge among the groups (see table 2.6). For example, Hispanic women are more likely than black women to be currently married, less likely never to have married, and less likely to be divorced. Hispanics were less likely than whites but more likely than blacks to live in married-couple

TABLE 2.6 Marital Status by Sex, Race, and Ethnicity: 1992

	Percent Distribution	
	Women	Men
All races	100.0	100.0
Never married	23.0	30.2
Married	52.7	57.1
Spouse absent	3.6	2.8
Widowed	11.2	2.7
Divorced	9.4	7.2
White	100.0	100.0
Never married	20.6	28.1
Married	56.0	59.9
Spouse absent	2.9	2.3
Widowed	11.3	2.5
Divorced	9.2	7.2
Black	100.0	100.0
Never married	39.1	45.0
Married	29.4	36.1
Spouse absent	8.6	6.4
Widowed	11.5	4.2
Divorced	11.5	8.4
Hispanic	100.0	100.0
Never married	28.6	37.3
Married	49.8	49.9
Spouse absent	6.9	5.8
Widowed	6.7	1.5
Divorced	8.0	5.5

Source: U.S. Bureau of the Census (1992c), table 1.

households, while Asians were more likely than whites to be married in 1990. Blacks were approximately twice as likely as Hispanics, and about four times as likely as whites and Asians, to live in female-headed households (see figure 2.5).

International Comparisons

The United States is comparable to other industrialized nations in the trend toward delayed first marriage. Common factors in delaying marriage among industrialized nations are the improved

FIGURE **2.5 Families with Own Children Under 18 by Race
and Ethnicity**

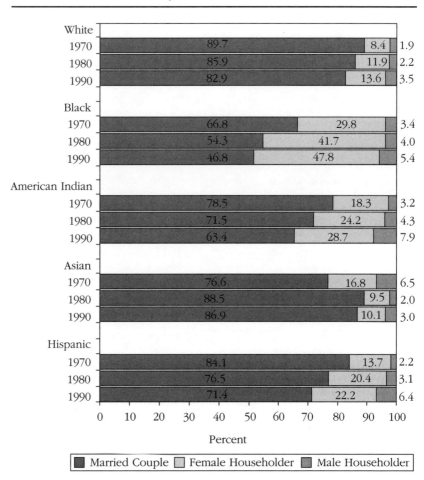

Source: Harrison and Bennett (1995), table 4A.1.

educational attainment and growing labor force participation
of women. Cohabitation, too, has played a similar role in the
United States and other countries. Living together before marriage is virtually universal in Sweden, and having a first child in a
cohabiting relationship is the norm (about one-half of all Swedish
births occur to cohabiting women). By 1980, 15 percent of all

Swedish households consisted of a cohabiting couple, compared with 2 percent in the United States (Cherlin 1992, p. 16).

Living together is also more common in France (6 percent of all households in 1982) than in the United States, but less typical than in Sweden. Cohabiting relationships last longer in France than in the United States, however, and partners report the only advantage of marriage is for the good of children; cohabitation is considered a "neutral" phase of life in which long-term decisions are postponed. Cherlin (1992, pp. 16, 17) predicts that U.S. patterns are more likely to follow the evolving French model than the Swedish one, which is steeped in a longer historical tradition.

The Canadian experience with cohabitation appears to resemble closely that in the United States. Ten percent of Canadian couples were cohabiting in 1991 (compared with 6 percent in the United States); Canadians who cohabit have higher rates of divorce than those who do not; and cohabitation is becoming more prevalent after marital dissolution (Hall and Zhao 1995; Wu and Balakrishnan 1994).

The United States leads the industrialized world in both rates of marriage and rates of divorce. The average marriage rate among the twelve countries listed in table 2.7 was six for every thousand women in the population in 1988. By comparison, the U.S. rate in 1988 was 9.7, more than 50 percent higher than the international average. As for the divorce rate, the U.S. rate of 21.2 divorces for every thousand women is by far the highest among industrialized countries (Kamerman 1995).

Over time, marriage rates have been declining worldwide, and divorce rates have risen dramatically. Between 1969 and 1985, divorce laws in nearly every industrialized country were liberalized, and civil divorce was introduced in Catholic countries like Italy, Spain, and Portugal. A dramatic rise in divorce immediately after the legislation was followed by a leveling off in the 1980s.

Crude divorce rates say little about the underlying cultural causes, or consequences, of divorce. In the United States, a woman's labor force participation appears linked to divorce, but Scandinavian countries have much higher proportions of employed women and far lower rates of divorce (due partially to lower marriage rates) (McLanahan and Casper 1995, p. 15). In

TABLE 2.7 Marriage and Divorce Rates in Selected Countries

Country	1960 Marriage	1960 Divorce	1970 Marriage	1970 Divorce	1984/88 Marriage	1984/88 Divorce
Austria	8.3	5.0	7.1	5.9	6.1	—
Canada	7.3	1.7	8.8	—	7.4	12.9
Denmark	7.8	6.0	8.0	7.5	5.6	12.8
Federal Republic of Germany	9.4	3.4	7.1	5.0	5.9	8.3
Finland	7.4	4.1	8.6	6.0	5.9	—
France	7.0	2.8	7.7	3.1	5.1	8.5
Italy	7.8	—	7.4	—	5.2	1.1
Netherlands	7.8	2.2	9.5	3.3	5.7	8.7
Norway	6.6	2.8	7.6	3.7	5.0	—
Sweden	6.7	4.9	5.4	6.7	4.4	10.7
United Kingdom	7.5	2.2	8.5	5.5	7.0	12.9
United States	8.5	9.4	10.7	14.9	9.7	21.2

Source: Kamerman (1995), tables 6.1 and 6.2.
Note: Rates are marriages and divorces per one thousand women.

addition, rates of growth in female labor force participation were as great or greater in many other countries as in the United States, without the accompanying rise in divorce rates. Finally, divorce can have more negative economic consequences for American women than for women in other (often social democratic) countries (McLanahan and Casper 1995, p. 31). In no other country, however, does divorce touch as many women's lives and have as serious economic effects as it does in the United States.

Summary

Although American women still marry, they are doing so with greater hesitation than in the past. The median age for women at first marriage is now almost twenty-five and for men almost twenty-seven. Delayed marriages have coincided with high divorce rates. The number of divorced persons for every married adult more than quadrupled between 1960 and 1992, and approximately one-half of all marriages are now projected to end in divorce. Women today thus spend fewer years married than their mothers did.

Cohabitation has become such a popular alternative to first and second marriages that the majority of marriages formed since 1985 began as cohabitation. Cohabiting couples now account for 6 percent of all households and help explain the recent declines in rates of first and second marriages. The greater incidence of children in cohabiting households suggests that many single parents may be choosing cohabitation over remarriage, although approximately two-thirds of divorced women and three-quarters of divorced men eventually remarry.

Wives continue to outlive their husbands, and women spend more time widowed than men. In 1990, almost one-half of women aged sixty-five and over were widowed, compared with less than one-fifth of elderly men. Such extreme differentials persist because of women's longer life expectancy, their tendency to marry older men, and elderly men's tendency to remarry sooner than elderly women. The majority of elderly widows live alone, many in homes that they inherited when their husbands died.

The growth of households headed by women, while not new, remains an important theme in women's changing lives. In 1994,

29 percent of all households were maintained by women, and single mothers are more numerous than single fathers despite the recent increase in father-child families. Recent estimates are that about one-half of mothers with young children will become a single parent by age thirty-five.

The proportion of households maintained by women constitutes the most significant racial difference in family status: nearly one-half of black families are maintained by women, compared with less than one-fifth of white families. Asian families are least likely to be headed by a single mother, and Hispanic families are intermediate between whites and blacks. Household structure also has important implications for poverty and the quality of life for women and their children. For example, fewer than one-half of single mothers own their own homes, compared with 79 percent of married couples. Nearly 80 percent of elderly female family householders owned their own homes in 1993.

The United States is similar to other industrialized nations in its delay in first marriage and growth of cohabitation. Despite their recent decline, American divorce rates remain high, however, by international standards.

Changing marriage patterns and living arrangements already deeply color women's economic and social roles in American society, as we have seen here and as we shall see in subsequent chapters. Perhaps most important, a woman's decision about marriage and childbearing directly affects her educational and occupational opportunities—delaying family formation gives a young woman more time to complete her education and lay the foundation for a job or career. A complex of factors influences each woman's decision, including her family background and socioeconomic expectations, her employment prospects, and those of her potential partner. In the end, the woman who delays marriage or childbearing structures her life very differently from the woman who marries or becomes a mother at a young age.

CHAPTER 3

Education

SHANNON FAULKNER BECAME A FEMINIST SYMBOL OF EDUCATIONAL equality in 1995 when she enrolled in the all-male military academy The Citadel after a lengthy legal fight. When Faulkner, citing exhaustion from her prolonged battle for admission, left The Citadel only several days into her orientation, her supporters were saddened while her classmates jubilantly celebrated. Both her hard-won admission and the starkly different reactions to her departure demonstrate the remaining tensions surrounding women's gains in education.

Such stories make the news in the 1990s because it is now rare for a state-supported university to be single sex. It is hard for young women to realize that higher education (even in privately funded colleges) once had to be justified for women. Mary Lyon, for example, founded Mount Holyoke College in 1837 with the words "Oh, how immensely important is the preparation of the Daughters of the land to be good mothers." The Reverend Dr. Todd expressed similar sentiments at the opening of Rutgers Female College in 1867 when he stated that women should be "educated to feel that the highest glory of woman is the paradise of the home" (Watson 1977, p. 134).

Attitudes like these are seldom expressed today. Most Americans now believe that women and men should have equal access to higher education for the intellectual and occupational opportunities it provides. In the mid-1970s, for example, two-thirds of Americans agreed with the statement that "It is much better for everyone involved if the man is the achiever outside the home

51

and the woman takes care of the home and family." By the early 1990s, 40 percent of Americans agreed with this sentiment (Farley 1996).

"Equal access" typically means coeducation in public institutions, where 79 percent of all college students were enrolled in 1990 (U.S. Bureau of the Census 1992d, table A-1). Many single-sex colleges became coeducational during the 1970s, and the last bastions of publicly funded male military colleges (The Citadel in South Carolina and Virginia Military Institute) have come under increasing legal pressure to admit women. These developments are significant, since throughout American history the more gender integrated the educational opportunities, the higher women's status relative to men's (Spain 1992).

Like motherhood and marriage, the institution of higher education has been transformed both by law and by women's choices. Title IX of the Education Amendments of 1972 prohibits sex discrimination in all public and private institutions receiving federal funding. This legislation occurred concomitantly with the introduction of the birth control pill and legalized abortion. Thus, as women gained the reproductive rights that made long-term commitment to jobs or careers possible—and as the economy shifted to demand more educated labor—higher education became an alternative to motherhood and marriage and an avenue into the labor force.

As this chapter will demonstrate, the proportions of American women completing high school and earning college degrees continue to rise.[1] Three-quarters of adult women now have a high school degree compared with one-half in 1970. In 1990, almost one in five American women had a college degree, compared with fewer than one in ten in 1970. Women's college *enrollment* rates reached those of men during the 1980s, and young women now are just as likely as young men to *graduate* from college. Women also are earning professional degrees in increasing numbers.

The data reveal a number of other trends in women's higher education. Where once, college was a transition from a parents' home to a home (and family) of one's own, a college education now frequently occurs at a later stage of life. Women aged thirty-five and over form a much larger proportion of all women students today than in 1972 (and significantly outnumber older male students). Women during the 1980s also were more likely to attend college part time than during the 1970s and were more likely than men to be part-time students (U.S. Bureau of the Census 1992d, tables A-5, A-6). These developments suggest that instead of a transition *between* two life stages, and two distinct roles, school enrollment simply adds to the burgeoning layers that characterize women's lives.

Despite the obvious strides that women have made in their access to and use of higher education, obstacles remain. There is evidence, for instance, that fields of study (college majors) became more gender segregated during the 1980s, after two decades of convergence. In addition, returns to higher education for women continue to be lower than those for men. This last fact may be due to the types of colleges women attend (two-year versus four-year institutions), the selection of different majors, occupational choices, employer discrimination, or women's choices about how to balance family and work.

Educational Attainment

It is now widely understood that a person's education increasingly determines his or her ability to compete in today's economy. Approximately three-quarters of adult women and men had a high school degree in 1990, a significant increase since 1960. And as high school completion rates have risen, so have the number of persons proceeding to a college education. Eighteen percent of women and 24 percent of men aged twenty-five and over had earned college degrees in 1990 compared with 6 percent and 10 percent, respectively, in 1960. Age differences are marked, however. Older persons are far less likely to have graduated from college. For example, fewer than 10 percent of elderly women had earned a college degree in 1990, compared with 23 percent of women aged twenty-five to thirty-four (see table 3.1).

College graduation rates vary with the economic and cultural forces facing each generation. College degrees were rare, for instance, among those born at the turn of the century, but among those who did go women were about equally as likely as men to *complete* their degree. Succeeding cohorts of women, however, did not keep pace with men. The female-male divide reached its widest point for persons born during the Depression: many women of this generation married early and stayed home to raise

TABLE 3.1 Education of Women and Men in Selected Age Groups

Education and Age Group	Women				Men			
	1960	1970	1980	1990	1960	1970	1980	1990
Elementary (8 years or fewer)								
Total, 25 and over	37.5	26.9	17.3	10.2	41.2	27.2	17.8	10.4
25–34	16.9	9.7	4.8	3.5	21.5	11.2	5.1	4.3
35–44	24.7	14.8	8.1	4.2	28.3	18.2	10.0	5.2
45–54	39.3	23.6	14.8	7.1	43.0	25.5	17.4	8.9
55–64	54.3	36.8	21.8	12.8	58.5	42.0	24.2	15.5
65–74	65.6	50.7	34.8	18.4	70.9	58.4	39.5	20.7
75 and over	70.1	60.1	50.0	32.1	75.8	67.6	57.0	35.5

(continued)

High school (12 years or more)

Total, 25 and over	43.0	52.9	66.4	75.0	40.0	52.0	67.9	75.6
25–34	60.2	71.3	84.5	85.3	57.1	72.4	85.3	83.1
35–44	53.1	62.6	76.9	85.8	50.7	61.0	77.5	84.8
45–54	40.1	54.4	66.3	77.7	36.0	53.3	65.6	77.9
55–64	29.1	42.2	57.6	68.0	25.5	37.6	57.1	67.3
65–74	21.3	32.0	44.0	60.7	17.6	26.2	41.7	58.5
75 and over	18.5	25.8	34.3	46.3	15.1	21.0	29.3	44.0

College (16 years or more)

Total, 25 and over	5.8	7.9	12.9	17.8	9.6	13.5	20.4	23.5
25–34	7.4	12.3	20.7	22.7	14.4	19.2	26.1	23.4
35–44	6.3	8.4	14.8	24.6	11.4	17.6	24.8	30.1
45–54	6.0	6.9	10.0	17.7	8.4	12.5	19.7	25.7
55–64	5.0	6.9	8.3	11.6	6.3	9.1	14.7	20.3
65–74	3.1	5.4	7.6	8.9	4.7	6.7	10.6	15.3
75 and over	2.8	4.1	5.7	8.6	3.5	5.5	8.1	11.8

Source: 1960, 1970, 1980, and 1990 census Public Use Microdata Sample.
Note: Percentage completing each level.

FIGURE 3.1 Percentage of Degrees Conferred on Women

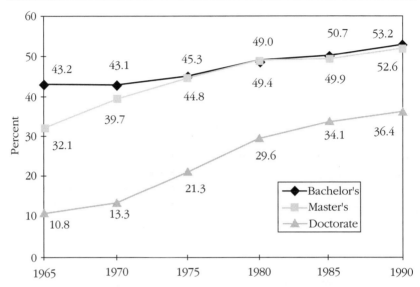

Source: National Center for Education Statistics, *Digest of Education Statistics,* selected years.

families, while their husbands enrolled in college courtesy of the G.I. Bill (Goldin 1992). When these women did attend college, they often went to earn the fabled "MRS" degree. (With so few occupational choices open to women, dropping out to marry a college-educated man, or to support his schooling, may have been a sound financial decision [Spain and Bianchi 1986].) For cohorts born since the 1950s, the gap has been narrowing. Among the youngest cohort, those born during the 1960s and later, the gap between women's and men's college completion rates has almost disappeared (Mare 1995).

Not only has the proportion of women completing college increased over time, but the proportion of all college degrees granted to women has increased. More than one-half of all bachelor's degrees now go to women, compared with 43 percent in 1965; the proportion of master's degrees granted to women rose from one-third to one-half. And the increase in the proportion of doctoral degrees awarded to women has shown the most dramatic increase rising from one-tenth to one-third since 1965 (see figure 3.1).

With regard to professional degrees, many women still enter traditionally female postgraduate programs, like the master's of education. However, growing numbers of women are competing for traditionally male degrees. A master's of business administration (MBA) was extremely rare for a woman in 1960, yet approximately twenty-five thousand women earned MBAs in 1990 (compared with more than fifty thousand men). Law and medicine also attracted more women during the 1970s and 1980s, with engineering showing a smaller rise (see figure 3.2).

Dentistry, medicine, and law schools have undergone significant transformations in the proportion of their enrolled and graduating students who are women. Almost no dentistry degrees were awarded to women in 1960 or 1970; by 1990, almost one-third of graduating dentists were women. The proportion of medical degrees granted to women rose significantly between 1960 and 1990 (from 6 percent to 34 percent), and the increased proportion of law degrees granted to women was truly remarkable—from 2 percent to 42 percent over the same period (see table 3.2). (Law, medicine, and dentistry are still overwhelmingly "male" professions, however, and will remain so until current levels of achievement persist for several generations. See chapter 4.)

Since law and business degrees are traditional routes to elective office, one would expect the proportion of women in politics to have risen over time. National data from the Center for the American Woman in Politics verify that women have become more politically active as their educational choices have expanded (see table 3.3). Women more than doubled their representation in Congress, statewide elective offices, and state legislatures between 1975 and 1995. In 1995, 8 percent of U.S. senators and 11 percent of U.S. representatives are women; 25 percent of these are women of color (Center for the American Woman in Politics 1995).

College Enrollment

More and more students attend college each year despite rising tuition costs. In 1990, one-third of young people aged eighteen to twenty-four were enrolled in college—13.6 million students compared with 7.4 million in 1970. By 1979, the number of women

FIGURE 3.2 Professional Degrees Conferred by Sex and Field: 1960–90

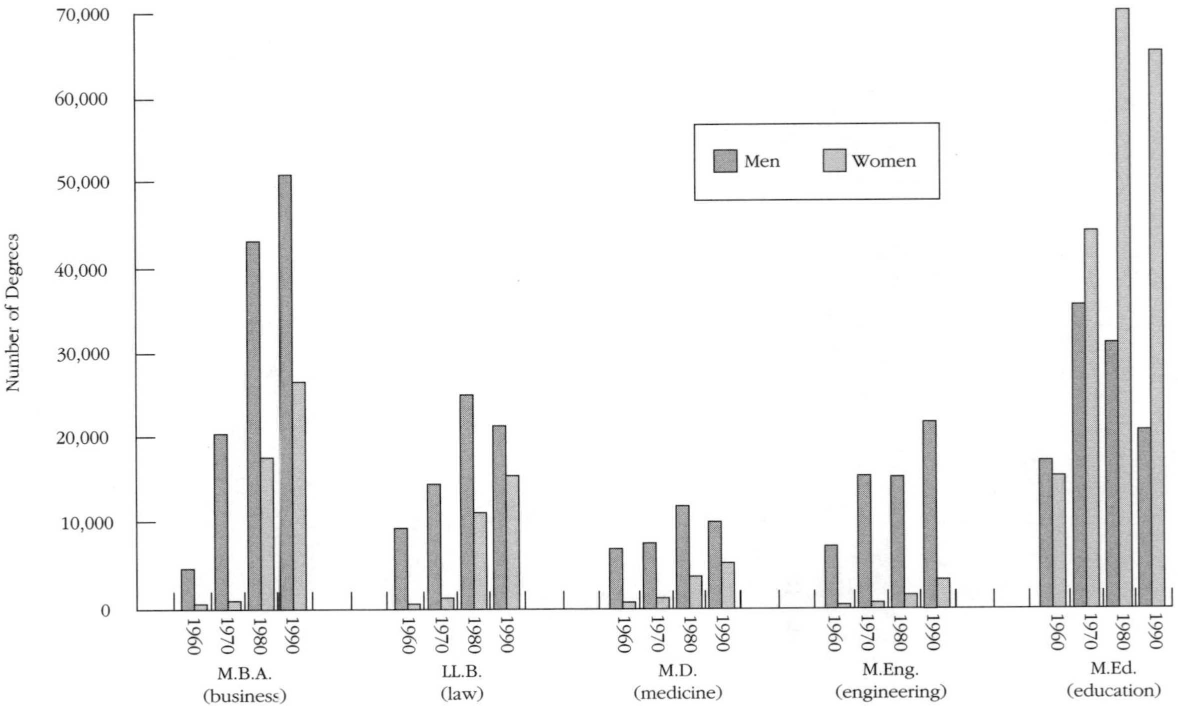

Source: U.S. Department of Education (1993).

TABLE 3.2 **Degrees in Dentistry, Medicine, and Law Granted to Women**

Year	Dentistry		Medicine		Law	
	Number	Percent	Number	Percent	Number	Percent
1960	26	0.8	387	5.5	230	2.5
1970	34	0.9	699	8.4	801	5.4
1980	700	13.3	3,486	23.4	10,754	30.2
1990	1,266	30.9	5,152	34.2	15,406	42.2

Source: National Center for Education Statistics (1994), table 249.

TABLE 3.3 **Percentage of Women in Elected Offices**

Office	1975	1985	1995
U.S. Congress	4	5	10
Statewide elective	10	14	26
State legislatures	8	15	21
County governing boards	3	8	—
Mayors and municipal councils	4	14	—

Source: Center for the American Woman in Politics (1995).

enrolled overtook the number of men, and women's edge continued to widen during the 1980s. In 1990, 7.4 million women were enrolled in college (compared with 6.2 million men) and women constituted 54 percent of the student body (U.S. Bureau of the Census 1992, table A-5). Much of this increase resulted from the expansion of community colleges. By the mid-1980s, community colleges enrolled almost one-third of all first-term students (Astin 1985, p. 80).

Women's enrollment rates have risen steadily since 1967, when they were 19 percent. Men's rates have fluctuated more—with atypically high rates at the height of the Vietnam War, when men could qualify for a draft deferment by attending college; then declining rates; and then a gradual rise to their current rate of 32 percent (U.S. Bureau of the Census 1992d, table A-4). By 1990, a young woman who graduated from high school was just as likely as a young man to enter college.

Female-male enrollment rates differ within the eighteen-to-twenty-four age group. For students aged eighteen and nineteen, men were more likely than women to enroll in college during the 1960s and 1970s, with the gap closing by the 1980s. Female and male students aged twenty and twenty-one have had consistently similar enrollment rates over time. And women students aged twenty-two and twenty-four actually have shown higher enrollment rates than men over the three decades (see figure 3.3).

The changing age structure of the student population is especially noticeable for women. In 1972 (the first year for which data on students aged thirty-five and over are available), women in their late thirties accounted for 11 percent of the female student body and men in their late thirties accounted for 7 percent of the male student body. By 1990, women aged thirty-five and over were 21 percent of all women in college, while men aged thirty-five and over were only 12 percent of all college men.

Part-time enrollment is one solution to the pressure of competing roles that older students may face. The proportion of women (and men) who attend college part time has increased during the past two decades and now stands at approximately 27 percent for women and 23 percent for men (U.S. Bureau of the Census 1992d, table A-6). Gender differences in part-time enrollment are not large, but since women students also are likely to be older than male students, the combination suggests that middle-aged women may be enrolling part time in an effort to juggle multiple roles. The advantage of such an approach is that one can work or raise a child while attending school. The disadvantage is that it takes longer to complete one's education, thus introducing the possibility that any hiring or promotion decisions influenced by age may penalize female college graduates more than male graduates.

Just as women are slightly more likely than men to attend college part time, they are also slightly more likely to attend two-year (community) colleges. In 1990, 35 percent of women students were enrolled in two-year colleges compared with 31 percent of male students (U.S. Bureau of the Census 1992d, table A-6). Community colleges are less expensive than four-year institutions and typically allow greater flexibility in scheduling classes (such as offering night courses). However, the returns to a community college degree—even among those who eventually transfer to, and graduate from, a four-year institution—are not as great

FIGURE 3.3 Percentage of Women and Men Enrolled
in College

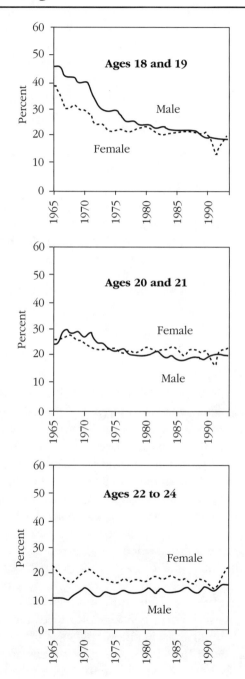

as those to a four-year college degree. In fact, community college attendance may translate into an occupational penalty for women and may perpetuate rather than ameliorate an already stratified system of higher education (Lee and Frank 1990; Monk-Turner 1990).

College Major

As college enrollment and completion rates for women have improved, new fields of study have opened as well. Traditionally masculine undergraduate majors, like architecture and business, have shown striking changes since 1970 in the proportion of degrees awarded to women: 39 percent of bachelor's degrees in architecture went to women in 1990 compared with only 5 percent in 1970, and nearly one-half of undergraduate business degrees were awarded to women in 1990 compared with less than 10 percent in 1970. Changes in the biological and physical sciences have been nearly as dramatic. Traditionally female fields of study, however, have remained largely female (such as the health professions, library sciences, and education), and engineering remains a male domain (see table 3.4).

The story is similar at the master's level: architecture and business have changed most dramatically, followed by the biological and physical sciences. An increasing proportion of master's degrees in psychology are going to women, as are degrees in mathematics. At the doctoral level, the proportion of doctoral degrees awarded to women in the biological sciences more than doubled between 1970 and 1990, as they did in mathematics, psychology, and the social sciences. Engineering, math, and the physical sciences grant the lowest proportion of such degrees to women.

Men's persistent dominance in mathematics (and fields dependent on math skills, like engineering and physical sciences) has roots that extend back to the secondary-school experiences of students. Whereas boys and girls in elementary school have equivalent math skills, significant gender differences emerge soon thereafter (Hyde, Fennema, and Lamon 1990; see Catsambis 1994, for a dissenting analysis). Ironically, the gap widens among the brightest students, as boys in middle school take advantage of neigh-

TABLE 3.4 Percentage of Degrees in Selected Fields of Study Conferred on Women: 1970 and 1990

Field of Study	Bachelor's		Master's		Doctorate	
	1970	1990	1970	1990	1970	1990
Architecture	5.2	39.1	6.5	36.3	9.1	29.1
Biological sciences	27.8	50.1	31.5	51.0	14.2	35.4
Business	8.7	46.8	3.5	34.0	1.6	24.9
Education	75.0	78.1	55.3	75.9	20.3	57.8
Engineering	0.7	13.8	1.1	13.8	0.6	8.9
English and literature	66.9	67.9	61.0	65.9	31.0	55.6
Fine and applied arts	57.2	61.0	47.0	56.3	19.3	44.4
Foreign languages	73.4	73.8	62.7	69.8	33.4	61.6
Health professions	78.0	84.3	52.0	77.6	16.2	54.2
Home economics	97.2	91.2	94.2	85.0	71.6	76.8
Library sciences	91.8	93.5	83.0	79.2	40.0	60.7
Mathematics	37.4	46.2	29.6	40.1	7.8	17.8
Physical sciences	13.6	31.3	14.2	26.6	5.4	19.4
Psychology	43.3	71.5	38.0	67.5	22.3	58.1
Religion (theology)	30.6	42.1	24.5	37.1	3.4	24.6
Social sciences	37.1	44.2	35.3	40.7	13.0	32.9

Source: National Center for Education Statistics, series P60, selected years.
Note: Biological sciences listed as life sciences for 1990. Fine and applied arts listed as visual and performing arts for 1990. Library sciences listed as library and archival sciences for 1990. Religion refers to study within the field of philosophy and religion for 1990.

borhood resources that improve their math skills (Entwisle, Alexander, and Olson 1994). Gender differences in math intensify in high school, a fact that influences the choice of college major and ultimately of a graduate's income potential (Wilson and Boldizar 1990).

Between the late 1960s and early 1980s, gender segregation by subject dropped significantly, but the pace of that convergence has since slowed considerably. In 1964, approximately one-half of women college students would have had to change majors to achieve the distribution of men's majors. By 1984, only one-third of women would have had to change majors to match men's majors. Between 1985 and 1990, however, the level of gender segregation among recipients of all postsecondary degrees declined only slightly. The slowdown occurred because of a decline in women entering traditionally male fields, since few men have entered traditionally female fields. Paralleling this change was a similar shift that occurred during the student's years in college, with students actually demonstrating a slight *increase* in the extent of segregation between their first and last years in school (Jacobs 1995).

Finally, enrolling, choosing a major, and graduating are the end results of a series of factors that determine who is most likely to attend college. Women and men who attend college probably have more in common with each other than they do with others of the same age who do not go to college, but gender differences in the path to college persist.

Paths to Higher Education

The more highly educated the parents, the more highly educated their children are likely to be. For example, children whose mothers graduated from high school are twice as likely to finish high school as those whose mothers did not graduate, and children whose mothers finished college are more likely to finish college themselves. The mother's educational attainment has a particularly strong effect for women, while the father's education has a strong influence on sons (Kalmijn 1994). Since women's college graduation rates are just now catching up with men's, it will take several generations for mothers to transmit higher educational goals to their daughters. As educational attainment increases for women and men, and as the similarities between husbands' and wives' educations increase, each successive generation constructs an "educational floor" below which children are unlikely to fall, providing a platform for further intergenerational attainment (Mare 1991, 1995, p. 181; Qian and Preston 1993).

Not surprisingly, family income affects the educational achievements of children. Affluent families tend to live in neighborhoods with the best public schools, or are able to afford private schools, that create opportunities for elite colleges (Persell, Catsambis, and Cookson 1992). They also can provide the shelter, food, and clothing that make success in school easier to achieve (Entwisle and Alexander 1995). And in an era of rising college tuitions, wealthy families are able to provide (or heavily subsidize) college costs and to forgo childrens' earnings (Mare 1995, pp. 177, 181; Steelman and Powell 1991).

One aspect of family background that affects children's likelihood of educational attainment, independent of parents' education or income, is the presence of a father. Children raised in female-headed families are less likely to finish high school or college than children raised in two-parent households because never married and divorced mothers tend to be economically disadvantaged, have more difficulty monitoring their children's activities, and have less access to community support networks (McLanahan and Sandefur 1994). Child-support payments do little to replace the income lost through divorce, and, as nonmarital childbearing increases, child support is becoming less effective in mitigating the negative effects of living in a single-parent family on the educational attainment of children (even though children are eligible for support until age twenty-one) (Hernandez, Beller, and Graham 1995). The growth of female-headed families may eventually slow rates of high school graduation, although that trend may be offset by smaller family size, since educational attainment is higher for children with fewer siblings (Mare 1995, pp. 178, 182).

Two factors associated with college completion for women are age at first marriage and fertility. Early marriage and higher education tend to conflict—the earlier the age at marriage, the lower the educational attainment—especially for women. Thus, partners in teenage marriages seldom complete college, although husbands are more likely to do so than wives. The negative correlation between age at marriage and educational attainment has been documented since the 1950s, but disagreement exists about the causality. Both early marriage and lower educational attainment may be a result of lower socioeconomic status, or marriage may act independently to lower educational levels.

Not all women end their schooling when they marry. One national sample found that one-fifth of married woman had attended high school or college since marrying, and that two-fifths intended to remain in school. Women who had attended some college before marriage were more likely to continue their education after marriage (Bianchi and Spain 1986, p. 125).

Women and men have other reasons besides marriage, of course, for interrupting their schooling. Taking time off between high school and college (or dropping out of college) to work or join the military are two possibilities. Attending school part time and working part time are other examples of the ways in which women and men make the transition from full-time schooling to full-time work. Increasing numbers of students are choosing this nonlinear path, and marriage before completion of schooling may be one of its components (Bianchi and Spain 1986, p. 126).

Early childbearing can also hinder a woman's educational achievement. The role of mother is even more time consuming than that of wife and can limit a woman's ability to continue in school. Young women who bear a child in their teens, for example, average 1.5 years less schooling than young childless women. Women with early first births also tend to have lower educational goals. The direction of causality in the relationship between education and fertility is unclear, however. Education may affect fertility by postponing the first birth and thus reducing the number of children ever born. Higher education also contributes to more effective contraceptive use, higher labor force participation, and preferences for fewer children, all of which result in lower fertility (Bianchi and Spain 1986, pp. 126–128).

Returns to Higher Education

The higher a woman's educational attainment, the more likely she is to be in the labor force and to work full time. This pattern has remained stable since 1960. In 1990, over three-quarters of women with postgraduate degrees were in the labor force compared with one-half of those with a high school degree (and less than one-third of those without a high school degree). About 40 percent of college-educated women worked full time and year round in 1990 compared with one-third of high school graduates and 15 percent of those without a high school degree (see table 3.5). The patterns are even more pronounced for younger women.

Table 3.5 also demonstrates that the proportion of all adult women without a high school degree who are in the labor force has remained stable at approximately one-third since 1960. By contrast, the proportion of women with high school or college degrees who are in the labor force has risen dramatically. Forty percent of female high school graduates were employed in 1960 compared with 55 percent in 1990; the comparable figures for college graduates are 48 and 72 percent.

TABLE 3.5 Labor Force Participation Rates of Women
by Education

Age and Years of School Completed	Percent in Labor Force				Percent Who Worked Full Time, Year Round			
	1960	1970	1980	1990	1960	1970	1980	1990
25 and over	35.3	40.8	48.4	55.8	14.9	17.3	22.3	31.0
Not high school graduate	30.8	33.3	30.8	31.0	12.0	13.1	12.4	14.7
High school, 4 years	39.1	46.7	53.6	55.1	19.5	21.9	26.6	31.3
College, 1 to 3 years	40.9	44.8	58.8	68.3	18.0	20.4	29.6	40.8
4 years	47.7	50.0	62.3	72.2	15.8	15.4	27.0	39.6
5 years or more	66.6	66.0	72.7	78.2	19.7	21.7	26.5	39.4
25–34	34.8	44.9	64.5	74.1	13.6	16.6	29.2	41.6
Not high school graduate	33.2	39.3	48.6	52.4	10.7	12.5	16.8	21.7
High school, 4 years	34.3	44.4	61.7	71.6	15.7	18.2	28.9	39.8
College, 1 to 3 years	35.5	46.4	69.5	79.3	14.6	20.4	34.6	46.6
4 years	41.6	53.4	74.8	83.1	14.6	14.9	35.0	50.6
5 years or more	58.6	70.6	79.6	87.2	17.6	21.9	30.3	47.8

Source: 1960, 1970, 1980, and 1990 census Public Use Microdata Sample.

Full-time commitment to employment shows a similar pattern by educational attainment. Women without a high school diploma were only slightly more likely to be working full time and year round in 1990 than in 1960, while participation increases for better educated women. Comparisons among younger women (aged twenty-five to thirty-four) show consistent gains in labor force participation over time, with even more pronounced differences by educational level (see table 3.5): those with a college degree more than tripled their representation as full-time employees (15 percent to 51 percent) and those with a high school degree more than doubled their proportions (16 percent to 40 percent).

Among women who are employed full time, year round, those with college or postgraduate degrees are more likely than those with less education to hold managerial or professional jobs (see table 3.6). Surprising in 1990, perhaps, is that women with some college education are as likely as high school graduates to

TABLE 3.6 Occupations of Full-Time, Year-Round Workers Aged 25 and Over by Education: 1990 (percent)

Occupational Group	High School, 4 Years		College, 1 to 3 Years		College, 4 Years		College, 5 Years or More	
	Women	Men	Women	Men	Women	Men	Women	Men
Total	100.0	100.0	100.0	100.0	100.0	100.0	100.0	100.0
Executive, managerial	11.9	8.4	18.5	16.7	26.7	32.0	22.5	27.7
Professional specialty	3.5	2.5	11.1	7.4	33.6	23.4	60.3	53.3
Technicians	2.8	2.4	5.8	6.8	5.9	5.9	4.8	4.2
Sales	10.9	10.0	9.6	14.0	10.7	17.8	4.0	6.5
Administrative support, including clerical	40.1	7.2	40.3	9.2	16.6	6.0	4.6	2.4

(continued)

Private household	0.3	0.0	0.2	0.0	0.1	0.0	0.0	0.0
Protective service	0.5	2.8	0.7	4.9	0.7	2.3	0.3	0.8
Other service	12.4	6.2	7.0	4.1	2.9	1.9	2.2	1.1
Farming, forestry, fishing	0.8	4.0	0.3	2.4	0.4	1.5	0.2	0.5
Precision production, including craft	3.8	29.2	2.1	21.6	0.9	5.8	0.7	2.4
Machine operators	9.7	11.8	3.1	5.9	1.0	1.4	0.3	0.4
Transportation workers	0.7	9.8	0.4	4.2	0.1	1.2	0.2	0.5
Handlers, laborers	2.5	5.9	0.7	2.8	0.3	0.8	0.1	0.2

Source: 1990 census Public Use Microdata Sample.

be clerical workers (40 percent). There is no comparable occupational concentration among men: about one-third of male high school graduates are blue-collar workers (operators, transportation workers, laborers) and those with some college are divided among precision production work, sales, and management. Among college-educated men, approximately one-third work as managers or executives, compared with one-quarter of well-educated women.

As one would expect given these occupational distributions, women with college degrees earn less than men with college degrees, partly because they work in jobs that pay less well. (The reasons for this disparity are discussed in greater detail in chapter 6.) In 1989, a woman with a college degree who worked full time, year round earned $27,000 annually—approximately what a man with a high school degree earned—compared with a male college graduate's median earnings of nearly $38,000. Whereas almost one-third of men with a college degree (and nearly one-half of men with postgraduate degrees) earn $50,000 or more annually, only 7 percent of women with a college degree and 19 percent of women with a postgraduate degree fall into that salary range (see table 3.7).

This differential return to education persists for various reasons. One is that women with some college education tend to work in lower-paid white-collar jobs (such as nonunionized secretarial positions), while men without a college degree tend to work in more highly paid blue-collar (unionized) jobs. Structural changes that have occurred in the economy in the 1980s and early 1990s, including the weakening of unions, may narrow men's advantage in the future. Although women initially tend to hold jobs with higher status (though not higher pay), men hold the advantage at midcareer. A self-fulfilling prophecy may also operate: not only do female college graduates earn less than their male colleagues, but they *expect* to earn less (Smith and Powell 1990). In other words, women may be less likely to negotiate a high starting salary or to push for significant raises as they progress in their career.

While differences in white-collar occupational categories partially explain the enduring earnings differentials between women and men with comparable educations, field of study

Table 3.7 Earnings of Full-Time, Year-Round Workers Aged 25 and Over by Education: 1989 (percent)

Earnings	High School, 4 Years		College, 1 to 3 Years		College, 4 Years		College, 5 Years or More	
	Women	Men	Women	Men	Women	Men	Women	Men
Total	100.0	100.0	100.0	100.0	100.0	100.0	100.0	100.0
Under $10,000	12.0	4.9	7.1	3.3	3.8	2.4	2.8	2.3
$10,000 to $14,999	25.6	10.1	17.2	7.1	7.7	3.5	4.0	2.6
$15,000 to $19,999	25.2	15.0	23.6	11.5	13.2	5.7	7.1	2.4
$20,000 to $24,999	17.2	16.5	19.9	13.8	18.9	9.4	11.7	5.0
$25,000 to $29,999	9.5	14.1	13.4	13.5	17.6	10.4	13.9	6.7
$30,000 to $34,999	4.7	13.3	8.9	13.9	14.0	12.1	14.0	7.5
$35,000 to $49,999	4.4	18.7	7.7	22.7	18.0	26.9	27.2	25.0
$50,000 and over	1.4	7.4	2.3	14.2	6.8	29.6	19.4	48.4
Median (1989 dollars)	17,454	26,249	20,536	30,282	26,812	37,698	33,780	49,285

Source: 1990 census Public Use Microdata Sample.
Note: Medians interpolated from distributions shown.

in college also accounts for some of the gap. Men still dominate the more prestigious and lucrative subject areas. Since the gender composition of the college major largely determines the subsequent gender composition of the occupation, skewed distributions of majors can have prolonged effects on lifetime earnings (Wilson and Boldizar 1990). Controlling for college major, however, reduces but does not eliminate the gender differences in returns to education (Bianchi and Spain 1986, p. 135).

Racial and Ethnic Comparisons

A high school diploma in the past, and a college diploma now, can provide upward mobility for economically disadvantaged minority and immigrant groups. Yet racial and ethnic groups vary greatly in the extent to which they achieve educational levels. Variation also exists between those members of an ethnic or racial group born in the United States and those born abroad.

All racial and ethnic groups, and women in those groups, have improved their rates of high school and college completion over time. Black, American Indian, and Hispanic students have made the greatest gains in high school graduation rates and are closing the gap with white and Asian students. About one-half of Hispanics had a high school degree in 1990 compared with one-third in 1970; about two-thirds of blacks and American Indians had high school diplomas in 1990 compared with one-third in 1970; and around 80 percent of Asians and whites were high school graduates in 1990 compared with two-thirds and one-half, respectively, in 1970 (see table 3.8).

Asian women had significantly higher rates of college completion in 1990 than women of any other racial-ethnic group (32 percent, double what it had been in 1970). About 20 percent of white women had completed college in 1990, compared with 12 percent of black women and less than 10 percent of American Indian and Hispanic women. Although non-Asian women in all minority groups doubled their rates of college graduation between 1970 and 1990, they still lagged far behind white and Asian women.

Table 3.8 Education of Women and Men Aged 25 and Over by Race and Ethnicity

	1970		1980		1990	
	Women	Men	Women	Men	Women	Men
All races						
Percent high school graduates	52.9	52.0	66.4	67.9	75.0	75.6
Percent college graduates	7.9	13.5	12.9	20.4	17.8	23.5
White						
Percent high school graduates	55.0	54.0	68.9	70.3	78.5	79.6
Percent college graduates	8.4	14.4	13.6	21.7	18.8	25.6
Black						
Percent high school graduates	32.5	30.1	51.6	50.8	64.0	62.3
Percent college graduates	4.6	4.2	8.3	8.5	11.8	11.0
American Indian						
Percent high school graduates	33.0	33.6	54.1	57.0	65.3	65.8
Percent college graduates	3.1	4.5	6.3	9.2	8.9	10.1
Asian						
Percent high school graduates	64.2	64.8	71.4	78.8	74.0	81.5
Percent college graduates	14.7	25.1	27.0	39.8	31.9	41.9
Hispanic						
Percent high school graduates	34.2	37.9	42.7	45.4	49.9	49.8
Percent college graduates	4.3	7.8	6.0	9.4	8.2	9.8

Source: Harrison and Bennett (1995), figure 4.5 and table 4A.1.

International Comparisons

Colleges and universities in the United States are among the most gender integrated in the world, although the United States is *not* ranked first in proportion of all college students that are women. That distinction belongs to Canada (at 55 percent), followed by France, Australia, the United States, and Denmark. Other industrialized countries report female enrollments of less than 50 percent (see figure 3.4).

The tendency for Western European men to predominate in higher education appears to be changing. Data for the European Union indicate that in the 1991–92 school year slightly more women than men went on to higher education (82 percent of women compared with 78 percent of men) (United Nations 1995, p. 93).

The representation of women in math, scientific, and engineering fields is typically low in industrialized nations, although it varies cross-culturally. The former Federal Republic of Germany, Japan, the Netherlands, Norway, Sweden, and the United Kingdom have low percentages of women in mathematical, scientific, and technical fields compared with France, Italy, Portugal, Spain, and the United States (United Nations 1995, pp. 96, 97). A cross-national study found that math scores among eighth-grade girls are higher in societies in which women have greater access to education and typically "male" occupations (Baker and Jones 1993).

The negative relationship between educational attainment and fertility demonstrated by women in the United States holds in other industrialized nations as well. In the Federal Republic of Germany, for example, women's extended school enrollment delays their transition to marriage and motherhood (Blossfeld and Huinink 1991). In general, across nations, more highly educated women marry later, want fewer children, and are more likely to use contraception effectively than women with less education (United Nations 1995, p. 92).

Summary

Women's enrollment in colleges and universities now exceeds that of men, and the youngest cohorts of women are graduating from college at rates equal to men's for the first time in history. Female college students are likely to be older than male students, however, and are more likely than men to attend college part time and to attend community colleges. Bachelor's and master's degrees are as likely to be awarded to women as to men, and one-third of doctoral degrees now go to women. One-third or more of profes-

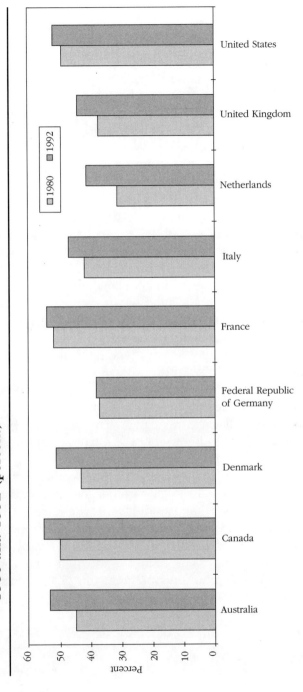

FIGURE 3.4 Women in Institutions of Higher Education for Selected Industrialized Countries for 1980 and 1992 (percent)

Source: United Nations (1994), table 13. France 1980 uses 1985 data. Netherlands 1992 uses 1988 data.

sional degrees in law, medicine, and business are now granted to women, and these specialties have helped propel women into public office in record-high numbers.

Paths to higher education are similar for women and men in that both daughters and sons benefit from being raised in affluent, well-educated, two-parent families. Women's education, however, is more likely than men's to be interrupted by early marriage or early family formation.

The more educated a woman, the more likely she is to work outside the home, although the returns to higher education for women generally lag behind those for men. Women with some college education are as likely to work as secretaries as women who stopped at a high school degree. In 1990, a college-educated woman who worked full time and year round earned only as much as a man with a high school degree. This could result from differences in the subjects that college women study, from a greater probability of their attending a community college, from different occupational choices, from employer discrimination, or from family choices that affect women's educational attainment. Women's greater likelihood of attending college part time and their older ages may also affect women's occupational and earnings profiles.

Racial and ethnic status influences high school and college graduation rates. Black, American Indian, and Hispanic students have made progress in high school graduation rates and are closing the gap with whites and Asians. Asian women have the highest college completion rates and Hispanic women have the lowest. The United States is similar to other industrialized nations in the proportion of its college students that are female.

A college degree may not yet open professional doors as quickly or as fully for women as for men but it clearly is doing so with greater frequency. The higher graduation rates for younger women, therefore, are an encouraging sign of women's progress in public and professional spheres.

CHAPTER 4

Labor Force Participation and Occupational Attainment

IN A SINGLE GENERATION, THE LIVES OF AMERICAN WOMEN HAVE UNDERGONE a remarkable transformation. Women who started families in the 1950s generally stayed home to raise their children; their daughters most often choose to work as they raise families. That such an enormous change in family lifestyle could occur in the span of a few decades testifies not only to changing attitudes about women's participation in the workforce but also to a labor market that has been able to attract and absorb women's labor.

Baby boom women have attended to the demands of jobs and babies simultaneously rather than sequentially for a variety of reasons. As previous chapters have shown, later age at marriage, rising educational attainment, the high divorce rate and women's ensuing realization that they must be able to support themselves (and their children) financially, the women's movement and changing attitudes about the desirability of working outside the home, the contraceptive revolution and the increased control these women had over the timing of their fertility, the stagnating wages of males after 1974 necessitating two-income families, and the relatively high consumption standards formed by a cohort raised in comfortable, often affluent, baby boom households all have shaped women's decisions over the past several decades.[1]

Trends in Labor Force Participation

Contrary to popular impression, the increased participation of women in *market* work—although it accelerated in the postwar decades (Goldin 1990) to reach the point where by 1994 59 percent of all women were in the labor force—is a story that has been unfolding since at least the early nineteenth century. As the United States began to shift from an agricultural to an industrial economy in the nineteenth century, the demand for factory workers grew. Women, most often young single women, filled some of that need. Then, as the service sector of the economy expanded in the early twentieth century, the demand for clerical workers increased, women again helped fill the demand. As a result, the employment of single women increased substantially between 1890 and 1920. When the supply of young, single women was not sufficient to meet demand, married women were accepted (Goldin 1990; Oppenheimer 1970). Although the Great Depression dampened employment generally, and women's employment particularly (Goldin 1990; J.G. Robinson 1988), married women's participation in the paid labor force grew slowly but steadily between 1920 and 1940. After 1940, the increase in married women's employment accelerated.

During the 1950s and early 1960s, older, married women returned to the labor force in great numbers after raising their children, filling jobs in the expanding clerical and service sectors of the economy, while younger women were occupied in the home rearing their relatively large, baby boom families. To quote from Gertrude Bancroft's monograph on the 1950 census:

> Typically, in the 1950s American girls seek jobs on leaving school, marry shortly thereafter, and continue working until they start having children, when they retire for a period of years. While they are in the labor force at the beginning of their working lives, they are probably doing clerical or secretarial work in an office or selling in a retail store. It is probable that after they send their last child off to school they will return to the labor force, voluntarily and with enthusiasm, not to pursue a career for which

they have been prepared by school and college but to supplement the family income at whatever kind of work is both available and agreeable. (Bancroft 1958, p. 38)

Bancroft did not anticipate the rise in age at first marriage, the decline in fertility, and the increase in educational attainment of women—all of which dramatically changed the labor force participation rates of young women over the ensuing decades. Nor did anyone predict that mothers of small children would remain in the labor force during their child rearing years. As a consequence, Bancroft's mid-1950 projections of labor force participation for women under age thirty-five proved much too low by 1975. Actual participation of women age twenty-five to thirty-four, projected by Bancroft to be 39 percent in 1975, stood at 55 percent in 1975 and increased to 74 percent in 1994 (see table 4.1). The story of the past two decades has been this rise in participation by younger women with families.

Many women now postpone family formation to complete education and establish themselves in the labor force (see chapter 1). Despite family obligations, a majority of women of all educational levels now work outside the home during the years they are raising children. Women's labor market involvement is still lower than men's, but there is no doubt that the economic activity of the two genders has become more similar in recent decades. Increasingly, it is viewed as "normal" for adult women, regardless of parental status, to be employed outside the home.

During this century, the number of women in the paid labor force increased dramatically—from about five million women in 1900 to more than sixty million by the mid-1990s (see table 4.2). At the turn of the century, only about one worker in five was a woman, and the pace at which the paid labor force "feminized" was fairly slow during the first four decades of this century. On the eve of American involvement in World War II, only one in four workers was a woman. But during the subsequent five decades, women's participation increased steadily and men's participation declined slightly, so that today we are approaching a situation in which one-half of the U.S. workforce is female.

During the 1980s, the female labor force grew at a rate that far exceeded the country's overall population growth. The number of

TABLE **4.1 Projected and Actual Labor Force Participation Rates for 1975 and 1994**

Sex and Age	Projected for 1975 in 1958	Actual in 1975	Difference (Actual-Projected)	Actual in 1994
Women	38.2	46.3	8.2	58.8
14–19	28.1	49.1	—	51.3
20–24	47.8	64.1	16.3	71.0
25–34	38.9	54.6	15.7	74.0
35–44	48.9	55.8	6.9	77.1
45–54	53.2	54.6	1.4	74.6
55–64	41.0	41.0	0.0	48.9
65 and over	11.6	8.3	−3.3	9.2
Men	78.9	77.9	−1.0	75.1
14–19	43.4	59.1	—	54.1
20–24	86.8	84.6	−2.2	83.1
25–34	96.8	95.3	−1.5	92.6
35–44	97.3	95.7	−1.6	92.8
45–54	95.6	92.1	−3.8	89.1
55–64	87.1	75.8	−11.3	65.5
65 and over	30.6	21.7	−8.9	16.9

Source: U.S. Bureau of Labor Statistics (1978, 1995), table 91; Bancroft (1958), table 3.
Note: Figures shown in the first column represent the average of four projections made by Gertrude Bancroft based on 1920 and 1950–55 data; the difference between the actual and projected labor force participation rate of the youngest age group is not calculated because the 1958 projection is for the 14–19 age group whereas the actual participation rates available for 1975 and 1994 are for the 16–19 age group.

women in the labor force increased by more than eleven million during the decade as women's commitment to paid employment intensified; by contrast, women workers would have increased by only five million if they were simply keeping pace with population growth. The seven million male workers added during the decade was actually 1.2 million *fewer* than might have been expected given population growth and men's participation rates at the beginning of the decade. (During the 1980s, men's rate of participation declined somewhat among all age groups [Wetzel 1995, table 2.1].)

Because table 4.2 focuses on the entire adult population, it includes many individuals whom we might not expect to be participating in paid work. For example, those over age sixty-five, and increasingly men between the ages of fifty-five and sixty-four, often have retired from the labor force. At the other end of the

TABLE 4.2 Women in the Labor Force

Year	Number in Thousands	Percentage of Total Labor Force	Percentage of All Women
1900	4,999	18.1	20.0
1910	8,076	21.2	23.4
1920	8,229	20.4	22.7
1930	10,396	21.9	23.6
1940	13,007	24.6	25.8
1950	18,389	29.6	33.9
1960	23,240	33.4	37.7
1970	31,543	38.1	43.3
1980	45,487	42.5	51.5
1990	56,554	45.3	57.5
1994	60,239	46.0	58.8

Source: U.S. Bureau of the Census (1976), series D11-25 and D29-41; (1979), table 1; (1989), tables 1 and 2; (1984), table 1; (1994), table 3.
Note: Labor force data for 1900–30 refer to gainfully employed workers aged 10 and over; data for 1940 include the labor force aged 14 and over; data for 1950–93 refer to the civilian labor force aged 16 and over. Figures for 1950–93 are based on annual averages derived from the Current Population Survey; figures for 1990–40 are based on the decennial census.

age spectrum, many of those between the ages of sixteen and twenty-four are still in school. Table 4.3, which is restricted to the population in the prime working ages of twenty-five to fifty-four, provides a better indication of just how pervasive market work has become for women in the United States. In 1950, 97 percent of men in this age range, compared with 37 percent of women, were in the labor force, a difference of 60 percentage points. By 1994, women's participation rate had jumped to 75 percent, compared with 92 percent of men, a difference of only 16 percentage points.

Women's labor force participation has increased in each decade since 1950, but there have been significant changes in the age groups accounting for this increase. Typically, men's patterns look like an arch or an inverted U (see figure 4.1). That is, rates increase as men finish school and enter the labor force. By their late twenties, most men are in the labor force and will remain there more or less continuously until they retire in their late fifties and sixties. Women's patterns, on the other hand, typically have dipped as women enter their childbearing years. That is, they are

TABLE 4.3 Gender Differences in Labor Force Participation for Prime-Working-Age Population

Year	Percent in Labor Force		Difference (M-W)	Ratio (W/M)
	Men	Women		
1950	96.5	36.8	59.7	.38
1960	97.0	42.9	54.1	.44
1970	95.8	50.1	45.7	.52
1980	94.2	64.0	30.2	.68
1990	93.3	74.2	19.1	.80
1994	91.7	75.3	16.4	.82

Source: U.S. Bureau of Labor Statistics (1989, 1991, 1995).

highest in the early twenties before women marry and start having children; they drop off as women leave the labor force to have children; and they increase as some of these women return to market work after their children enter school. This is the sort of pattern Bancroft refers to as typifying women's participation in the 1950s.

This pattern is apparent in 1950 1960, and 1970, and it is clear that the biggest increases in labor force participation in the 1950s were for women in their forties and fifties, women beyond the years of most intensive child rearing responsibilities. But by the late 1960s, this pattern began to change. Since then, the largest increase in labor force participation has been among women in their twenties and thirties—women most likely to be raising small children. The increased participation of young women in the 1970s, when the first wave of baby boom women was entering the labor force, was particularly dramatic (figure 4.1; Wetzel 1995, figure 2.1).

By 1990, labor force participation rates no longer dipped for women in their twenties. Younger women's labor force participation rates were still lower than men's rates and rose less steeply, but in 1990 women's age pattern of participation looked more like men's than it did like women's patterns in the 1950s or 1960s.

All the numbers we have examined thus far refer to whether an individual was in the labor force—that is, had a job or was looking for work—in a given week. The previous year also forms the reference period for the decennial censuses and the Current

FIGURE 4.1 Labor Force Participation by Age and Sex

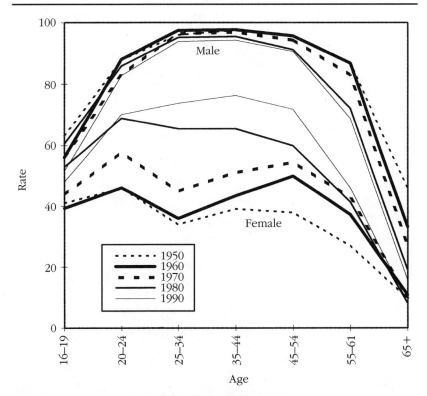

Source: U.S. Bureau of Labor Statistics (1989), table 5; (1991).

Population Survey (CPS), the two main data sources for employment and unemployment trends in the United States. The decennial censuses and the March CPS surveys also ask about the number of weeks a person actually worked in the previous year and
the number of hours per week. In the United States, year-round
employment has typically been defined as working fifty to fifty-
two weeks a year, and full-time employment is usually defined as
working at least thirty-five hours a week.

From these employment data, three trends emerge that point
to a narrowing of the gender difference in employment. Figure 4.2
helps illustrate each trend. First, the percentage of women who
did *not* work during the preceding year declined precipitously

FIGURE 4.2 Weeks Worked per Year for Women and Men

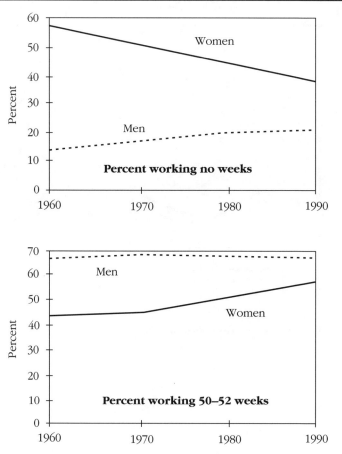

Source: 1960, 1970, 1980, and 1990 census Public Use Microdata Samples.

between 1960 and 1990—from 57 to 38 percent. Second, the percentage of men who did *not* work during the year increased from 14 to 21 percent. Finally, women's commitment to year-round work increased. The percentage of female workers employed fifty to fifty-two weeks a year increased from 43 to 57 percent between 1960 and 1990. Women workers in 1990 were working more weeks a year but not necessarily more hours a week than women workers in 1960, so that women workers in 1990 continued to work fewer hours a week than male workers.

Perhaps as much as 40 percent of the overall increase in women's labor force participation in the 1970s and 1980s was related to the continued shift toward those more likely to be employed—that is, better educated, unmarried, and childless women (Lichter and Costanzo 1987; Zhan 1992). But behaviors and normative conditions in society were also changing, either as cause or, perhaps more often, as consequence of demographic change, educational upgrading, and market demand. Whether women were wives and mothers came to matter less and less.

Throughout the 1970s and 1980s, the group with the lowest rate of labor force participation historically—married women with children—increased their participation most rapidly. By 1990, almost three-quarters of married women with children under age eighteen worked in the paid labor force, and one-third of married mothers worked full time and year round (Hayghe and Bianchi 1994). By 1990, most married mothers with young children had some involvement in market work, and many worked year round, although the majority of married mothers were part-time workers.

Stresses at the bottom and middle of the income distribution assured that employment became more "normal" for all women, not just the college educated. Women with a high school education or less, who might have discontinued market work when they had children because their wages were relatively low, were married to similarly educated men who were increasingly challenged to support a family on their earnings alone. Having two breadwinners became more important to less educated couples who hoped to own their own home (Myers 1985; Myers and Wolch 1995). Young wives, even those who could not command high salaries, worked outside the home to supplement the household income, or, in some cases, provide the bulk of it. Also, as more women and men divorced, paid work became an economic necessity for the growing number of single mothers, many of whom received inadequate child support from absent fathers.

In 1950, a woman pushing a baby carriage on a Monday morning was most often out for a stroll with her child. By 1990, a similar woman encountered on a Monday morning was quite likely delivering her baby to a child-care provider before catching a bus to her job. A normative transformation took place in the United States in the 1970s and 1980s, one that was occurring in other industrialized nations as well. As a society, our view of women's proper place—at home with their young children—shifted to one that considers it normal for married women with children to work and to leave their children in the care of others while they do so. The welfare reform debates of the 1980s and 1990s reflect the pervasiveness of this behavioral and normative change. As more married mothers work outside the home, the right of single mothers to stay at home with children (and collect welfare) has been increasingly called into question. As a nation, we began to lament what might be happening to the care of children (Presser 1989), but we also began to view as "normal" the labor force participation of all working-age adults, regardless of gender, marital, or parental status.

Changing Lifetime Work Experience

Changes in labor force participation,weeks worked, and hours of employment tell only part of the story of increasing gender equality in the labor market. To understand trends in the ratio of women's to men's earnings (addressed in chapter 5), it is necessary to determine the likelihood of women and men working continuously throughout adulthood and to assess how their lifetime work experiences have been changing.

The relation between labor force participation and lifetime work experience helps explain why women's wages failed to increase relative to men's in earlier decades. In the first part of this century, married women rarely worked outside the home, but those who did tended to work continuously throughout their adult lives, although overt discrimination kept their wages low relative to men's. This situation changed after World War II, as the most blatant forms of discrimination were gradually eradicated and married women's labor force participation accelerated (Goldin 1990).

During the 1950s and 1960s, as older, married women returned to the labor force after raising their children, they found themselves at a disadvantage. While out of the labor force, these women seldom were able to upgrade or even maintain the skills demanded in the paid labor market. Nor were they accruing seniority or tenure with an employer, another basis for salary, retirement benefits, or wage increases. The large influx of workers with limited recent experience in the labor market in the 1950s and 1960s effectively diluted the average work experience of the female labor force and held down average wages of working women.

Beginning in the late 1960s, the character of female labor force participation began to shift; younger women, who entered the labor force after completing school, decided to remain employed even after they married and had children. Longitudinal surveys suggest that the proportion of women who chose to work while raising their families—or, more technically, those displaying continuous labor force attachment—increased during the 1970s and 1980s among women from all educational and family backgrounds (Hill and O'Neill 1992; O'Neill and Polachek 1993; Wellington 1993). However, because young, less experienced workers earn lower wages than older, more experienced ones, the entry of a large cohort of baby boom women beginning in the late 1960s and early 1970s did not immediately raise the relative wages of women workers. It took a number of years before the salutary effect of their increased educational attainment and work experience began to narrow the wage gap.

Decennial censuses do not collect employment *histories* of the population. Rather, they collect more limited information on attachment to the labor force in the year preceding the census: did a person work in the year prior to the census; if so, how many hours a week and how many weeks was he or she employed? The percentage of women employed full time and year round gives some perspective on the attachment of those who moved into and out of the labor force in the 1970s and 1980s. It also affords a picture of the increase in work experience of young women and the growing similarity in the labor force attachment of men and women.

Table 4.4 shows changes in the full-time and year-round work of cohorts born between 1906 and 1965. Our data for the baby boom generation come directly from the 1980–90 censuses; data on the older generations are captured by looking at the information provided by earlier censuses about the parents and grandparents of the baby boom generation. These cohorts are described in table I in the introduction. As the table shows, each

TABLE 4.4 Percentage of Full~Time, Year~Round Workers by Age, Sex, and Birth Cohort

Birth Cohort	Ages 25–34	35–44	45–54	55–64
Women				
1956–65 Late baby boom	42			
1946–55 Early baby boom	29	43		
1936–45 World War II	18	30	41	
1926–35 Parents of baby boom	14	21	29	25
1916–25 Parents of baby boom		18	25	21
1906–15 Grandparents of baby boom			20	20
Men				
1956–65 Late baby boom	66			
1946–55 Early baby boom	62	72		
1936–45 World War II	68	71	70	
1926–35 Parents of baby boom	66	71	68	51
1916–25 Parents of baby boom		70	68	51
1906–15 Grandparents of baby boom			65	55
Ratio, women/men				
1956–65 Late baby boom	.63			
1946–55 Early baby boom	.47	.60		
1936–45 World War II	.27	.42	.58	
1926–35 Parents of baby boom	.21	.30	.42	.49
1916–25 Parents of baby boom		.26	.37	.42
1906–15 Grandparents of baby boom			.31	.36

Source: 1960, 1970, 1980, and 1990 census Public Use Microdata Samples.

succeeding cohort of women was more likely to work full time and year round than the previous generation, but the pace of change accelerated among baby boom women.

For example, whereas 14 percent of mothers of the baby boom (aged twenty-five to thirty-four) worked full time and year round, 18 percent of the World War II cohort, 29 percent of the early baby boom cohort, and 42 percent of the late baby boom cohort did so. Women in the early baby boom cohort had a rate of full-time participation (29 percent) at ages twenty-five to thirty-four that was not achieved by those in the World War II cohort until they were thirty-five to forty-four And at ages thirty-five to forty-four, years during which child rearing responsibilities are still great, 43 percent of the early baby boom cohort, compared with 30 percent of the World War II cohort, were full-time, year-round workers.

The participation rates shown in table 4.4 index the increased labor force attachment of women in the 1970s and 1980s. (Table I specifies the time periods of entry and departure for each cohort.) As the early baby boom cohort of women moved into prime working age (twenty-five to thirty-four) in 1980, with a full-time, year-round labor force participation rate of 29 percent, they "replaced" the oldest generation of women shown in the table, grandmothers of the baby boom, who aged out of the labor force completely. In the 1980s, as the early baby boom women reached ages thirty-five to forty-four, with a full-time, year-round participation rate of 43 percent, they replaced their mothers born in 1916–25, only 18 percent of whom had been full-time workers when they were in their late thirties and early forties.

The bottom panel of table 4.4 shows how this "replacement of generations" affected the gender differences in labor force attachment. Men's full-time participation rates have not changed much over time: historically work peaks at ages thirty-five to fifty-four, when about 70 percent of all men are employed full time and year round. Ironically, women's lower rates of full-time attachment are often implicitly, if not explicitly, measured against a false perception that virtually all men work full time, year round. A very high percentage of men (more than 90 percent) work during the census year but a substantial fraction of them also experience unemployment or underemployment (less than full-time work) at some point during the year.

The acceleration in labor force attachment among baby boom women—and the steady attachment rates among men—produced profound movement toward gender equality among those in their late twenties and early thirties by 1990. At ages twenty-five to thirty-four, the full-time attachment of women of the World War II cohort was only 27 percent that of similarly aged men and only a little higher than that of the cohort before them (see first column, bottom panel of table 4.4). Among the early baby boom cohort, the full-time attachment of women jumped to 47 percent of men's and then rose to 63 percent for those of the late baby boom generation. Women's full-time labor force participation rates have not yet reached parity with men's, but they are moving rapidly in that direction.

Other researchers provide corroborating evidence of a significant shift in labor force attachment of women that occurred around 1970 (Hill and O'Neill 1992; Rexroat 1992). For example, the overall rate of labor force participation (the rate for all workers and job seekers, not just those successful in finding full-time, year-round work) clearly indicates that the increase in labor force participation at ages twenty-five to thirty-four was exceptionally great for the early baby boom cohort compared with the preceding World War II cohort (Wetzel 1995, figure 2.1).

Trends in Occupational Sex Segregation

In addition to gender differences in labor force attachment, men and women are differentiated by what they do in the labor market and the sectors of the economy in which they work. These differences continue to be of great interest because they at least partly explain women's inability to earn as much as men.

Job growth in capitalist countries like the United States results in large part from consumer demand and is often regulated by competition. As discussed in depth elsewhere (Levy 1995; Wetzel 1995), the 1980s were years of intensified competition between domestically produced and foreign produced goods. Increasingly, imported goods met consumer demand. Many manufacturing jobs, typically filled by semiskilled, high school–educated male workers, disappeared as industries restructured to stay competitive. The "good jobs" for high school–educated men became increasingly scarce as the baby boom generation began to raise their families. Strenuous debate about the destruction of "good jobs" and the creation of "bad jobs" characterized the 1970s and 1980s. In the end, it appears that both kinds of jobs were created by the U.S. economy.

One-half of newly created jobs in the 1980s were in professional services and in finance, insurance, and real estate (FIRE) industries—"good" jobs in that they offered average wages or better, full-time employment that was year round, and excellent benefits. The group poised to enter these jobs were the relatively well educated baby boomers. Women, a group exhibiting increased commitment to market work and holding the skills required in the expanding industries, particularly health care, were especially well positioned. During the 1980s, 50 percent of

TABLE 4.5 Percentage Female in Occupational Groups

Occupational Group	1970	1980	1990
Executives, managers	19	31	42
Professional specialty	44	49	54
Technicians	34	44	46
Sales	41	49	49
Administrative support, including clerical	73	77	77
Private household	96	95	95
Protective service	7	12	16
Other service	61	63	63
Farming, forestry, fishing	9	15	16
Precision production, including craft	7	8	10
Machine operators	40	41	40
Transportation workers	4	8	10
Handlers, laborers	17	20	20
Total labor force	38	43	46

Source: 1970, 1980, and 1990 census, published tabulations.

the job growth for women was in professional services, compared with 40 percent of the job growth for men. At the other end of the spectrum, one-third of female job growth but one-half of male job growth was in much less well paid lower-level retail and service sector jobs (Wetzel 1995).

How differentiated by gender was the occupational distribution by the end of the 1980s after two decades of increased participation by younger women? Table 4.5 shows the gender composition of the thirteen major occupational groupings used to classify workers in the decennial censuses of 1970–90.[2] Between 1970 and 1990, the experienced civilian labor force increased from 38 to 46 percent female. Women greatly increased their representation in white-collar occupations; in particular, the proportion of managers who were women jumped from 19 to 31 percent in the 1970s and then to 42 percent by the end of the 1980s.

Nonetheless, women and men continue to do quite different jobs. In 1990, women held 77 percent of clerical administrative support positions. In fact, such positions were more often filled by women in 1990 than in 1970. Service occupations (except protective service) were more often filled by women than men, although the percentage of the male labor force in service jobs increased as this sector of the economy expanded. On the other hand, women held only 10 percent of skilled craft (or precision production) and transportation jobs in 1990.

Why occupations are so differentiated by gender has been a subject of considerable debate. Human capital theorists emphasize the role of choice, arguing that women's expectations about spending time outside the labor force to rear children leads them to choose occupations compatible with child rearing—such as part-time or temporary clerical or sales jobs that may not penalize them for time out of the labor force. Women supposedly look for jobs that are less demanding because they anticipate the need for flexibility in their lives. They pay a price because they "choose" jobs with lower age-earnings profiles, fewer benefits, lower returns to seniority, and little on-the-job training.

Some aspects of the human capital explanation have been debunked; for example, the original formulation argued that women choose jobs with higher starting salaries but a less steep rise in wages over time, but no research has demonstrated the existence of higher starting wages for women in female-dominated jobs (England 1992). Still, the possibility persists that women contribute to their own occupational "ghettoization" because they view job choice and time for child rearing as more important than do men and act accordingly.

Causes of occupational segregation also are traced to job discrimination, past and present—explanations that point more to constraints than to choice as the reason for gender segregation. For example, when women are crowded into female-dominated occupations, it increases the supply of workers for these jobs and ultimately lowers the wages an employer can pay to get workers to fill such positions (Bergmann 1986). An alternative explanation for the lower age-earnings profiles of women is that some jobs have strong career trajectories, while others do not, and that women and minorities have been systematically excluded from the former. Perhaps the best circumstantial evidence that women's occupational "choices" are constrained is that predominantly female jobs pay less well than male jobs. If increased wages motivate market work, it is unclear why women would continue to *choose* occupations that are relatively low paid.

If the reason for gender segregation is choice, then the choice results, in part, from lifelong socialization that attracts men and women to different jobs. The occupational goals of boys tend to be more highly sex typed than those of girls, and even preschoolers express sex-typed occupational preferences. Men tend to place higher value on status, power, money, and freedom from supervision, and men may be more willing to take risks. Women more often value working with people, helping others, and creativity. Job choice may also reflect a preference for working with one's own sex (Beutel and Marini 1995; England and Brown 1992).

Knowledge of available jobs also influences "choice." The channels of information by which people find jobs differ by gender, especially for women in predominantly female occupations. Women hear about jobs from other women, while men find out about jobs from other men. Thus occupational segregation is perpetuated locally by the different networks used by job-seeking women and men (Hanson and Pratt 1991, 1995).

Some of the historical reasons for occupational segregation may change as more women view labor force participation as a lifelong activity. For example, female high school seniors continue to place less emphasis than male high school seniors on "having lots of money," but the proportion who thought it very important tripled from 10 to 30 percent between 1972 and 1992. (The comparable increase for men was from 26 to 45 percent.) By 1992, 89 percent of these young women (87 percent of men) reported that steady employment was very important in life, up from 74 percent in 1972 (82 percent for young men). In fact, in 1992, young women were more likely to report that steady employment was very important (89 percent) than they were to report that marrying and having a happy family were very important (82 percent) (Green 1993).

In the decennial census, workers are classified into about five hundred detailed occupations, far more detail than allowed by almost any other data source. A common measure of gender segregation is the index of dissimilarity, which measures the percentage of the male or female labor force that would have to change categories in order to equalize the gender distribution across occupations. An index of 100 means that women and men are completely segregated from each other, whereas 0 means that they are similarly distributed across all occupational categories.

In 1970, the index of dissimilarity stood at 68 percent—two-thirds of the women (or men) in the labor force would have had to change jobs to achieve equal representation in all occu-

TABLE **4.6** **Index of Occupational Dissimilarity of Women and Men**

	Index Number	Percentage
1970	67.7	
Change in 1970s due to		
Desegregation	−6.7	80
Structural shift	−1.7	20
1980	59.3	
Change in 1980s due to		
Desegregation	−4.3	69
Structural shift	−2.0	31
1990	53.0	
Total change,1970–90	−14.7	
Desegregation	−11.0	75
Structural shift	−3.7	25

Source: 1970, 1980, and 1990 census, published tabulations.
Note: Decomposition calculations by Prithwis Das Gupta.

pational categories (see table 4.6). In 1990, the degree of concentration by gender remained high: over one-half of the labor force would have had to be redistributed. However, the decline of almost fifteen index points over the 1970–90 period was quite remarkable, especially in light of so little change prior to 1970.[3]

The index of dissimilarity, or occupational segregation, can decline in one of two ways. One is that gender-segregated occupations—for example, machinists, who are primarily men; or clerk-typists, who are primarily women—can grow more slowly than integrated occupations. Such a "structural" shift occurred throughout both decades. As shown in table 4.6, this component accounted for 20 percent of the decline in the 1970s and 31 percent in the 1980s.[4] This implies that employment in gender-segregated occupations grew more slowly than in more integrated ones. Relatively slower growth in gender-segregated occupations accounted for 25 percent of the increased integration of men and women in the workplace over the twenty-year period. The other source of change—less segregation within specific occupations—accounted for the other 75 percent.

One troublesome aspect of the decline in occupational segregation in the 1970s was a tendency for some occupations that desegregated to rapidly resegregate—from mostly male to mostly female. Case studies suggest that these occupations were often ones in which wages were declining even before women entered them. As an occupation became less attractive, men left and women filled the void. Women who entered occupations that were rapidly desegregating—for example, pharmacists, editors, public relations specialists, insurance, and real estate sales—earned more than the average woman worker in female-dominated occupations. But their wage increases relative to men's were due more to declining earnings for men than to large wage gains for women. Four-fifths of the increase in the female-to-male earnings ratio among editors in the 1970s was attributable to men's loss in real earnings (Reskin and Roos 1992).

During the 1980s, some of the occupations that had been predominantly male "tipped" to predominantly female. By 1990, for example, insurance adjusters shifted from 30 to 72 percent female and typesetters from 17 to 70 percent female. In some of the most rapidly desegregating occupations, either women were "ghettoized" in the lower-paying specialties and firms or industrial changes were occurring to deskill jobs or make employment less attractive and less financially rewarding than it had been in the past (Roos and Reskin 1992).

The conclusion that occupations tend to resegregate might be premature, however, because there is contrary evidence for selected high-paying, high-status occupations. Women have increased their representation in computer work with no commensurate decline in earnings or massive exit of men from this field (Wright and Jacobs 1994). Women have also become more integrated into the high-status professions of law and medicine without a decline in the status of these occupations (Jacobs 1989). And women have moved into management and narrowed the gender wage gap without an exit of men from these positions (Jacobs 1992).

Even the detailed occupational categories used in the decennial census may not fully capture dissimilarity in the work that men and women do. Women are more likely to be in small firms in industries with labor-intensive production and relatively low levels of unionization and profit (England 1992). The five hundred detailed occupational categories are aggregations of jobs, within which women often specialize in different fields than men. For example, women doctors tend to concentrate in specialties such as pediatrics, which do not pay as well as male-dominated surgery or cardiology.

More detailed data on job titles and firm characteristics would no doubt show more occupational segregation than suggested above. Using a sample of business and manufacturing establishments in California studied by the U.S. Employment Service between 1959 and 1979, Bielby and Baron (1994) showed that the vast majority of women workers held completely different job titles than men. Rather than indexes of dissimilarity of 60 to 70 percent as found with the three-digit census occupational categories, the mean index for the establishments data was 93. That is, 93 percent of women would have had to change jobs in the late 1960s and early 1970s to have the same job titles as men. Using data from a U.S. Department of Labor Area Wage Survey, Peterson and Morgan (1995) report similarly high levels of segregation within firms for the 1972–83 period.

Is gender segregation of jobs still so pervasive in the early 1990s? Given the changes in women's market participation, probably not. Recent data, collected in the state of North Carolina in 1989, suggest that job segregation has declined: about 77 percent of women would have had to change jobs in North Carolina to have the same distribution as men (Tomaskovic-Devey 1993, 1995). Although still extremely high, this level of segregation is considerably lower than the 93 percent reported by Bielby and Baron (1984) and the 90 percent reported by Peterson and Morgan (1995).

Unfortunately, data like those for North Carolina are scarce. Only a few studies are able to provide statistical evidence for what casual observation suggests: the workplace is substantially segregated by gender. A female construction worker still elicits a double take; a male nurse or secretary still evokes comment.

Racial and Ethnic Comparisons

Black women experienced the same changes that accompanied other women's increased labor force participation—the delay in marriage, decline in fertility, and educational and occupational upgrading. But, perhaps because black women's labor force participation was already quite high in 1970, they did not increase their participation in paid work as rapidly as did white women in the 1970s and 1980s. Labor force differentials between black and white women narrowed substantially during the 1970s and 1980s. Between 1965 and 1992, the participation rate for white women rose twenty percentage points to reach 58 percent, while the rate for African American women rose by only nine percentage points to reach a similar level (U.S. Department of Labor 1993).

To give some idea of the diversity in labor force participation, table 4.7 shows the percentage of men and women age sixteen and over who were in the labor force in 1970 1980, and 1990. Data are shown for whites, blacks, Hispanics, Asians, and American Indians. In 1970, not only black women but also Asian women were considerably more likely than white, Hispanic, or American Indian women to be in the labor force. During the subsequent two decades, labor force participation rates increased for all groups of women but, if anything, increased somewhat faster for those with lower levels of participation in 1970. The end result was more similarity in participation across racial and ethnic subgroups of women by 1990: between 55 and 60 percent of each group were working.

The second panel of the table shows trends for men. Hispanic, Asian, and white men are more likely to be in the labor force than black or American Indian men. For both black and white males, there was a small decline in participation between 1970 and 1990. The rates of Asian and Hispanic men changed little over the two decades whereas American Indian men increased their participation.

The bottom panel of the table shows the gender difference in labor force participation. For all groups, given the significant rise in female labor force participation, the gender difference narrowed substantially. By 1990, blacks had the smallest gender gap in participation, only seven percentage points. Greater gender equality among blacks resulted both from the relatively high rate of labor force participation of black women and the relatively low rate of black men.

Asian and American Indian women had labor force participation rates about fourteen or fifteen percentage points

TABLE **4.7** **Labor Force Participation, Persons Aged 16 and Over by Race and Ethnicity**

	1970	1980	1990	Change, 1970–90
Women				
White	40.6	49.4	56.3	+15.7
African American	47.5	53.3	59.6	+12.1
Hispanic	39.3	49.3	55.9	+16.6
Asian	48.5	57.7	60.1	+11.6
American Indian	35.3	48.1	55.1	+19.8
Men				
White	77.4	76.1	75.2	−2.2
African American	69.8	66.7	66.5	−3.3
Hispanic	78.2	78.0	78.7	+0.5
Asian	75.4	76.5	75.5	+0.1
American Indian	63.4	69.6	69.4	+6.0
Difference (M-W)				
White	36.8	26.7	18.9	
African American	22.3	13.4	6.9	
Hispanic	38.9	28.7	22.8	
Asian	26.9	18.8	15.4	
American Indian	28.1	21.5	14.3	

Source: Derived from tabulations of 1970, 1980, and 1990 Censuses of Population and Housing by Harrison and Bennett (1995), table 4.6.

lower than men. Asian women and men have very high participation rates. In fact, at all points in time Asian women's participation was as high or higher than black women's. American Indian women, on the other hand, significantly reduced the gender gap because they dramatically increased (twenty percentage point) their own levels of participation in the paid labor force and because participation rates for American Indian men are relatively low when compared with any other group except blacks.

The gender gap among whites in 1990 was half what it was in 1970 but remained higher than among blacks, Asians, and American Indians. The largest remaining gender gap is found among Hispanic men and women. Although Hispanic women greatly increased their labor force participation over the two decades and participation changed little for Hispanic men, thus narrowing the gap, men's participation rates were still twenty-three percentage points higher than women's in 1990.

Table 4.7 describes participation in the labor force but does not distinguish between the employed and the unemployed, since those who actively seek work are counted as part of the labor force. Because this distinction can be important, especially when discussing ethnic and racial differences, figure 4.3 shows the employed and unemployed separately as percentages of the population in 1990. According to the Current Population Survey, unemployed persons comprise all civilians who were not employed during the reference week of the survey, who had made efforts to find a job within the previous month, and who were available for work during that week. Persons laid off from a job and expecting recall are also classified as unemployed.

As the figure shows, some groups suffer higher unemployment than others. Whites and Asians are much less likely to be unemployed than blacks, Hispanics, and American Indians. Black women have relatively high rates of labor force participation, but many more are looking for work than among Asian and white women. Hence, the actual percentage employed is higher among Asian and white women than among black, Hispanic, and American Indian women.

This general pattern holds for men. The main exception is Hispanic men, who experience more unemployment than white and Asian men but paradoxically enjoy relatively high rates of employment as well. This seeming contradiction arises from their high rates of participation in the labor force.

International Comparisons

Table 4.8 affords a comparison between labor force participation trends in the United States and those in selected industrialized countries: Australia, Canada, France, Germany, Italy, Sweden, and the United Kingdom, which are arranged in the table by female/male participation ratios. We restrict our comparisons to these economies because they display many of the same macroeconomic trends affecting the United States and because data

FIGURE 4.3 Percent Who Are Employed and Unemployed by Race and Ethnicity: 1990

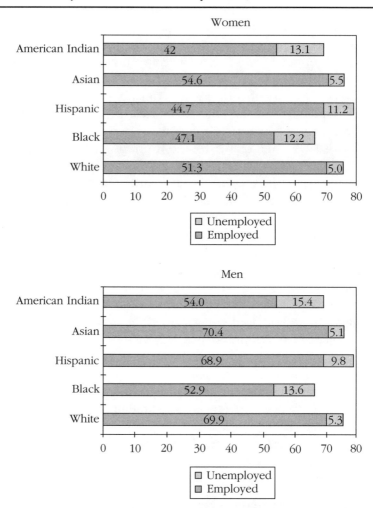

Source: Derived from tabulations of 1970, 1980, and 1990 Censuses of Population and Housing by Harrison and Bennett (1995), table 4.6.

TABLE **4.8** Labor Force Participation of Women and Men, Selected Countries: 1960 and 1990

	Women			Men			Ratio (W/M)	
Country	1960	1990	Change, 1960–90	1960	1990	Change, 1960–90	1960	1990
Australia	33.8	53.1	+19.3	85.3	76.5	−8.8	.40	.69
Canada	30.1	58.4	+28.3	82.8	75.9	−6.9	.36	.77
France	38.2	47.0	+8.8	82.4	68.4	−14.0	.46	.69
Germany	41.1	43.6	+2.5	82.4	68.4	−14.0	.50	.64
Italy	32.3	32.7	+0.4	82.4	63.1	−19.3	.39	.52
Sweden	46.1	63.6	+17.5	87.1	72.8	−14.3	.53	.87
United Kingdom	40.1	53.1	+13.0	86.8	75.6	−11.2	.46	.70
United States	37.7	57.5	+19.8	83.3	76.1	−7.2	.45	.76

Source: "Comparative Labor Force Statistics: Ten Countries: 1959–1993," supplied by Constance Sorrentino, U.S. Bureau of Labor Statistics (1994a).
Note: Sweden 1960 uses 1961 data. France 1960 uses 1962 data. German data cover Federal Republic of Germany as defined before unification.

going back to 1960 are available from the U.S. Bureau of Labor Statistics (BLS). International comparisons are always fraught with comparability problems, but the BLS, using U.S. definitions of the labor force, has attempted to standardize labor force data for these countries.

The Scandinavian economies are known for their generous social welfare policies and emphasis on gender equality (Esping-Anderson 1990). Hence it is not surprising that Sweden registers the highest rate of labor force participation for women over the age of sixteen in 1990, a rate of 64 percent. Swedish women's participation rates, already much higher than other women's in 1960, increased by eighteen percentage points between 1960 and 1990.

Because the BLS series includes the elderly population, most of whom are no longer active in the labor force, the rates shown in table 4.8 are lower (by ten to fifteen percentage points) than if the population were restricted to the working-age population. For example, based on data for persons age fifteen to sixty-four, compiled by the Organisation for Economic Cooperation and Development (OECD 1992), the participation rate of Swedish women stood at 79.1 percent in 1992. Finnish and Norwegian women also have high rates of labor force participation, though not as high as in Sweden (Casper, Peltola, and Bianchi 1995; Gornick 1995). However, in Sweden, many women are part-time workers (55 percent in 1987) whereas the vast majority of employed Finnish women work full time (90 percent in 1984) (Gornick 1995). Swedish social policy has been geared toward keeping women involved in paid employment during their child rearing years by allowing generous paid absences after the birth of a child and by encouraging part-time work (that is, six-hour days) for parents of children under eight years old (Hoem 1990). Occupational segregation exists in Sweden despite these policies, however. Professional women hold fewer supervisory positions and earn less money than professional men (Mueller, Kuruvilla, and Iverson 1994).

Women's participation in paid employment also increased substantially in Australia, Canada, the United Kingdom, and the United States between 1960 and 1990. Canada is perhaps most noteworthy in this regard. Starting from a relatively low level of female labor force participation in 1960 (30 percent of women over age sixteen), Canadian women increased their presence in the paid labor force by twenty-eight percentage points over the next three decades. Their rate of participation in market work of 58 percent, though not quite as high as Swedish women's, was similar to that for U.S. women in 1990 and significantly higher than the rates of Australia, France, Germany, Italy, and the United Kingdom, all of which had higher rates of female labor force participation in 1960. In all Western countries, as in the United States, the labor force participation of younger women increased substantially in the 1970s and 1980s (Sorrentino 1990).

Despite somewhat different rates of increase in female labor force participation, the ratio of women's to men's rate of participation rose in all countries, indicating a heightened similarity in the labor market roles of adult men and women. In the United States, but also in Australia and Canada, this convergence resulted primarily from the increase in women's participation in the paid workforce, and to a much lesser extent from the decline in men's participation. The fall in male participation was a much more important factor in narrowing the gender employment gap in Europe. In Germany and Italy, for example, where women's participation rates did not change much between 1960 and 1990, men's rate of participation declined in both countries; as a result, virtually all of the increase in the ratio of women's to men's participation could be attributed to the decline in male participation in market work. French men's participation rate also reached the relatively low rate of 68 percent by 1990, although in France women's almost nine percentage point increase in participation was a more significant factor in narrowing the gender gap than in Germany and Italy. Even in Sweden, the decline in male participation was almost as great as the increase in female participation.

What do we know about occupational sex segregation in the United States as compared with other countries? Between 1960 and 1980, such segregation lessened in North America, but in Europe segregation more often increased than decreased. Interestingly, because female labor force growth has been rapid in most countries, men's probability of sharing the same occupation as women has increased, but women in 1980 were more likely than in 1960 to work with other women (rather than men). This differential may fuel dueling perceptions—the first by men that women are making great inroads into the labor force and the second by women that change is slow and that the labor force is still quite segregated (Jacobs and Lim 1995).

Also, countries that have incorporated traditionally "female work," such as care of children and the elderly or food and personal services, into the formal economy are typically characterized by higher female labor force participation. Although this kind of economic structure provides more paid work for women, it simultaneously contributes to greater occupational segregation by gender (Charles 1992). For example, Sweden, which has a large service sector and a very high rate of female labor force participation, also has a high level of occupational segregation, higher than that in the United States and other countries with lower labor force rates for women (Blau and Ferber 1992; Blau and Kahn 1992; Mueller, Kurivilla, and Iverson 1994).

Summary

Women's labor force participation has increased dramatically over the century, and in recent years the continuity of women's careers also has risen. What brought about these changes?

Perhaps the most important factor has been the increase in wages paid to women working outside the home. Also significant has been the rising educational attainment of women, which has fueled women's preferences for market work and increased the costs to them of *not* working outside the home. Moreover, as the clerical and service sectors grew over this century, well-educated, skilled women increasingly met demand (Goldin 1990; Wetzel 1995).

The importance of World War II—and the demand it created for women workers—has been noted as another catalyst for the accelerated participation of women, particularly married women. The role of the war in facilitating women's movement into paid work remains controversial, however. During the war years, women filled not only traditionally female jobs but also male-dominated ones because of the increased production demands and the absence of men who were serving in the military. However, upon demobilization, returning servicemen displaced many of the women employed in the more highly paid manufacturing sector, since they were given preference for these jobs. Some argue that the war had little permanent effect on women's employment. Rather, women found that the wartime elevation of their employment prospects was only temporary (Goldin 1991).

Yet World War II may have raised women's "taste" for market work, which, in turn, facilitated the increase in paid employment among women in later decades. That is, for some women who worked during the war and subsequently left paid employment to marry and raise children, the experience may have contributed to the greater likelihood that they would return to the labor force after their children were grown. Hence, World War II may have been a factor in the acceleration in employment among older married women during the 1950s and 1960s.

Delayed marriage and fertility are part of the story in the 1970s and 1980s, but the sharpest growth in market work was among married women with children. Later marriage and child-bearing offer women more time to earn a degree and get a job, the same things young men do. And because the economic prospects for less educated workers declined, particularly in the 1980s, it was not just well-educated women who delayed marriage and childbearing and who failed to leave employment once they married and had children. Women's paid employment became an important component of family income, especially among young couples with limited education.

Although women and men are still concentrated in different jobs, the level of occupational segregation has dropped. In 1970, two-thirds of women (or men) would have had to change jobs to achieve similar representation in all occupational categories; by 1990, that proportion had fallen to one-half. This was a significant reduction given the slow pace of change prior to 1970. The lower level of occupational segregation is a result of the slower growth of gender-segregated occupations compared with gender-integrated occupations and the decline of segregation within specific occupations.

Labor force differentials between white and black women narrowed substantially during the 1970s and 1980s, primarily due to white women's higher participation rates. By 1990, from 55 to 60 percent of women in all racial and ethnic categories were in the labor force. Unemployment rates for black, Hispanic, and American Indian women, however, were higher than those for white and Asian women. The gender gap between participation rates is lowest among blacks, where women's rates are high and men's rates are relatively low. Hispanics have the greatest difference in labor force participation between women and men.

International comparisons place the United States in the middle ranks in women's labor force participation. Among the industrialized countries, Sweden has the highest rate, with 64 percent of women in the labor force, and Italy has the lowest with 33 percent (the U.S. rate was 58 percent in 1990). The United States was comparable to Australia, Sweden, and the United Kingdom in the growth of women's labor force participation between 1960 and 1990, but lagged behind Canada.

Changing attitudes about gender roles in the workplace and society at large have no doubt influenced women's propensity to earn higher degrees and enter the world of paid work. Additionally, legislative protections have opened doors previously closed to women. Greater attachment to paid work provides women more independence and marital choice—they can delay marriage or leave an unhappy one more easily. Working also provides women with more financial security when they are propelled by circumstance into providing for a family on their own.

Historically, we have not considered it puzzling that men work for pay, nor have we asked what motivates their high rates of participation. The assumption has been that paid work is what adult men do: they support themselves and those who depend on them. Women may still see more "choice" than men when it comes to decisions about work. But choice is tied to issues of economic dependence and independence. As women increasingly view themselves as independent, as responsible for themselves and frequently for their dependent children, they too see little choice in whether to work for pay. They work because that is what adult women do: they support themselves and those who depend upon them.

CHAPTER 5

Earnings

THE COVER STORY OF THE FEBRUARY 1996 ISSUE OF *WORKING WOMAN* magazine, on women's salaries, asked readers "Do You Make What You're Worth?" and "Do You Know How to Get It?" The article inside revealed that "women typically earn 85% to 95% of what men in similar jobs do—far better than the 74-cents-on-the-dollar cited by the Bureau of Labor Statistics as the difference between women's and men's wages" (Harris 1996, p. 27).

How can such discrepancies exist between government statistics (including the ones used in this book) and those produced by *Working Woman?* A large part of the answer lies in the use of different data. Whereas BLS and the Census Bureau rely on nationally representative samples, *Working Woman* used reports from professional associations, such as Advertising Age, the National Society of Professional Engineers, and the National Restaurant Association, in addition to some national data. The wage gap calculated with BLS and Census data is based on earnings alone, while *Working Woman* sometimes includes bonuses, commissions, or profit sharing benefits. Finally, the average wage ratios calculated by the federal agencies encompass all nonagricultural occupations, whereas *Working Woman's* survey reflects only the white-collar occupations of greatest interest to its readers.

Whether generated by the public or private sector, however, statistics on wage equality by gender show that the gap has recently narrowed but has not been eliminated. "Fifty-nine cents on the dollar"— for decades the ratio of women's to men's earnings among full-time, year-round workers—was a rallying cry of the women's movement during the late 1960s and 1970s. And, even though that ratio has now risen to 71 cents on the dollar, the wage gap continues to be an important barometer of gender equality.

Although earnings are important in their own right—they largely determine a woman's economic well-being—they also, like education, reflect how much women's lives have changed. Age, education, and the presence of children (to the extent that child care influences occupational choice) all affect earnings, just as earnings, in turn, affect schooling and family structure. This chapter looks at the changing pattern of women's earnings and why it is important to understanding American women's lives.

The Gender Earnings Gap

Very little change occurred in the ratio of women's to men's earnings throughout the 1960s and 1970s, although the difference in their labor force participation rates narrowed steadily and dramatically after World War II. Women's earnings hovered around 60 percent of men's throughout the 1955–80 period, despite the fact that by 1980 the college enrollment rates of women and men were virtually identical and that women had increased their share of law, medical, and dental school degrees and moved into managerial positions in record numbers.

During the 1980s, however, the gender wage gap finally narrowed in response to women's increased labor force participation and educational attainment. This increase in the female/male earnings ratio is in large part a story about the baby boom generation of young women. As this well-educated group of women moved into midcareer and as their mothers, who had spent many years at home raising children before returning to work, retired from the labor force, the average earnings of women increased and the wage gap narrowed. The 1990 census data, in conjunction with data from prior censuses, provide the raw material for an analysis of the economic activity of men and women in the United States. More important, the data provide a perspective on how the experiences of birth cohorts have evolved.

Women born after World War II were raised by parents whose ability to finance their children's college education increased to an unprecedented level. Baby boom women marched forward to obtain college and advanced degrees in record numbers at the same time that they were protesting the sexism of college course offerings and content. They inundated executive offices, law firms, hospitals, and finally the armed forces, voicing great skepticism as to whether their abilities and credentials would be rewarded to the same extent as those of their male counterparts. Nevertheless, as individuals, they acted as if they would be the exception rather than the rule. If they worked assertively, diligently, *and continuously*, the inherently sexist, unfair system would somehow recognize their individual talents and promote them as readily as their equally well-trained male counterparts.

For another group, however, those with a high school education or less, life did not seem so "fair" in the 1980s. In the past, men with a high school education had been much better able than women to secure a high-paying job, even than women with a college education. Increasingly, those high-paying semiskilled jobs for men have disappeared, however, as massive restructuring occurred in the manufacturing sector. Because men were more concentrated in shrinking job sectors, they were hurt more than women, who more often worked in the expanding service sector. The ultimate result is that the gender wage gap has narrowed across the board, with less well-educated women workers closing the gap primarily because they worked longer hours and because the wages of men stagnated and then declined.

So how much do women earn relative to men? The answer depends on who is included in the comparison (all workers, full-time workers, wage and salary workers) and the measure used to create the comparison (annual, weekly, or hourly wages). In 1992, for example, according to CPS data, the hourly earnings of female wage and salary workers were 79 percent those of male workers, on average. On the other hand, among all men and women who worked in 1992, the earnings ratio was only 61 percent. The most commonly used indicator of the gender wage gap, average earnings of full-time, year-round workers, stood at 71 percent in 1992.

Although the level of earnings equality varies widely depending on weeks worked and hours per week worked, the story told by each time series graphed in figure 5.1 is the same. Something rather dramatic happened in the 1980s, perhaps beginning in the late 1970s. After at least two decades in which the ratio of women's

FIGURE 5.1 Women's Earnings as a Percentage of Men's Earnings

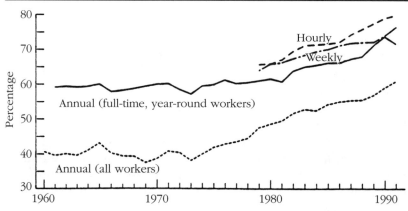

Source: U.S. Bureau of the Census and Bureau of Labor Statistics, published and unpublished tabulations.
Note: Median hourly earnings and median weekly earnings of wage and salary workers and median annual earnings of all workers and full-time, year-round workers.

to men's earnings fluctuated but remained at about the same level, the ratio increased steadily during the 1980s. Between 1979 and 1992, women's hourly wages as a percentage of men's increased from 64 to 79 percent, weekly earnings from 63 to 75 percent, annual earnings of full-time, year-round workers from 60 to 71 percent, and annual earnings of all workers from 46 to 61 percent.

Table 5.1 shows year-to-year variation in the real dollar amounts earned by men and women. The figures show a fairly steady progression for women so that by 1992, their real earnings were 50 percent greater than in 1960. For men, average earnings increased steadily until 1973 but stagnated (or declined) in the late 1970s and 1980s. By 1992, the average real earnings of men were 91 percent what they were in 1973, the peak in men's earnings. Because of the steady rise in women's earnings and the decline in men's earnings, the ratio of women's to men's earnings moved upward throughout the 1980s and stood at 70 to 72 percent in the early 1990s.

Despite this progress, women have by no means achieved parity with men: in 1992 employed women who worked full time and year round earned an average of $21,440, compared with $30,358

TABLE 5.1 Ratio of Women's to Men's Earnings Among Full-Time, Year-Round Workers (1992 dollars)

| | Median Annual Earnings | | |
| | Women | Men | Ratio (W/M) |
Year			
1960	14,191	23,389	.61
1961	14,311	24,153	.59
1962	14,595	24,612	.59
1963	14,852	25,195	.59
1964	15,275	25,824	.59
1965	15,704	26,206	.60
1966	15,728	27,327	.58
1967	16,040	27,759	.58
1968	16,587	28,521	.58
1969	17,723	30,108	.59
1970	18,083	30,458	.59
1971	18,206	30,596	.60
1972	18,653	32,237	.58
1973	18,831	33,250	.57
1974	18,842	32,069	.59
1975	18,733	31,850	.59
1976	19,129	31,780	.60
1977	19,131	32,469	.59
1978	19,434	32,695	.59
1979	19,246	32,258	.60
1980	19,088	31,729	.60
1981	18,687	31,548	.59
1982	19,099	30,932	.62
1983	19,601	30,822	.64
1984	19,958	31,532	.63
1985	20,372	31,548	.65
1986	20,779	32,330	.64
1987	20,886	32,044	.65
1988	20,880	31,613	.66
1989	21,236	30,924	.69
1990	21,278	29,711	.72
1991	21,172	30,307	.70
1992	21,440	30,358	.71

Source: U.S. Bureau of the Census, series P-60, published tabulations.

earned by men. Common explanations for women's lower earnings are that they enter and leave the labor force more frequently than men, resulting in less work experience; that their skills and educational background are not equal to those of men; and that they are discriminated against in hiring, promotion, and pay. Research conducted in the 1970s and 1980s has tried to explain why earnings differences persist in light of the fact that more and more women are earning college degrees, women's attachment to the labor force is increasing, and discrimination is lessening. Although it is possible to quantify some of these variables—such as work experience, on-the-job training, and educational attainment—it is difficult to measure hiring and promotion practices, motivational factors, and qualitative differences in the jobs of men and women, a topic to which we return later in this chapter.

Earnings of Cohorts

As discussed in the preceding chapter, the continuity of women's labor force attachment increased greatly among the baby boom cohorts. The movement into midcareer of a cohort of women with educational credentials and work experience more similar to men's than those of previous cohorts was a potent force affecting the female-to-male earnings ratio during the 1980s. Already by 1981, when the overall ratio of women's to men's earnings still stood at 59 percent (see table 5.1), there were signs that the wage gap was beginning to narrow among younger workers.

Table 5.2 shows two series of ratios for young workers age twenty-five to thirty-four: median annual income from 1970 to 1992 and mean annual earnings from 1975 to 1992. The series are shown for all workers and for those with a college education. Between 1970 and 1981, the annual income of young women increased from 65 to 70 percent that of young men with most of the increase coming in the latter 1970s. Among college-educated young workers, the ratio increased from 68 to 73 percent.

As the baby boom cohorts moved into their prime working ages in the late 1970s and 1980s, the ratio of women's to men's annual income among those aged twenty-five to thirty-four increased to 82 percent in 1992 (79 percent among the college educated). Earnings ratios were slightly lower than income ratios, which include sources other than earnings, such as interest income.

TABLE 5.2 **Ratio of Women's to Men's Income and Earnings Among Full-Time, Year-Round Workers Aged 25–34**

	All Workers		College-Educated Workers	
Year	Median Annual Income	Mean Annual Earnings	Median Annual Income	Mean Annual Earnings
1970	.65		.68	
1971	.65		.68	
1972	.65		.67	
1973	.63		.68	
1974	.63		.69	
1975	.66	.65	.71	.69
1976	.68	.65	.71	.68
1977	.68	.65	.71	.66
1978	.66	.64	.70	.66
1979	.66	.65	.71	.68
1980	.69	.69	.74	.71
1981	.70	.69	.73	.71
1982	.72	.71	.75	.72
1983	.73	.73	.74	.73
1984	.74	.73	.73	.72
1985	.75	.74	.74	.73
1986	.75	.74	.75	.73
1987	.74	.74	.74	.74
1988	.75	.74	.77	.74
1989	.79	.76	.78	.75
1990	.78	.77	.79	.76
1991	.80	.78	.77	.74
1992	.82	.79	.79	.76

Source: U.S. Bureau of the Census, series P-60, published tabulations.

To better understand how the earnings of baby boom women differ from those of earlier cohorts, it is helpful to examine real earnings of full-time, year-round workers. Each succeeding cohort of women tended to earn more at a given age than preceding cohorts. For men, on the other hand, the baby boom cohorts earned somewhat less at young ages than the World War II cohort that came before them. While it is "good news" for women that their earnings have been increasing in real terms, and many would applaud greater equality of outcomes between the sexes, it is not

TABLE 5.3 Annual Earnings of Full-Time, Year-Round
Workers by Age, Sex, and Birth Cohort
(1989 dollars)

Birth Cohort	Ages			
	25–34	35–44	45–54	55–64
Women				
1956–65 Late baby boom	21,337			
1946–55 Early baby boom	19,004	23,876		
1936–45 World War II	18,024	19,641	22,965	
1926–35 Parents of baby boom	13,734	17,582	19,369	20,898
1916–25 Parents of baby boom		13,919	18,169	19,258
1906–15 Grandparents of baby boom			13,784	17,892
Men				
1956–65 Late baby boom	28,739			
1946–55 Early baby boom	29,407	38,210		
1936–45 World War II	30,506	37,943	42,904	
1926–35 Parents of baby boom	23,163	37,228	38,919	40,643
1916–25 Parents of baby boom		26,936	36,104	35,960
1906–15 Grandparents of baby boom			25,871	32,487
Ratio, women/men				
1956–65 Late baby boom	.74			
1946–55 Early baby boom	.65	.62		
1936–45 World War II	.59	.52	.54	
1926–35 Parents of baby boom	.59	.47	.50	.51
1916–25 Parents of baby boom		.52	.50	.54
1906–15 Grandparents of baby boom			.53	.55

Source: 1960, 1970, 1980, and 1990 census Public Use Microdata Samples.

necessarily "good news" for young women that the men they marry may do less well in the labor market than previous cohorts.

The bottom panel of table 5.3 shows the ratio of women's to men's earnings. At ages twenty-five to thirty-four, the World War II cohort of women who were working full time and year round had average earnings that were about 59 percent those of men, the same as the generation before them. The ratio increased to 65 percent for early baby boom women and to 74 percent for late baby boom women, more of whom worked full time, year round because fewer were married and rearing children at these ages.

For fathers of the baby boom (born between 1926 and 1935) who settled into midcareer during the 1960s when the economy was booming, real earnings increased by a phenomenal 61 percent over their earnings during their twenties and early thirties. By contrast, among the World War II cohort of men who entered midcareer during the 1970s (a decade of sluggish economic growth), the increase in earnings still averaged 24 percent in real terms. And for both cohorts of men, the percentage increases realized by full-time, year-round workers greatly outstripped those for women.

Early baby boom men also experienced a sizable increase in average earnings as they made the same transition in the 1980s. Hence, their real earnings at ages thirty-five to forty-four were comparable to, or even slightly higher than, the World War II cohort before them. Late baby boom men had not yet reached their late thirties by 1990, so it is unknown whether their age-earnings profile will be as steep as for men in the early baby boom cohort. What is different about early baby boomers is that as they made the transition from age thirty to age forty, the increase in earnings—the steepness of the age-earnings profile—was more similar for women and men than it had been for previous cohorts. The increase in mean earnings among full-time, year-round workers was greater for men (30 percent), but only a little greater than for women (25 percent).

Earnings by Education

Table 5.4 uses decennial census data on the ratio of women's to men's real earnings within levels of educational attainment to illustrate how different the experience of baby boom women was from the two cohorts that came before. Not only did college-educated *mothers* of the baby boom who worked full time start their careers at lower salaries relative to men than later cohorts, the wage gap between men and women workers widened considerably between their early thirties and early forties. Among women in the World War II cohort with some college education or more, the earnings ratio among full-time, year-round workers declined steeply between their early thirties and early forties. For the early baby boom women with a college education, on the other hand, there was much less change in the ratio of women's to men's earnings between their early career and midcareer.

TABLE 5.4 Ratio of Women's to Men's Earnings from Early Career to Midcareer by Education and Cohort

	Late Baby Boom	Early Baby Boom	World War II	Parents of Baby Boom
Less than high school				
25–34	.74	.66	.56	.55
35–44		.64	.56	.53
Change		−.2	.0	−.2
High school				
25–34	.71	.63	.59	.63
35–44		.65	.55	.51
Change		+.2	−.4	−.12
Some college				
25–34	.73	.66	.63	.59
35–44		.67	.56	.49
Change		+.1	−.7	−.10
College graduate				
25–34	.78	.68	.62	.57
35–44		.67	.52	.45
Change		−.1	−.10	−.12
Postgraduate professional				
25–34	.73	.69	.68	.64
35–44		.66	.57	.52
Change		−.3	−.11	−.12

Source: 1960, 1970, 1980, and 1990 census Public Use Microdata Samples.

The sharpening of the earnings divide with age among the older cohorts reflects,in part, their more discontinuous pattern of labor force participation. But it is also likely that among earlier cohorts, when the norm for women was to stay at home when children were young, those who defied that norm and worked full time, year round faced limited occupational mobility and wage discrimination to a much greater extent than did the early baby boom women, who entered the workforce after passage of the 1964 Civil Rights Act and the 1963 Equal Pay Act.

Part of what bolstered the relative earnings of women of the baby boom generation—and led to a narrowing of the gender wage gap—was that women were poised by 1980 to advance in the labor force, and the decade turned out to be a phenomenal one in terms of earnings improvement for the well educated. In addition, and somewhat perversely, it was a very poor decade for young, unskilled workers, and this fact also contributed to greater gender equality in earnings.

During the 1980s, the earnings of less skilled, less educated workers declined relative to those of more skilled, more highly educated workers.[1] Further, among those with a high school education or less, average wages of younger workers fell relative to those of older workers. As a consequence, during the 1970s and 1980s, the proportion of less educated men with low earnings–lower than the poverty level for a family of four–rose sharply, after having declined dramatically during the 1950 and 1960s. The trend was similar but not nearly so pronounced for better educated young men (Danziger and Stern 1990).

Why did the earnings of those with a high school education or less deteriorate relative to those with a college education? The causes include the large shifts out of low-technology industries and basic manufacturing and into professional and business services, a shift that favored college graduates (Levy 1995). In part, the revolution in computer and information technologies and the expanding health care industry drove the increased demand for highly educated workers (Davis and Haltiwanger 1991; Krueger 1991; Mincer 1991; Wetzel 1995). Simultaneously, large deficits and the globalization of trade pushed low-skill production jobs overseas (Borjas, Freeman, and Katz 1992; Murphy and Welch 1992). The large budget deficits in the 1980s raised interest rates and strengthened the dollar, both of which made products produced overseas more competitive (Katz and Murphy 1992). The adverse effects on American workers were concentrated among high school dropouts.

Other studies argue that the declining fortunes of the high school educated *relative* to the college educated can be explained by the decline in unions, erosion in the real value of the minimum wage, and supply factors, such as the slower growth in the number of college graduates in the 1980s than in the 1970s (Blackburn, Bloom, and Freeman 1991; Katz and Murphy 1992). Still others observe that even among workers of the same age and educational attainment, wages became more unequal in the 1980s. Why some

TABLE 5.5 Annual Earnings of Workers Aged 25–34 with a
High School or College Education: 1980 and
1990 (1989 dollars)

	1980	1990	Percentage Change
High school graduate (or less)			
All workers			
Women	10,810	11,443	+6
Men	22,537	20,443	−9
Ratio, women/men	.48	.56	
Full-time, year-round workers			
Women	16,591	16,318	−2
Men	26,018	22,525	−13
Ratio, women/men	.64	.72	
College graduate (or more)			
All workers			
Women	17,889	22,905	+28
Men	31,111	33,513	+8
Ratio, women/men	.58	.68	
Full-time, year-round workers			
Women	23,566	27,559	+17
Men	34,728	36,432	+5
Ratio, women/men	.68	.76	
Birth cohort, aged 25–34	Early baby boom	Late baby boom	

Source: U.S. Bureau of the Census, Current Population Survey, published tabulations.

high school graduates fared much worse than others, and why some college graduates did much better than other college graduates is not well understood (Levy and Murnane 1992).

Given the increase in earnings inequality, the conditions that contributed to gender equality in the 1980s were distinctly different at the two ends of the educational distribution. Table 5.5 arrays mean real earnings of young women and men, in 1980 and 1990, for those with and without a college education.[2]

Women did well relative to men in the 1980s across the educational spectrum. Among workers with a high school education or less, however, women's gains resulted primarily from the deterioration in the real earnings of men rather than from any increase in their own wages. The average earnings of full-time, year-round workers declined for both sexes, but the percentage change was much greater for men. Among all workers (part time and full time), women with a high school education or less did *not* experience a decline in earnings, primarily because they worked more weeks a year in 1990 than in 1980.

Among young college-educated workers, on the other hand, the average earnings of men and women increased, but the percentage increases for women were over three times as large as those for men. Women continued to earn much less than men, but gained on men in relative terms. The ratio of women's to men's earnings increased for workers with a high school or college education, but the ratio was higher for college-educated workers. Among full-time, year-round workers, the differences by educational attainment were less striking–women with a college education earned 76 percent as much as men, whereas women with a high school education earned 72 percent as much as men.

The changing earnings gap in the 1980s among young workers entails a comparison of two cohorts, the early and late baby boom men and women. A somewhat different view is provided by asking what happened to the earnings differentials among a single cohort—the early baby boom—during the 1980s.

Table 5.6 shows average real earnings for these men and women by educational level. That is, the average earnings of early baby boom men and women with a high school or college education are tracked as they aged from early career to midcareer, roughly from age thirty to age forty, over the decade of the 1980s.

Among high school–educated workers, men's earnings did *not* decline during their thirties, although the percentage increases were small relative to college-educated men of the same cohort. The earnings of women with a high school education rose more than those for men, in part because they were more likely to work full time as they grew older. This is indicated by the fact that the rise in relative earnings of high school–educated women was greater among *all* workers than among full-time, year-round workers: women's earnings as a percentage of men's rose (as the cohort moved from age thirty to age forty) from 48 to 56 percent among all workers but from only 64 to 66 percent among full-time, year-round workers.

TABLE 5.6 Annual Earnings of the Early Baby Boom Cohort
with a High School or College Education: 1980
and 1990 (1989 dollars)

	Aged 25–34 in 1980	Aged 35–55 in 1990	Percentage Change
High school graduate (or less)			
All workers			
Women	10,810	13,597	+26
Men	22,537	24,324	+8
Ratio, women/men	.48	.56	
Full-time, year-round workers			
Women	16,591	18,269	+10
Men	26,018	27,563	+6
Ratio, women/men	.64	.66	
College graduate (or more)			
All workers			
Women	17,889	25,745	+44
Men	31,111	48,276	+55
Ratio, women/men	.58	.53	
Full-time, year-round workers			
Women	23,566	32,185	+37
Men	34,728	50,945	+47
Ratio, women/men	.68	.63	

Source: U.S. Bureau of the Census, Current Population Survey, published tabulations.

What about the college educated of this cohort? In contrast to
the implication from table 5.5, while both men and women of the
early baby boom realized sizable percentage increases in earnings
during the 1980s, the gains for college-educated men were greater
than those for women. College-educated men started with an
advantage, in that they were earning significantly more than college-educated women when this cohort was about age thirty. In
1980, young women's earnings averaged around $18,000 (in 1989
dollars) compared with young men's earnings of $31,000. And as
this cohort aged, the relative position of women declined. For
example, the ratio of women's to men's earnings among all work-

ers with a college degree was 58 percent in 1980, but only 53 percent in 1990. For full-time, year-round workers, the ratio was 68 percent at age thirty and 63 percent at age forty.[3]

The cross-cohort picture of dramatic improvement in the relative earnings of women (shown in table 5.5) must therefore be qualified in at least two ways. First, the "improvement" for women at the lower end of the educational distribution resulted mainly from a deterioration in men's earnings. Second, at the high end of the educational distribution, the relative improvement for women when viewed within the cohort does not indicate a rapid move toward gender equality in earnings in the 1980s. What happened at that more educated end was that a cohort in which the women were more equal to men in work experience and educational attainment replaced a cohort in which there was less equality. This process progressed during the 1980s to the point where it was occurring not only at the entry level but also at midcareer, when earnings are relatively high. A final illustration of what happened in the 1980s is provided by figure 5.2. In 1982, college-educated women did not earn as much, on average, as high school–educated men. Among full-time, year-round workers, women with a college degree earned 85 percent what a man with a high school degree earned. A milestone was reached by college-educated women in the 1980s. By the end of the decade, a college-educated woman earned more when she worked full time and year round than a man with a high school education—not a lot more, but a little more. By 1992, women with a bachelor's degree earned 11 percent more, on average, than a man with a high school degree. A college-educated woman still earned far less, on average, than a college-educated man, but this ratio also improved in the 1980s.

By 1992, a college-educated woman outearned her high school–educated sister by considerably more than in 1982: a college-educated woman earned 58 percent more than a high school–educated woman in 1992 whereas she had earned 33 percent more in 1982. Similarly for men, the premium for a college education increased. In 1992, a college-educated man earned 64 percent more than a high school–educated man; in 1982, the premium for a college education had been a considerably smaller 44 percent.

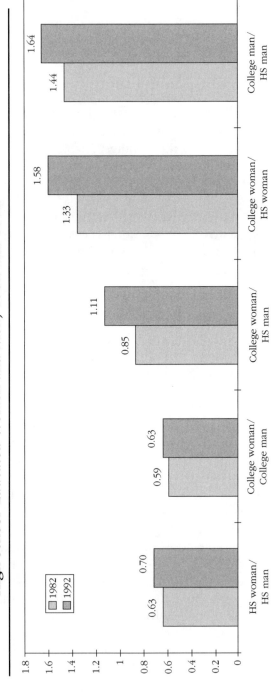

FIGURE 5.2 Ratio of Earnings of Full-Time, Year-Round Workers, College- and High School-Educated Women and Men, 1982 and 1992

Source: U.S. Bureau of the Census, series P-60 (1983b, 1993a).

122

Why Women Earn Less Than Men

A frequently voiced concern about overall earnings comparisons, even comparisons that control for education, is that they are really not comparisons of men and women doing similar jobs. Chapter 4 presented evidence that women and men are concentrated in different industries and types of occupations. The suspicion is that if we compared women and men in similar lines of work, we would find lower, perhaps nonexistent, pay differentials.

Thus women may narrow the gender wage gap but remain occupationally segregated. If relatively high-paying occupations dominated by women, such as nursing, are growing and high-paying jobs dominated by men, such as unionized, semiskilled jobs in manufacturing, are disappearing—as seems to have been the case in the 1980s (Wetzel 1995)—the gender wage gap can narrow with relatively little decline in occupational segregation. On average, however, female-dominated occupations pay less well than male-dominated ones. Hence, it would seem that the decline in occupational segregation, experienced primarily by recent cohorts of women, is necessary to ensure continued, sustained narrowing of the gender wage gap (see chapter 4 for a more detailed discussion).

To provide some perspective on earnings differentials by occupation, table 5.7 displays the average hourly earnings for women and men within major job groupings. The table is restricted to workers in their prime working ages. During the 1980s, the percentage increase in women's earnings tended to outstrip the increase in men's earnings (or declines in average earnings were not as severe for women as for men). In most instances, women's hourly earnings were closer to men's in 1990 than in 1980. Particularly among managers, women increased their average earnings by 16 percent, although they still earned only 62 percent of similarly employed men by 1990. Women achieved the greatest parity with men in service and transportation jobs. In these groups, women's average hourly earnings were more than 80 percent of men's earnings. However, convergence in these groups occurred primarily because men expe-

TABLE 5.7 Hourly Earnings of Workers Aged 25–64 by Sex and Occupational Group: 1980 and 1990 (1989 dollars)

Occupational Group	Women			Men			Ratio, Women/Men	
	1980	1990	Percentage Change	1980	1990	Percentage Change	1980	1990
Managers, executives	12.27	14.27	+16	22.45	23.03	+3	.55	.62
Professionals	14.61	15.51	+6	20.72	22.85	+10	.71	.68
Technicians	10.48	11.66	+11	17.11	17.42	+2	.61	.67
Sales	9.36	10.83	+16	17.59	19.32	+10	.53	.56
Administrative, clerical	10.23	10.11	−1	14.64	13.51	−8	.70	.75
Protective service	10.13	12.21	+21	14.68	14.03	−4	.69	.87
Other service	8.03	7.96	−1	12.16	9.70	−20	.66	.82
Farming, forestry, fishing	7.09	7.20	+2	13.07	10.95	−16	.54	.66
Precision production, craft	9.56	9.25	−3	15.25	14.86	−3	.63	.62
Machine operators	8.43	8.13	−4	13.89	12.49	−10	.61	.65
Transportation workers	10.11	10.31	+2	14.78	12.57	−15	.68	.82
Handlers, laborers	9.69	8.06	−17	12.86	12.65	−2	.75	.64
Total employed workers	10.44	11.20	+7	16.71	16.65	0	.62	.67

Source: 1980 and 1990 census Public Use Microdata Samples.

rienced real declines in average hourly earnings between 1980 and 1990.

Research using the 1980 and 1990 censuses' detailed occupational data suggests that about one-third of the decline in the gender wage gap in the 1980s might be attributed to the decline in occupational segregation (Cotter and others 1995). This is in line with other studies that have tended to find between 20 and 40 percent of the gender pay gap "explained" by occupational segregation (Jacobs 1989; Reskin 1984; Sorenson 1989; Treiman and Hartmann 1981).

As noted in the last chapter, even detailed occupational categories are aggregations of disparate *jobs.* If we had more information on specific jobs, we would find gender occupational segregation more closely tied to the earnings gap than the occupational data suggest. Women in the occupational category of "baker," for example, tend to hold jobs in store bakeries while male bakers are concentrated in more lucrative production baking jobs. Women in real estate sales tend to sell homes and men dominate the more expensive commercial sales (Reskin 1988, p. 69). Using data on a 1989 sample of North Carolina employees, Tomaskovic-Devey (1995) estimates that, after controlling for education, work experience, industry, size of firm, and job characteristics, such as supervisory authority, task complexity, unionization, and hours of work—that is, after controlling for an array of factors that might explain the gender gap—job segregation explained almost half (46 percent) of the earnings differential between women and men. If he had not had information on jobs but merely on occupational groups, the effect of sex segregation would have accounted for about one-third of the gender wage gap, a figure similar to that obtained in other studies. A consistent finding in studies of the gender wage gap is that workers in occupations with a higher percentage of female employees earn less than those in occupations with a lower percentage.

Knowing that women earn less than men because of occupational segregation merely refocuses the issue. The more general question remains: Why do women earn less than men? Why are women in lower-paying occupations and firms?

There are at least two competing explanations of why women are concentrated in less well-paid occupations. One focuses on the choices women make; the other on the constraints they face. Perhaps the most influential framework for analyzing earnings differences has come out of the neoclassical human capital tradition in economics.[4] Drawing parallels with the theory of firms (and firms' investments in physical capital in order to enhance productivity and profits), the human capital tradition as developed by Gary Becker (1975), Theodore Schultz (1960), Jacob Mincer (1962), and others emphasizes that individuals make investments in themselves, in their "human capital," in order to increase their productivity and earnings (Blau and Ferber 1992, chap. 6). Investment in formal schooling (number of years in school and type of education, such as college major) and in continued learning on the job, via training or experience, is key to understanding why some workers are more productive than others and therefore why they are paid more.

In 1974, Mincer and Polachek laid out an argument for why women might come to invest less in themselves than men, and, hence, why they might reap lower financial rewards when they participate in paid work. They theorize that because women do not expect to work as much as men throughout their lives, they invest less in education and in acquiring labor market skills. Women anticipate having children and leaving the labor force to raise them and therefore take jobs that have relatively high initial wage rates but offer little on-the-job training or potential wage growth. When women leave the labor force to rear children, the skills they have deteriorate and they suffer a wage penalty when they reenter. Employers may also choose to invest less in women workers because they believe women will work less continuously than men, and, hence, they, the employers, will not realize the return on investment in women workers that they will in male workers.

Mincer and Ofek (1982) revised Mincer and Polachek's argument by postulating that human capital that depreciates during periods of nonparticipation in the labor force can be, and often is, restored rather quickly and fairly extensively once women reenter the labor force. There is still a cost to spending time outside the labor force, but the short-run costs are much greater than the long-run costs.

To the average person, the conception of workers, specifically women workers, as machines whose productive value depreciates but then, with some reinvestment, is restored, may seem a bit strange. Nonetheless, the human capital explanation has been useful in understanding both changes in the gender gap over time and the persistence of a sizable difference in earnings between women and men.

Neoclassical economic theory predicts that as women's commitment to market work increases, women will invest more in education and training. Employers also will be more willing to provide on-the-job training to female workers because they are more likely to realize the return on their investment. Neoclassical economists highlight the increased work experience of younger women as the most important reason for the narrowing of the wage gap in the 1980s (O'Neill and Polachek 1992).

Human capital theory, with its emphasis on investment in education and accumulation of work experience, provides a somewhat convincing story about the narrowing of the earnings gap in recent decades, at least among college-educated women and men. However, it is a less complete explanation of earlier time periods (such as the 1930s and 1940s) when overt discrimination against women in the paid labor force, particularly married women, kept women's wages low (Goldin 1990). Human capital factors also only partially explain the rather large gender differential in earnings that persists into the 1990s.

The competing argument about why the earnings gap has narrowed, and why the remaining gap is so large, focuses more on the role of constraints facing women, in particular discrimination and exclusionary practices in the labor market. Here, the recent narrowing of the wage gap is interpreted as the result of a decline in discriminatory practices against women workers. Discrimination has lessened because norms about women's abilities and opportunities have changed in the wake of civil rights and equal opportunity legislation.

Sociologists more often than economists embrace the "constraint" argument. As Jacobs and Steinberg (1995) point out, human capital theory has largely evolved as an analysis of supply-side factors—differences in earnings among individuals largely result from the choices individuals make about investment in labor market skill and commitment to paid employment. Neoclassical economists are skeptical that discrimination can persist in the long run because market forces should eradicate discriminatory barriers. Sociologists more often focus on the context within which work is done, the social construction of gender relations within work settings and the relative power differentials between advantaged and disadvantaged groups. Their focus on context, politics, and culture, Jacobs and Steinberg (1995) argue, leads them to the view that discriminatory practices can and do persist in organizations.

Sociologists also are more likely than economists to recognize underlying power structures that support pay differentials. If the earnings gap is due, not to occupational segregation, but to men's desire to preserve their advantaged position, they will establish rules to distribute income in their favor. Thus, the devaluation of women's work leads whatever jobs women perform to be defined as unskilled, and women's relative powerlessness prevents them from redefining the work they do as "skilled" (examples being caring for children and the elderly, entering data, or assembling microelectronic circuits). Wages will remain low in women's jobs under such circumstances (Reskin 1988).

Where do these two competing theories meet? Recent studies have suggested that while human capital variables can explain part of the wage gap, a sizable residual remains (Kilbourne and others 1994; O'Neill and Polachek 1993; Wellington 1993). This residual is sometimes pointed to as a measure of labor market discrimination, but must be used cautiously. Taking the residual as a measure of discrimination can overstate the effect of discrimination if an important variable is overlooked and excluded from the equation. On the other hand, the unexplained residual can also underestimate discrimination if discriminatory practices somehow distort the human capital variables. In other words, to allow that certain wage differences are deserved because of productivity differences between male and female workers, one must assume that no discrimination exists in the acquisition of education and training and that no discrimination has entered into promotions and selection for certain jobs. To the extent that women have faced such discrimination, existing wage differentials explained by differences in education, on-the-job training, or job tenure are not solely due to productivity differences.

It may be that the wage and occupational differentials between women and men are the result of women's choices concerning family roles, choices that negatively affect their market equality with men. It is also easy to believe that there is less discriminatory treatment of women in the workplace today than there was twenty years ago. But it is just as easy to believe that discrimination continues to exist, perhaps in subtler forms than in the past, and that its existence is part of the reason that repeated attempts to explain male-female wage differentials have been incomplete.

Pay Equity

When the gender gap in earnings seemed permanently stalled in the 1970s and early 1980s, the concept of comparable worth held out hope that the gap could be narrowed or even eliminated. Now comparable worth is rarely mentioned, although public employees in several states successfully negotiated re-evaluations of their job performance systems, which, in some cases, improved the wages paid for predominantly female jobs (England 1992).

Cases of women being paid less than men for the identical job, although once quite common (Goldin 1990), have become rare and are explicitly illegal under the 1963 Equal Pay Act and Title VII of the 1964 Civil Rights Act. The problem, as explained in the preceding chapter, is that women and men are often *not* in identical jobs. In Tomaskovic-Devey's (1995, p. 26) North Carolina sample, for example, the average man was in an *occupation* that was 27 percent female but held a *job* that was only 8 percent female. The average woman was in an *occupation* that was 65 percent female but a *job* that was 88 percent female.

Two basic strategies have been used to address gender inequality in jobs and pay. First, attempts were made, supported by the courts, to alter the opportunity structure facing women entering the labor market—to guarantee equal, or in some cases even preferential, access to educational and employment opportunities. Until the early 1990s, this strategy was seldom questioned, had fairly widespread compliance if not enthusiastic acceptance, and created programs aimed at enhancing the entry (and retention) of women and minorities into most large work settings. Requirements for reporting to the Equal Employment

Opportunity Commission about the pool of applicants for positions, the means of advertising, and the numbers of women and minorities at various levels within organizations also heightened awareness of the goal of ensuring equal representation. There is little question that many women and minorities benefited from these measures; the major issue is whether they would have been included without such programs. These procedures began to be challenged in the 1980s by those who argued either that they were no longer necessary or that they constituted a new form of discrimination, against white men, and resulted in unqualified candidates being hired for positions.

In addition, a second strategy, advocated by some but always more controversial than the first, was to pay workers in dissimilar jobs but with equivalent skills the same salary. Proponents of this pay equity notion argued that women were not being paid fairly for the work they did and that the intended scope of the Civil Rights Act was far broader than had been interpreted. The idea behind pay equity, or comparable worth, was that wages paid should be based on the skill, effort, responsibility, and working conditions of a given job. Jobs that were dissimilar in content but similar in productivity requirements should be paid comparably. Women should be the primary beneficiaries of such a reevaluation because, its proponets contended, female-dominated jobs were systematically undervalued and underpaid. A popular example was that daycare workers (typically female) earned less than parking lot attendants (typically male); comparable worth would ensure both sets of workers the higher of the two wage rates.

Opponents of comparable worth objected to the fact that a system of remuneration based solely on job content would ignore external market forces, which affect the supply of labor and the price employers must pay to attract and retain workers (Waldauer 1984). In response, proponents argued that institutional factors, such as unionization and discrimination, systematically subverted the market by undervaluing certain jobs deemed "women's work" and so disregarded productivity-related factors. Despite opposition to the pay equity issue, considerable legislative activity took place at the state and local levels during the 1970s and 1980s. The issue is receiving little attention in the 1990s, however. In the absence of new legislation, federal courts are unlikely to address the comparable worth issue in the coming decades (England 1992).[5]

All in all, the research suggests that a wage gap will persist for the foreseeable future and that it is at least possible that traditionally "female" skills are not valued as highly as "male" skills. With little prospect of a reevaluation of reward structures, women workers will improve their market wages primarily by becoming more like men: in the subjects they study in school, the skills they hone on the job, and the years they spend in paid employment.

Racial and Ethnic Comparisons

Information on the economic position of black Americans exists for a much longer time period than for other minority groups. Table 5.8 shows the ratios of median annual earnings of black, white, male, and female workers employed full time, year round from 1967 to 1992. Black women have been (and continue to be) at the bottom of the earnings hierarchy just as white men continue to be at the top. The relative improvement of black women's economic position throughout this period was substantial, however. In 1955, the annual income of black women was only about half that of black men's income and one-third that of white men's income. By 1992, black women earned two-thirds what white men earned and nine-tenths what black men earned.

In 1980, black women's earnings seemed to be rapidly approaching white women's: in the late 1970s, the ratio of their earnings fluctuated between 94 and 96 percent. But the expected convergence did not occur; in fact, the gap reopened. Throughout the 1980s, the ratio fluctuated around the somewhat lower level of 90 to 92 percent. Why did the move toward racial parity stall among women?

First, as we have seen, during the 1970s and 1980s younger woman became more committed to market work, a change that was greater for whites than blacks. Black women were already quite committed to full-time, year-round employment by the 1970s, and hence the increase in labor force attachment was greater for white than black women in the 1980s. The wage premium associated with age increased more rapidly for white women as they increased their work experience (Harrison and Bennett 1995, table 4.5).

TABLE 5.8 Ratios of Median Annual Earnings of White and Black Women and Men

Year	Black Female/ White Male	Black Female/ Black Male	Black Female/ White Female	White Female/ White Male	White Female/ Black Male	Black Male/ White Male
1967	0.43	0.67	0.75	0.58	0.90	0.65
1968	0.44	0.66	0.76	0.58	0.86	0.68
1969	0.46	0.68	0.79	0.58	0.86	0.67
1970	0.48	0.70	0.82	0.59	0.85	0.69
1971	0.52	0.75	0.89	0.59	0.85	0.69
1972	0.49	0.70	0.86	0.57	0.82	0.69
1973	0.48	0.70	0.85	0.56	0.82	0.68
1974	0.54	0.75	0.93	0.58	0.81	0.72
1975	0.55	0.75	0.96	0.58	0.77	0.74
1976	0.55	0.76	0.94	0.59	0.81	0.73
1977	0.54	0.78	0.93	0.58	0.83	0.69
1978	0.55	0.71	0.94	0.59	0.76	0.77
1979	0.54	0.75	0.92	0.59	0.81	0.73
1980	0.56	0.79	0.95	0.58	0.83	0.71
1981	0.54	0.76	0.92	0.61	0.82	0.71
1982	0.56	0.78	0.92	0.63	0.85	0.72
1983	0.57	0.79	0.90	0.62	0.87	0.72
1984	0.57	0.82	0.92	0.63	0.90	0.69
1985	0.57	0.82	0.91	0.63	0.90	0.70
1986	0.57	0.80	0.90	0.63	0.90	0.71
1987	0.59	0.82	0.92	0.64	0.89	0.72
1988	0.61	0.81	0.93	0.65	0.87	0.75
1989	0.61	0.85	0.92	0.66	0.93	0.72
1990	0.62	0.85	0.90	0.69	0.95	0.73
1991	0.62	0.85	0.90	0.69	0.94	0.73
1992	0.64	0.89	0.92	0.70	0.97	0.72

Source: U.S. Bureau of the Census (1993a), table B-17.
Note: Data are for full-time, year-round workers.

Second, during the 1950s 1960s, and 1970s black women completed their shift out of poorly paid, private household work into clerical and service sector jobs. The movement of black women out of private household work began earlier in the century—the proportion of black women in private household work dropped from 60 percent in 1940 to 36 percent in 1960. In the 1960s, passage of the civil rights legislation enhanced the occupational (and earnings) opportunities for black women. By the end of the 1970s, the gradual transition out of household service was virtually complete and there was no more narrowing of the racial gap from this source in the 1980s. (By 1990, only 2 percent of black women were in private household service.)

During the 1980s, it was lower educational attainment that kept black women's earnings below those of white women. Within educational attainment categories, black women tended to earn the same or more than white women in 1989 (Farley 1996, table 7.6; Harrison and Bennett 1995, figure 4.7).

Table 5.9 broadens the racial and ethnic focus to include Hispanics, Asians, and American Indians. The tabulations are from the decennial censuses and show median income of full-time, year-round workers. Ratios for whites and blacks differ somewhat from table 5.8 because the data are for income rather than earnings.

Annual income of women workers increased in the 1970s and 1980s among all racial and ethnic groups. However, except for black women in the 1970s, the improvements for white women tended to equal or surpass those of other women. By 1990, an Hispanic woman's average income was 81 percent of a white woman's (compared with 90 percent in 1970). American Indian women earned 83 percent of what white women did (down from 94 percent). Largely because of their better educations, Asian women outearned white women in 1990, but by less than they did in 1970.

Trends are similar among men except that the ratios of minority to white men's income are consistently lower than similar ratios among women. In 1990, only Asian men, a relatively well-educated group, had an average income similar to white men. (According to Farley [1996], when employment, region, language ability, and educational attainment are controlled, only one group

TABLE 5.9 Median Annual Income of Full-Time, Year-Round Workers by Race and Ethnicity (1989 dollars)

	1970	1980	1990	Percent Change		Ratio (to White)		
				1970–80	1980–90	1970	1980	1990
Women								
White	15,910	17,700	20,050	+11	+13	1.00	1.00	1.00
African American	12,760	16,070	18,020	+26	+12	.80	.91	.90
Hispanic	14,330	14,950	16,310	+4	+9	.90	.84	.81
Asian	18,900	19,270	21,340	+2	+11	1.19	1.09	1.06
American Indian	14,960	15,560	16,680	+5	+7	.94	.88	.83
Men								
White	28,510	30,430	30,760	+7	+1	1.00	1.00	1.00
African American	19,060	21,240	21,690	+11	+2	.67	.70	.71
Hispanic	22,210	21,730	20,320	–2	–6	.78	.71	.66
Asian	27,880	29,160	30,080	+5	+3	.98	.96	.98
American Indian	21,890	23,360	22,080	+7	–5	.77	.77	.72
Ratio, women/men								
White	.56	.58	.65					
African American	.67	.76	.83					
Hispanic	.65	.69	.80					
Asian	.68	.66	.71					
American Indian	.68	.67	.76					

Source: Derived from tabulations of (1970, 1980, and 1990 Censuses of Population and Housing by Harrison and Bennett (1995), table 4A.1.

of men earned as much, on average, as white men—native-born Asian men.) Hispanic male workers averaged only 66 percent what white male workers averaged in 1990, and this ratio had declined substantially in the 1970s and 1980s. Black and American Indian men averaged a slightly higher 71 or 72 percent of white men's income in 1990.

Among all racial and ethnic groups, the gender gap in income narrowed: for blacks during the 1970s and 1980s; for others during the 1980s. Within the groups themselves, black women had the highest female-male income ratio (83 percent in 1990)—the lowest wage gap of any group. Hispanic, American Indian, and Asian women also had higher income ratios than white women: 80 percent among Hispanics, 76 percent among American Indians, and 71 percent among Asians, versus 65 percent among whites. Although Asian and white women had relatively high incomes when compared with other groups of women, Asian and white men had such high incomes relative to other men that the gender gap was widest among Asians and whites. In some sense, it was easier for working Hispanic, black, and American Indian women to earn relatively high incomes because the men in each of these groups earned far less than the average for white men.

Particularly among black men, the gap with white men remained sizable in the 1980s. Blau and Beller (1992) note three problematic trends for black men in the 1980s: younger cohorts stopped doing better relative to older cohorts; the narrowing of racial differences in earnings and wages that had characterized the 1970s stopped; and the amount of time black men spent in the labor force declined, perhaps because of industrial restructuring (which has affected the less skilled) and the movement of jobs out of central cities (where residentially segregated poorer blacks have been concentrated) (Kasarda 1995).[6]

Finally, the types of jobs that women and men hold also affect the racial and ethnic gender gap in earnings. Cotter and others (1995) estimate the importance of occupational segregation in explaining the wage gap between women of various racial-ethnic groups and white men. They show that all minority women have tended to be more occupationally segregated from white men than have white women. Hence, the recent decline in occupational segregation tends to explain more of the narrowing of the earnings gap for minority women: whereas for white women, they estimate that 38 percent of the narrowing of the wage gap in the 1980s was due to declining segregation, the estimate is 45 percent for Hispanic women, 55 percent for black women, and 61 percent for American Indian women. Only among Asian women is declining occupational segregation *not* a factor (explaining only 3 percent) of the narrowing gender differential.

In sum, increased gender wage equality has touched all Americans, regardless of race or ethnicity, but changes in women's commitment to market work, their gains in occupational attainment, and their relative earnings vary by racial and ethnic subgroup.

International Comparisons

Figure 5.3 shows the ratio of women's to men's wages in selected industrialized countries. Blau and Kahn (1992) note that the pay gap has narrowed in many countries since the 1950s. By the late 1980s, the earnings ratio was highest in Australia, France, New Zealand, and the Scandinavian countries (in the 80–90 percent range) and somewhat lower in Canada, the other European countries, and in the United States (in the 65–75 percent range). Gornick (1995), using the Luxembourg Income Study data base, which contains income surveys from a number of countries, also finds relatively high ratios of women's to men's earnings among full-time workers in Scandinavian countries and in Belgium and Italy. However, in the latter two (as well as in other continental European countries like the Netherlands and Luxembourg), women's labor force participation rates are quite low.

The wider gender gap in the United States is not a result of a lag in legislating equal employment opportunity in the United States. Blau and Kahn (1992, table 1) show that equal employment opportunity (EEO) legislation was enacted relatively early in the United States, dating back to the 1963 Equal Pay Act. Many European countries, including the Scandinavian countries, did not pass explicit EEO legislation until the 1970s and 1980s. What may be important, however, is that many of these countries have much more generous maternity and parental leave benefits than the United States (Blau and Kahn 1992, table 2). Kamerman and Kahn

FIGURE 5.3   Ratio of Women's to Men's Earnings, Selected Countries

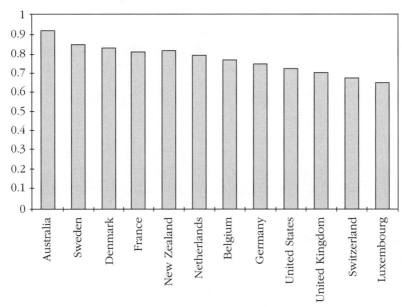

Source: International Labour Office, *1993 Year Book of Labor Statistics,* data for 1990, 1991, or 1992. Swedish data taken from Gornick (1995); U.S. data from U.S. Bureau of the Census (1993a).

Note: Average hourly earnings for all countries except Sweden and United States. Median annual earnings of full-time, year-round workers in Sweden and the United States.

(1988) show that the tradition of generous social security and family support was well established in Europe in the early twentieth century, far sooner than in the United States, where most such legislation can be traced to the New Deal.

Another factor in the relatively large gender earnings gap in the United States is the country's much more unequal wage distribution. Wages in many European countries are less variable because of strong industrywide unions and centralized wage-setting mechanisms, such as government tribunals, which set wages for an entire industry or occupation (Blau and Kahn 1992).

Blau and Kahn (1992) estimate that in the United States the average female worker is at the thirty-third percentile of the male earnings distribution, a percentile ranking that is actually higher than in many other countries. In countries where a big earnings gap separates the middle (the fiftieth percentile) from the top (the seventy-fifth, ninetieth, or one-hundredth percentile), it takes a substantial earnings improvement to close the gap with those at the high end of the distribution. Given the increase in income inequality that was occurring in the United States throughout the 1980s, the relative improvement in women's average earnings in the United States is all the more striking. American women were swimming upstream, and the current was far stronger here than in other countries.

The comparative work by economists like Francine Blau and Larry Kahn helps to shift the debate on the gender gap away from the narrow focus on supply-side factors. Their assessment of the macroeconomic forces at work in the United States and other countries includes ones outside individual workers' control: factors such as how centralized the wage-setting mechanisms are in a country and how much wage dispersion is tolerated. There is more than one path to gender equality. The U.S. path, with its emphasis on individualism and equal opportunity in the labor market and its deemphasis on public support of family responsibilities, has led to a situation in which women's labor force participation is high—not as high as in Scandinavia but higher than in many continental European countries—in which women's occupational segregation is relatively low and declining (Blau and Ferber 1992), even when compared with Scandinavian countries; and in which the gender wage gap is relatively large but narrowing, perhaps in ways that will be quite long-lasting (through increased lifetime commitment to market work and through the succession of ever more equal cohorts of male and female workers).

Summary

The wage gap between men and women closed during the 1980s, from 59 to 71 percent, with much of the movement resulting from a gradual process of cohort replacement. The women of the baby boom generation saw profound changes in educational attainment, occupational choice, labor force attachment, and earnings. With that generation, a tide rose and swept through the economic landscape of the 1970s and 1980s, leaving the economic, if not the domestic, roles of women and men far more similar by 1990 than they had been at any other time in this century.

During the 1980s, as the early baby boom women graduated into midcareer, their mothers who had interrupted their work to raise them, retired from the labor force. This particular generational replacement added substantially to the narrowing of the gender wage gap. In addition, young workers at the bottom of the skill distribution found an increasingly hostile labor market. Their economic insecurity propelled the less educated to remain unmarried and delay having children. It also ensured that wives without particularly high earnings would continue to work even after starting a family.

Women's wages relative to men's improved across the educational spectrum during the 1980s. Among full-time, year-round workers, women with a college degree earned 76 percent as much as men, and women with a high school education earned 72 percent as much as men. The average earnings of women with a college degree improved, mainly because younger women are now more equal to men in educational attainment and work experience. Among those with a high school education or less, however, women's gains resulted primarily from a deterioration of men's earnings.

Black women continue to be at the bottom of the earnings hierarchy, just as white men continue to be at the top. Gender wage parity is greater among blacks than whites, however, partly because black men's pay is so low. By 1992, black women earned nine-tenths of what black men earned, while white women earned seven-tenths of what white men earned. Among all racial and ethnic groups, the gender gap in income narrowed during the 1980s, mostly because of declining gender segregation across occupations. Women's gains relative to men's losses vary by racial and ethnic group.

The ratio of women's to men's earnings was highest in Australia, France, New Zealand, and Scandinavian countries and somewhat lower in Canada, some European countries, and the United States. The U.S. gender gap is larger than that in many European countries, partly because the U.S. wage distribution is more unequal. Another difference is that the United States has emphasized equal access to the labor market for women, while many European countries have emphasized family support mechanisms that enable women to combine paid work and child rearing.

In sum, women continue to earn less than men for a variety of reasons: occupational and job segregation, lower human capital investment, the possible devaluation of women's work, and discrimination in the workplace. Two strategies for redressing gender inequality in jobs and pay have been affirmative action and the notion of comparable worth, or equal pay for jobs with equivalent skills. Comparable worth is no longer even discussed nationally as a policy option, and affirmative action is losing its political appeal as an avenue toward equality. These developments suggest that little further progress will be made in pay equity until younger cohorts of women with skills similar to men's replace older cohorts of women. Even then, there is no guarantee that the earnings gap will decline further. To the extent that women's work is devalued, to the extent that there exists the potential for a backlash against women's progress, and to the extent that labor market conditions are unfavorable for women and minorities, women's future gains remain uncertain.

CHAPTER 6

Family Well~Being: Wives and Single Mothers

OF ALL THE TRENDS WE HAVE REVIEWED IN PRECEDING CHAPTERS, TWO developments—the movement away from marriage and the increase in women's labor force participation—have most affected the economic position of women by revolutionizing the financial contribution women make to families. Although a husband still earns more among most couples, the importance of a wife's earnings has increased. In addition, a growing proportion of families rely solely on a female wage earner. Thus, more and more adult women are now acting as their family's "breadwinner" in addition to its "caregiver."

In this chapter, we examine the economic activity of working wives and working single mothers. In particular, we are concerned that the income gap between these two groups of women has been growing. Unmarried women and their children are becoming more economically disadvantaged relative to dual-income, married-couple families. Increasingly, poverty is a condition of life for single mothers and their children.

Income and Poverty

Most women still marry and spend a large part of their adult lives with a spouse; over two-thirds of people between the ages of thirty-five and sixty-five were married in 1990. During the years in which they are married, the financial well-being of a couple and their children are inextricably tied. Any given individual's quality of life depends not only on how well he or she does in the labor market but also on the earnings of those with whom income and assets are pooled. Old-age security, provided by social security and pension income, also is determined not only by an individual's own labor force participation but by his or her marital history.

Over a lifetime, economic well-being, more so than earnings, should ideally be independent of gender. In reality it is quite difficult, if not impossible, to quantify economic well-being well enough to compare the lifetime standard of living of women and men. However, to provide a somewhat more complete picture of the economic situation of adult women and men, we look at per capita, family, and household income and poverty (see table 6.1).[1]

The gender gap in *income* was much smaller than the gap in *earnings* in 1990. (For earnings data, see chapter 5.) Whereas the ratio of women's to men's earnings among full-time, year-round workers was about 70 percent in 1990, household, family, and per capita income levels of women averaged about 90 percent those of men.[2] The relative level of women's income did not change greatly over the 1960–90 period, although women's income declined somewhat between 1960 and 1980 as a greater percentage lived apart from a spouse and had sole financial responsibility for dependent children. Even those women living with men or other wage earners may not share equally in the total income of that household, however, and there is some evidence that employed women have more control over shared resources than nonemployed women (Treas 1993).

Gender disparities in income differ with the age of the cohort. Female-male ratios of per capita income are lower among those aged fifty-five and older than among those of younger ages (see table 6.2). There also was some deterioration in the relative well-being of women to men over time, although it seems to have halted and may even be reversing for the baby boom cohorts.

Public policy debates have focused more on the changing gender composition of the poverty population than on the relative well-being of women and men in the middle or upper end of the income distribution. The term *feminization of poverty* gained

TABLE 6.1 Household, Family, and Per Capita Income of Women and Men (1989 dollars)

| | 1960 | 1970 | 1980 | 1990 | Percentage Change | | |
					1960–70	1970–80	1980–90
Household income							
Women	26,913	35,601	36,008	40,680	+32.3	+1.1	+13.0
Men	28,635	38,696	39,959	45,128	+35.1	+3.3	+12.9
Ratio, women/men	.94	.92	.90	.90			
Family income							
Women	25,903	34,642	32,734	39,212	+33.7	−5.5	+19.8
Men	27,535	37,585	35,968	43,178	+36.5	−4.3	+20.0
Ratio, women/men	.94	.92	.91	.91			
Per capita income							
Women	8,458	11,484	12,633	14,916	+35.8	+10.0	+18.1
Men	8,850	12,331	13,886	16,478	+39.3	+12.6	+18.7
Ratio, women/men	.96	.93	.91	.91			

Source: 1960, 1970, 1980, and 1990 census Public Use Microdata Samples.
Note: Mean income assigned to all persons aged 16 and over living in households.

Table 6.2 Per Capita Income Ratio of Women to Men by Age and Birth Cohort

Birth Cohort	Ages					
	25–34	35–44	45–54	55–64	65–74	75 and Over
Late baby boom	.90					
Early baby boom	.87	.92				
World War II	.85	.89	.93			
Parents of baby boom	.89	.94	.94	.87		
Parents of baby boom		.99	.99	.89	.87	
Grandparents of baby boom			1.02	.91	.93	.89

Source: 1960, 1970, 1980, and 1990 census Public Use Microdata Samples.

popularity in the late 1970s and early 1980s when mother-child families began to constitute a larger proportion of the poor (as husband-wife couples moved out of poverty due to a strong economy and social programs like the War on Poverty). Many of the poor now are children, and the likelihood of being poor is much higher for children in mother-child families (Hogan and Lichter 1995).

Adult women's poverty rates were higher than men's at every age in 1992 (see figure 6.1). Poverty rates between men and women were closest for individuals aged thirty-five to fifty-four, the ages with the highest proportion of men and women married and living together. But even at these ages, women's poverty rates were 25 to 35 percent higher than men's. Among those aged sixty-five and older, women's rates were 75 percent higher than men's.

What do such gender disparities among the working-age population reflect? What determines women's likelihood of living in poverty? First, women are less likely to be employed than men, and they earn considerably less than men when they do work. Gender differences in labor force attachment and earnings leave women more vulnerable to poverty, particularly when they do not share a household with a male wage earner. Second, women who

FIGURE **6.1 Poverty Rates by Gender and Age: 1992**

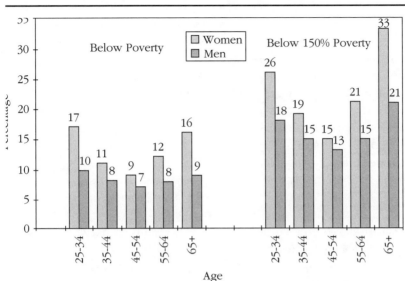

Source: U.S. Bureau of the Census, Current Population Survey, published tabulations.

are not living with a husband are much more likely than men who are not living with a wife to be caring for and supporting dependent children. These women must share their own (often meager) income with children, which drives the family's living standards below the poverty level. One of the largest gender differentials affecting women's economic well-being is the much greater responsibility women assume for children both within, but also outside, marriage.

Women also are more likely than men to be "near poor"— with incomes above the poverty line but not more than 50 percent above it (see figure 6.1, second panel). The proportion of women aged thirty-five to fifty-four who had incomes less than 1.5 times poverty was 20 to 23 percent higher than it was for men of the same age. Among the elderly, 33 percent of women and 21 percent of men were poor or near poor. That is, the likelihood of elderly women having low incomes was 60 percent greater than for elderly men.

Poverty among elderly women (and men) declined in the 1970s and 1980s, in large part because social security benefits, upon which many poor or near-poor elderly rely, have risen with inflation. Yet those who depend solely on social security remain more likely to live in poverty or just beyond it. The elderly who fare best are those who also have earnings from part-time employment and income from pensions or investments; elderly men remain more likely than elderly women to have income from these sources (Treas and Torrecilha 1995).

Elderly women are less likely than men to have pension income in their own right because of their limited labor force histories and relatively low wages. Many women share their husband's pension but can lose access to that income upon his death if they do not have survivor's benefits. Also, as divorce increases, claim on an ex-husband's pension is sometimes bargained away, often in exchange for the family home. The price many women pay for discontinuous labor force participation and low wages continues long after they retire from the labor market, and the long-term economic cost of marital disruption can be great (Holden and Smock 1991). The likelihood of living in poverty increases the longer a woman lives: in 1990, more than one-half of poor elderly women were over age seventy-five (Treas and Torrecilha 1995, table 2.4).

Single Mothers and Their Children

Although father-child families have been increasing in number, only 1.4 million such families (compared with six million mother-child families) were counted in the 1990 census. As we discussed in chapter 2, the formation of mother-child families slowed in the 1980s, but the increase that occurred was more concentrated among never married mothers (Bianchi 1994).

During the 1980s, the employment rates of married women with children essentially caught up with the rates of unmarried women rearing children alone (see figure 6.2). As more two-parent families had two breadwinners, one-parent families with one earner—or frequently no earners, given the increase in young, less educated, never married mothers—became relatively more disadvantaged.

FIGURE 6.2 **Employment Rates of Married and Unmarried Mothers with Dependent Children**

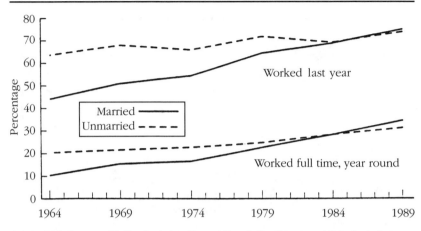

Source: U.S. Bureau of Labor Statistics. Current Population Survey, published tabulations.

Poverty rates declined in mother-child families in the 1960s, leveled in the 1970s, and increased in the early 1980s; they remained at higher levels throughout the 1980s than during the 1970s (see figure 6.3) Throughout the period, the chances of living in poverty were dramatically higher for persons who lived in mother-child families than among those in other types of families.

As discussed in the previous chapter, earnings of less educated workers declined or, in the case of women, rose only marginally during the 1980s. The profile of single mothers also shifted toward the never married—those least likely to have the education and skills to become (and stay) employed or to find jobs that pay more than the minimum wage. Part of the reason the increase in never married mothers is so controversial is that these mothers have problems supporting themselves and their children at a standard above the poverty level. The economic circumstances of young, never married mothers are much worse than those of divorced mothers, although the psychological consequences for the children may differ because there is not the same loss of a father (McLanahan and Sandefur 1994).

Never married mothers are young and less well educated because unmarried childbearing often occurs before women fin-

FIGURE 6.3 Percentage of Persons in Mother-Child
Households Who Live in Poverty

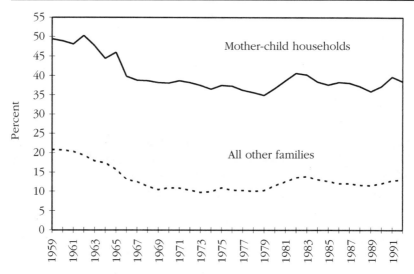

Source: U.S. Bureau of the Census (1993b), table 2.

ish high school (Hofferth and Moore 1979). A never married
mother is only half as likely to be employed as a divorced
mother. The median family income of never married, mother-
child families is only one-half that of the families of divorced
mothers. Consequently, two-thirds of never married mothers and
their children were in poverty in 1991, compared with a little
more than one-third of divorced mothers and their children
(Bianchi 1994, table 6).

In addition to their own low levels of education and employment, never married mothers' ability to garner income from the
father of their children is also much lower than among women
who are formerly married (see table 6.3). In 1991, nearly three-
quarters of divorced women with children under twenty-one had
an agreement or court award of child support from the absent
father, compared with around one-half of separated women and
just over one-quarter of never married mothers. Twenty percent
of never married mothers received at least some child support in
1991, compared with 34 percent of separated mothers and 57 per-

TABLE 6.3 **Child Support Received by Divorced, Separated, or Never Married Mothers: 1991**

	Divorced	Separated	Never Married
Child support in 1991			
(1) Percent of mothers with award	72.8	46.4	27.0
(2) Percent with award who receive support	78.3	74.2	74.1
(3) Percent receiving support [(1) × (2)]	57.0	34.4	20.0
Mean annual amount per recipient (dollars)	3,623	2,753	1,534

Source: Scoon-Rogers and Lester (1995), tables 1, 2.
Note: Separated includes a small number of women whose spouse is absent for reasons other than marital discord. The denominator in (2) is those who have an award (or agreement) and were supposed to receive support in 1991.

cent of divorced mothers. The average amount received by never married mothers was less than one-half of that received by divorced mothers ($1,534 versus $3,623 a year).

Only about one-half of custodial mothers receive the full amount of child support awarded them by the court, regardless of marital status (Scoon-Rogers and Lester 1995, table 1). Compliance by noncustodial fathers can vary substantially from month to month, and many parents make informal adjustments to custodial and support arrangements that are not reflected in CPS data (Peters and others 1993). Unpredictable child support makes it difficult for single mothers to achieve financial security, however, and can contribute to higher welfare dependency. Receiving regular child support can reduce the probability of returning to welfare once divorced mothers have left welfare rolls (Meyer 1993).

Unlike social security, welfare income such as Aid to Families with Dependent Children (AFDC) was not indexed to rise with inflation, so the income on which poor single mothers often rely declined in value in the latter 1970s and 1980s (Sawhill 1988; Bianchi 1993). And while social security benefits are the same across the United States, AFDC benefits vary regionally. Even so, welfare benefits tend to be similar to earnings from a minimum wage job but have the advantage of providing Medicaid benefits for mothers and their children (Moffitt 1992). Once receiving AFDC, earnings from a job (as well as income from child support) reduce those benefits, and hence many young mothers with little education and job experience may embark on a strategy of cycling between paid work and welfare in order to support themselves and their children (Spalter-Roth and Hartmann 1994). A significant proportion (one-third) of single mothers on welfare are employed, and they eventually move off welfare as their job skills improve (Harris 1993).

The relationship among welfare, nonmarital childbearing, and the feminization of poverty is hotly debated. Some argue that the welfare system has encouraged irresponsible parenting on the part of both women and men (Murray 1984). Others argue that welfare has been a bit player in the larger drama of industrial restructuring and loss of "good jobs," and it is these economic factors that have kept young men and women from marrying and having children within marriage (Wilson 1987).

It is likely that there would be a smaller gender poverty gap, at least at younger ages, if adult men and women were more likely to marry and stay married throughout adulthood and if childbearing occurred within stable marriages (Casper, McLanahan, and Garfinkel 1994). Whether men and women will form more stable marriages in the future is uncertain, but a large shift toward more marital stability seems unlikely. As documented in chapter 2, the divorce rate remains high and the trend toward later marriage shows no signs of reversal.

Gender differences in poverty might also be reduced through continued movement toward equality in the labor force behaviors of women and men. If women's labor force participation and earnings were more like men's, the gender differential in poverty would be reduced. The paradox—and why we are unlikely to see any policy to address gender equality in the labor market—is that women's growing equality is intertwined with their move away from marriage and toward more independence from men. The movement toward equality was lopsided—women added the responsibility of providing economically for a family but continued to provide most of the caregiving for children and perform the majority of household work—and this disrupted the balance of the marital division of labor.

FIGURE 6.4 Labor Force Participation of Husbands and Wives

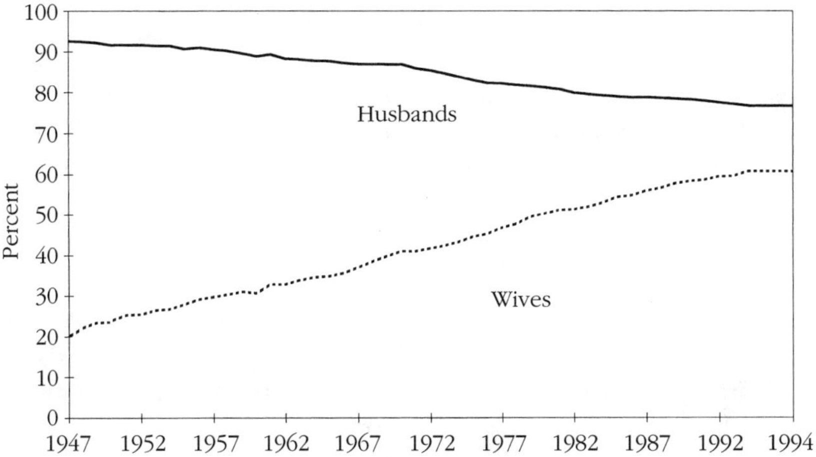

Source: U.S. Bureau of Labor Statistics (1988), table C-3; (1989), table 55; and unpublished tabulations.

It is possible, as some argue, that we are shifting toward more egalitarian marriages (Goldscheider and Waite 1991). It is also possible that as rules about marriage change, we may see greater diversity in marriages—with some very "high-quality," long-lasting unions but many more "low-quality," short-lived matches occurring as individuals "search" for the optimal partner (Oppenheimer 1988 1995). If this view is correct, increased divorce and later marriage are "rational," to be expected, and do not signal the decline of the American family, although there are societal costs as well as benefits. The one thing that is certain is that roles of husband and wife are changing as women attain more labor market experience and earn a substantial portion of the family's income.

Economic Roles of Wives and Husbands

Women's employment and the relative earnings of husbands and wives affect the balance of power in marriages (England 1992; England and Kilbourne 1990; Treas 1993). The increased employment of *married* women has accounted for much of the rise in labor force rates among women throughout the post–World War II period. Labor force participation rates of married women remain much lower than those of married men, but there has been a distinct convergence in these trends over time (see figure 6.4).

TABLE 6.4 Married Mothers' Labor Force Attachment

	1970	1980	1990
With children under age 18			
Percentage who worked last year	51	63	73
Percentage who worked full time, year round	16	23	34
With children under age 6			
Percentage who worked last year	44	58	68
Percentage who worked full time, year round	10	18	28
With children aged 6–17			
Percentage who worked last year	58	68	78
Percentage who worked full time, year round	23	29	40

Source: U.S. Bureau of Labor Statistics, Current Population Survey, unpublished tabulations.

Throughout the 1970s and 1980s, the group with the lowest rate of labor force participation historically—married women with young children—increased participation rapidly. In 1970, 44 percent of married women with young children worked during the year and only 10 percent worked full time, year round (see table 6.4). By 1990, 68 percent of married women with young children worked outside the home and 28 percent worked full time, year round. By 1990, most married mothers of young children had some involvement in market work, although they typically were employed part time (Hayghe and Bianchi 1994).

In the 1980s, wives' proportional contribution to family earnings increased because more wives had earnings: 71 percent in 1990 compared with 61 percent in 1980.[3] In both the 1980 and 1990 censuses, in about one-quarter of couples in which the wife was a wage earner, she contributed more earnings to the household than her husband. On average, working wives contributed about 30 percent of their family's income—40 percent in those families in which the wife worked full time, year round (Hayghe and Bianchi 1994). By the early 1990s, wives' economic contribution to the family represented much more than "pin money," and, presumably, their bargaining power within marriage was rising in proportion to their financial ability to leave it (or not enter one in the first place).

Not surprisingly, these labor force trends have affected cohorts of women differently. Whereas 25 percent of wives born in the early 1930s (mothers of the baby boom) spent *no* years working outside the home between ages twenty-two and thirty-one, only 5 percent of late baby boom wives did not work at this age. Conversely, only 14 percent of mothers of the baby boom had earnings from their employment in all (or all but one) of the years between age twenty-two and thirty-one, but over 50 percent of late baby boom wives had such earnings. In 20 percent of the late baby boom couples, wives' earnings were equal to or greater than their husbands', and another 26 percent had earnings that were 50 to 99 percent of their husbands'. These percentages were far higher than among their parents' generation (Iams 1993).

Census data allow one to compute a wife's proportional contribution to family income and assess how it varies with certain family characteristics. The first column of table 6.5 shows how the age of a married woman's children, her age or birth cohort, her education, and her family income (minus her own earnings—a measure of how affluent the family is relative to other families if she contributes no earnings) affect a wife's chances of working for pay. For example, the chances that a married woman without children under age eighteen in the household is a family earner are three times those of a woman who is similar in age, education, and other family income but who has a preschooler at home. The second column shows how these characteristics affect whether a wife contributed a greater than average percentage of income to the household. Full-time, year-round attachment is added as a predictor of above-average contribution to family income.

Not only were married women without children at home more often family earners, but mothers with school-age children were more than twice as likely to contribute to family earnings as mothers of very young children (under age six). Each younger cohort of married women had higher odds of being a family breadwinner relative to older cohorts. For example, the odds that married mothers among the late baby boom were earners in 1990 were six times those of their mothers.

The chances that a married woman was an earner rose steeply with her education; the likelihood of paid employment for women with a postgraduate degree was almost six times greater than for those who dropped out of high school. Also, other things being equal, the odds were two to one that wives in less affluent families were earners (other income less than $40,000), compared

TABLE 6.5 Odds of a Married Woman Contributing Earned
Income to the Family: 1990

	Odds Ratios	
	---	---
	Contributes Earnings	Earns More than 30 Percent of Family Income
Children (relative to children under age 6)		
No children under age 18	3.0	1.7
Children 6–17	2.4	1.2
Children under age 6	*1.0*	*1.0*
Cohort/Age (relative to ages 55–64)		
Ages 25–34 (late baby boom)	5.8	3.0
Ages 35–44 (early baby boom)	4.5	2.2
Ages 45–54 (World War II)	2.9	1.4
Ages 55–64 (mothers of baby boom)	*1.0*	*1.0*
Education (relative to not high school graduate)		
High school graduate	2.0	1.2
Some college	2.9	1.6
College graduate	3.5	2.7
Postgraduate education	5.7	5.8
Not high school graduate	*1.0*	*1.0*
Other family income (relative to $40,000 or more)		
Less than $15,000	1.8	6.6
$15,000–24,999	2.1	9.9
$25,000–39,000	1.8	4.9
$40,000 or more	*1.0*	*1.0*
Full-time, year-round worker (odds relative to part year/part time)	—	15.1

Source: 1990 census Public Use Microdata Samples.
Note: Numbers shown are relative odds ratios. Regressions of likelihood of contributing more than 30 percent of family income are restricted to wives with $1 or more of earnings in 1989.

with wives in the highest income quartile. Since we are describing married couples, most of this other family income was from the husbands' earnings. This suggests that economic need continued to be an important factor in married women's decision to participate in the paid labor force.

Marriage and Gender Differences in Paid Work

In the discussion of earnings, one aspect of the narrowing of the gender gap was that well-educated early baby boom women's earnings did not keep pace with men's as they aged from their thirties to their forties. They were less likely than earlier cohorts of women to lose substantial ground vis-à-vis men, but they still did not experience earnings increases as large as the well-educated men of their cohort. Why were these women—who gained immensely on men in terms of education and occupational attainment and who participated in the labor force in far greater numbers and with more continuity than prior generations—unable to sustain earnings improvements into midcareer?

As they aged, many of these women married and, more important, had the children they postponed in order to obtain an advanced education. Well-educated women tended to marry well-educated men, who earned more than they did. Hence, if and when the question arose about who should cut back on their work to accommodate the needs of children, the women of this generation did so more than their husbands.

Labor force and earnings differences continued to distinguish men and women of the early baby boom cohort in 1990 (see table 6.6). Married men continued to have higher employment rates, stronger year-round attachment to the labor force, more hours of work, and higher earnings than other workers. Although the gap separating the most attached workers (married men) from the least attached workers (married women) of this generation shrank compared with the gap that existed for the World War II cohort in 1980, the labor force activity and earnings of these women and men continued to diverge.

For example, the proportion of married men employed in the year preceding the 1990 census was 96 percent compared with 77 percent of married women, a 19 percentage point differential. In 1990, the full-time, year-round employment rate of married women of the early baby boom cohort was 39 percentage points lower than that of married men of the same cohort. Married women averaged almost nine hundred fewer hours of market work than married men and earned $11.60 for each hour of that work compared with $17.42 among married men.

TABLE 6.6 Employment and Earnings of Married and
Unmarried Women and Men Aged 35 to 44:
1980 and 1990 (1989 Dollars)

	1980	1990	Difference, 1980–90
Percentage who worked last year			
Married women	65	77	+12
Unmarried women	80	84	+4
Unmarried men	89	87	−2
Married men	97	96	−1
Percentage who worked full time, year round			
Married women	27	38	+11
Unmarried women	47	54	+7
Unmarried men	61	59	−2
Married men	78	77	−1
Annual hours worked (including none)			
Married women	951	1,250	+299
Unmarried women	1,394	1,567	+173
Unmarried men	1,759	1,729	−30
Married men	2,124	2,138	+14
Hourly earnings (workers)			
Married women	9.84	11.60	+1.76
Unmarried women	10.78	11.99	+1.21
Unmarried men	14.37	15.29	+0.92
Married men	17.77	17.42	−0.35
Birth cohort, age 35–44	World War II	Early baby boom	

Source: 1980 and 1990 census Public Use Microdata Samples.
Note: Hourly earnings calculated for those with $1 or more of earnings in 1980 (or 1990).

It is difficult to determine whether these women's labor force involvement and earnings failed to keep pace with their male peers because of choices they made about family or because of discrimination in the workplace. It is also hard to know why these women started their labor force career with earnings that were, at most, 70 percent of comparably educated men's earnings, although gender differences in college major and occupational selection were probable factors.

The data for the early baby boom cohort suggest that men and women allocate their time between family and market work differently. Any assessment of the pace of further movement toward gender equality in earnings must consider differences in the domestic roles men and women perform in the American family. The balance between paid market work and work in the home is a topic we address in the next chapter.

Racial and Ethnic Comparisons

The increase in mother-child families is characteristic of all racial and ethnic groups except Asians (Harrison and Bennett 1995, table 4A.1). Except among blacks, the majority of families with children were still two-parent families in 1990. For black families, more children were being raised by their mother alone than by both parents (see figure 6.5).

As discussed in chapter 4, across all racial and ethnic groups the labor force participation of women has increased, although rates of increase have been particularly large for white married women with children. At the beginning of this chapter, we suggested that the increase in single-parent families combined with the increase in dual-earner, married-couple families has resulted in a growing polarization among women and children—with some doing ever better because of the increased earnings of families with two earners and others doing far worse because of one or no earner in mother-child families.

Is there evidence of growing differences among women by family type within each racial and ethnic group? Trends in the median income do suggest growing dissimilarity (table 6.7). Average income increased in the 1970s and 1980s for families with two earners, with the increases in the 1970s tending to outstrip those in the 1980s (the exception being Hispanics for whom income in two-earner families rose less in the 1970s than among other groups). Except among Asians, income in families with one earner declined in real terms in the 1980s. Increasingly, to stay ahead of inflation, families need at least two earners (Levy 1987).

The result is that the income ratio between families with two earners versus those with one earner increased. By 1990, families with two earners had incomes between 1.6 and 2.4 times greater

FIGURE 6.5 Two-Parent and Mother-Child Families by Race and Ethnicity: 1990

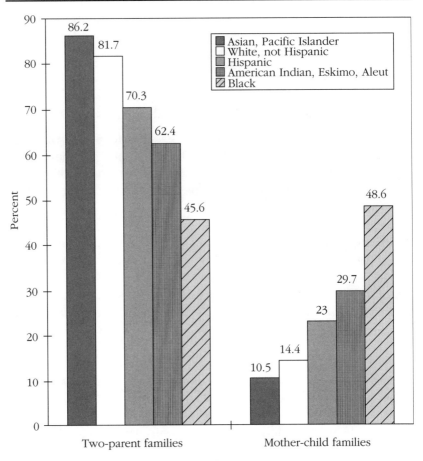

Source: U.S. Bureau of Census (1993c), table 40.
Note: Figures are for households with children under 18. Persons of Hispanic ethnicity may be of any race.

than families with only one earner. This ratio was lower (under 2.0) among whites and Asians, groups in which more of the one-earner households were traditional husband-wife couples with only the husband working. The ratio was higher (above 2.0) among Hispanics, American Indians, and blacks, groups in which many single-earner households were mother-child households.

Similarly, among all groups except whites, these ratios increased substantially in the 1980s.

Poverty rates were much higher at each point in time among mother-child families than among married couples with children. Those with the lowest poverty rates among mother-child families, whites and Asians, still had a far higher likelihood of poverty than married couples. In 1990, more than one-third of white and Asian mother-child families and over one-half of black, Hispanic, and American Indian mother-child families lived in poverty.

The ratio of the poverty rates of mother-child families to those of husband-wife families with children indicates that the economic situation of low-income white and black single mothers deteriorated relative to mothers in married-couple families. By 1990, white mothers raising children alone were over six times more likely to live in poverty than white married mothers with children. Among blacks, single mothers were 4.5 times as likely to be poor as black married mothers.

On the other hand, among the other three racial and ethnic groups, poverty did *not* increase more in mother-child households than in other types of families. The *relative* position of single mothers was better by 1990 among Hispanics, Asians, and American Indians. By 1990, single mothers in these racial and ethnic groups had poverty rates around three times those for married mothers, but this ratio was lower than in 1970 (and in 1980 among Hispanics, but not Asians and American Indians). Part of the reason was that the likelihood of poverty increased between 1970 and 1980 among Hispanic and American Indian married-couple families, and between 1980 and 1990 among Asian married-couple families, whereas poverty rates declined for black and white married-couple families.

In sum, most (but not all) indicators of economic well-being suggest greater disparity in the income and poverty of single mothers as compared with married mothers over the 1970s and 1980s. This was particularly true among blacks, the group for which the move toward more single-parent living was most accentuated. Debate continues over how much these changes in family structure have contributed to the poverty of mothers and their children (Sawhill 1992). Some suggest that as much

TABLE 6.7 Median Family Income by Family Type and by Race and Ethnicity

	White			Black		
	1970	1980	1990	1970	1980	1990
Median income in families						
w/two earners	35,120	40,240	46,120	25,670	31,450	36,990
Income ratio for families with						
Two earners/one earner	1.3	1.4	1.6	1.7	1.9	2.4
Two earners/no earner	3.8	2.7	2.6	4.7	4.5	7.0
Poverty rate						
Married couples						
w/children	8.2	5.5	5.4	19.1	14.3	12.0
Mother-child family	35.7	30.5	34.4	59.5	52.5	53.9
Poverty ratio, mother-child/						
married couple	4.4	5.6	6.4	3.1	3.7	4.5

Source: Derived from tabulations of 1970, 1980, and 1990 Censuses of Population and Housing by Harrison and Bennett (1995), table 4A.1.

as 50 percent of the rise in child poverty in the 1980s was due to the movement away from raising children within married-couple households, particularly among blacks (Eggebeen and Lichter 1991). Others emphasize that poverty increased among children living in two-parent families in which the household head had a high school education or less (Blank 1990). Low educational attainment was far more common among black, Hispanic, and American Indian householders than among whites (Blank 1990; Harrison and Bennett 1995). In the early 1990s, gender of the householder, even more so than race, differentiated who was poor and who was not: those who lived in mother-child families had a much higher likelihood of growing up poor than those who lived in a household with a male wage earner.

International Comparisons

International evidence suggests that single mothers fare worse than married mothers in all countries for which we have information (McLanahan and Casper 1995). However, the relative

TABLE 6.7 *(continued)*

	Hispanic			Asian			American Indian	
1970	1980	1990	1970	1980	1990	1970	1980	1990
28,820	31,120	34,880	32,980	41,420	42,260	22,210	30,220	32,980
1.4	1.7	2.1	1.6	1.5	1.8	1.3	1.7	2.1
4.3	4.3	5.8	4.7	4.9	5.6	3.4	3.9	5.4
11.3	16.4	18.2	12.2	9.5	10.7	17.2	18.9	20.6
57.4	56.3	54.7	44.4	34.8	35.6	61.4	51.8	57.6
5.1	3.4	3.0	3.6	3.7	3.3	3.6	2.7	2.8

deprivation of mother-child families in the United States tends to be far greater than in many European countries, which have a more generous social safety net. European countries have tended to tolerate far higher taxes and accept far greater public provision for all citizens. However, the paths taken by different countries diverge. Some, like France, provide child allowances regardless of family structure or employment status of mothers. Such non-means-tested transfers work to the benefit of both lower- and higher-income households (and thus are more politically feasible). The Scandinavian countries, Sweden in particular, tend to provide generous benefits but also encourage women to work. They tend to be relatively unconcerned with whether parents marry. Countries like the Netherlands do not have poor single mothers because of a generous safety net for all citizens but neither do they encourage work on the part of mothers, single or married. Italy has a relatively low gender poverty gap because marriage rates are very high and most childbearing occurs within marriage (Casper, McLanahan, and Garfinkel 1994).

FIGURE 6.6 Labor Force Participation of Wives in Selected
Industrialized Countries: 1985

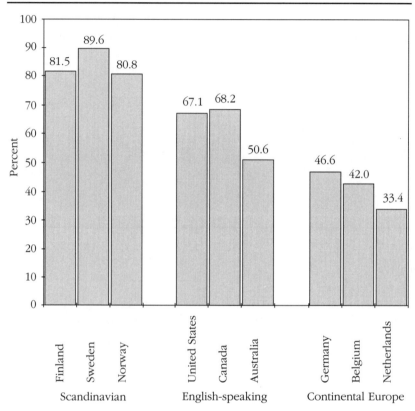

Source: Tabulations from the Luxembourg Income Study.
Note: Sample includes all couples in which the wives are age 20–60.

The variation in women's roles is reflected in the labor force participation rates of *wives* (under age sixty) in various countries (see figure 6.6). Rates are extremely high in Sweden (90 percent), Finland (82 percent), and Norway (81 percent)—countries that encourage similarity in gender roles and encourage labor market involvement of wives and mothers through paid maternity leaves, public provision of child care, and part-time work (in the case of Sweden).

More liberal "free market" economies, such as the United States and Canada, have adopted equal opportunity measures to ensure inclusion of women in the labor force but do not do much to encourage or discourage labor participation of wives and mothers. The participation rates of married women in these countries are lower than in Scandinavia but higher than in many continental European countries.

Wives' engagement in market work is quite low in countries like the Netherlands and Belgium, which have a more traditional family structure than the English-speaking or Scandinavian countries. The "traditional" couple with a wage-earning husband married to a homemaker wife has all but disappeared in Scandinavia and may be vanishing in the United States and Canada, but it is less scarce on the continent of Europe.

Consequently, if we calculate how much wives depend on husbands' earnings, with a measure that ranges from 1.0 (a wife completely dependent on a husband's earnings) to -1.0 (a husband completely dependent on a wife's earnings) with zero indicating equality, we find that wives are somewhat dependent on husband's earnings in all countries but are much closer to equality in Finland and Sweden than in Germany, Belgium, or the Netherlands (see figure 6.7).[4] U.S. wives have intermediate levels of dependency. Dependency of wives on husbands is greatly reduced in the continental European countries when the sample is restricted to dual-earner couples, but in a country like the Netherlands we eliminate over 70 percent of married couples with such a restriction (Casper, Peltola, and Bianchi 1995).

To a great extent, employment expectations for single mothers in a given country parallel those for married mothers. In the United States, one of the reasons the collection of welfare by single mothers has become increasingly suspect is that married mothers often work outside the home to support their families, and taxpayers think single mothers should work also (Bianchi 1993). In a country like Sweden, children do not sever a woman's ties with the labor force, though they do mean working part time rather than full time (Hoem 1990). Married and unmarried mothers work for pay in Sweden as well as receive guaranteed child allowances and this ensures that the cost of raising children outside marriage is lower in Sweden than in the United States. In a country like the Netherlands, where relatively few married mothers work for pay, adequate public support of unmarried

FIGURE 6.7 Mean Earnings Dependency of Wives in Selected Industrialized Countries: 1985

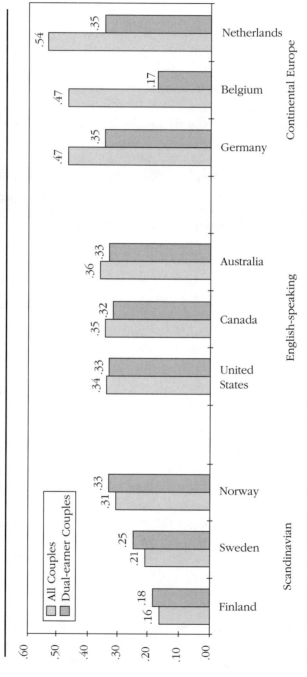

Source: Tabulations from the Luxembourg Income Study.
Note: Sample includes all couples in which wives are age 20–60. Earnings dependency is the proportion of the total earnings (husband's plus wife's) contributed by the husband *minus* the proportion contributed by the wife. For example, if the husband contributes 70 percent of total earnings and the wife 30 percent, earnings dependency is .4. If both contribute 50 percent, earnings dependency is zero.

mothers does not require labor force participation (McLanahan and Casper 1995).

The U.S. system is an individualistic one requiring market work. In the absence of work, or even in the presence of low-paid work, the alternative is public support, but at a level that is likely to be below the poverty level. Most women and children, particularly white women and children who are in married-couple families, do *not* live in poverty. But many single mothers and their children (including more than half of black, Hispanic, and American Indian single mothers) do. The situation of these two groups is more divergent in the United States than in other industrialized countries: women at the top may do better here, but those at the bottom do much worse.

Summary

When measured by household, family, or per capita income, women's economic well-being over a lifetime is more equal to that of men than are their earnings. But women are less well off than men because they have lower incomes during the years they spend outside marriage, because they spend a somewhat greater proportion of their lives living on their own, and because they are often supporting children during those years. Further, the long-term shift among single mothers from widows (supported by social security) to the never married (dependent on more modest AFDC benefits) has reduced women's economic well-being relative to men's.

Poverty rates are higher for women than for men in every age category. Persons living in mother-child families have over twice the poverty rate as those living in married-couple or father-child families. Part of this higher incidence of poverty is due to low and unpredictable child support payments from absent fathers.

Husband-wife couples have come to rely on the earnings of both partners. The proportion of family income contributed by working wives is now about 30 percent (40 percent when wives work full time). As husband-wife couples have come to rely on combined earnings, mother-child families have become more likely to have no earners given the rise in young, never married single mothers. The income of single-mother families thus has declined relative to married-mother families, at least among whites and blacks.

An increasing share of the poor live in single-parent families. In 1990, more than one-third of white and Asian mother-child families and more than one-half of black, Hispanic, and American Indian mother-child families lived in poverty. International evidence suggests that the cost of growing up in a single-parent family is greater in the United States than in most other industrial countries because public support of the low-income families is less generous in this country and has eroded over time.

CHAPTER 7

Combining Employment and Family

THE MAJORITY OF AMERICAN WOMEN HAVE ALWAYS BEEN MOTHERS, AND now a majority of mothers are also employees. The dual responsibilities of child care and paid employment are particularly problematic for the growing number of single mothers. The economic realities of women's lives—that they earn less than men and are more likely to live in poverty—mean that the balancing act between motherhood and employment is less often a choice than a necessity. The purpose of this chapter is to examine the ways in which women combine these competing obligations.

Doing It All

A woman's paid commitments can be part time, full time, or even time-and-a-half if she has a career or moonlights on a second job. Many of the demands and rewards of paid employment have been discussed in preceding chapters. Her unpaid commitments typically include housework, child care, and occasional volunteer activities. For many women, these unpaid commitments are as consuming as their "paid" jobs.

Although the physical demands of housework are less strenuous for each generation of women, the total amount of housework to be done has remained fairly constant throughout this century, with the first sign of decline occurring in the past two decades. "Labor-saving devices" did little to reduce the number of hours women spend on housework since rising standards of cleanliness accompanied improved technology (Cowan 1988; Vanek 1974). In most households, women still bear the large brunt of housework. The persistence of employed wives' primary responsibility for child care and domestic tasks has been labelled the "stalled revolution" (Hochschild 1989) because of its seeming intransigence in the face of additional market work by women. A wife's employment may, perversely, reinforce the traditional division of labor if housework becomes the primary way in which gender is defined by the couple in the rare instance when a wife earns more than her husband (Brines 1994).

A house can remain dirty and dishes can sit in the sink while couples negotiate their division of labor, but children must be cared for continuously. Actual child care takes place less and less frequently within the homes of employed women, however. In the 1950s, one-half of children whose mothers were employed full time were cared for in their own homes; by the 1990s, fewer than one-third of children with full-time employed mothers received care in their own home. Although affordable child care is the most important issue for families with employed mothers (U.S. Department of Labor 1994), the United States is the only industrialized nation that does *not* provide child care and parental leave policies supportive of families (married couples or others) in which mothers work (Kamerman and Kahn 1991).

An additional time constraint is the time spent ferrying children from one activity to another. The expansionary post–World War II economy that allowed many couples to form large families also created suburban sprawl more heavily dependent on cars than on public transportation. Dolores Hayden (1984) observes that Americans frequently complain about a lack of time, yet rather than blame the zoning regulations that ensure home, work, school, shopping, and leisure are separated by long distances most people blame their demanding lifestyle. Since few mothers of the baby boom generation were in the labor force, the time costs of such development patterns were initially invisible. Now that the majority of mothers work outside the home, the price is more apparent. Children's activities have become more formally organized as there are fewer mothers at home to supervise unstructured play, and the more formal organization has created the demand for transportation that requires additional labor from parents.

Gender Equality in Domestic Tasks

"Man's work ends at set of sun. Women's work is never done." This is a cliche most girls hear while growing up, but few appreciate until they try to combine employment and family responsibilities. Women find that a twenty- or forty-hour work week outside the home does not excuse them from tasks inside the home. Individual couples may resolve the "chore wars" differently over the life course, but employed wives typically do more housework than employed husbands.

Given the increasing amount of time women spend in market work (men's traditional domain), it is reasonable to ask how much time men spend in housework and child care (women's traditional sphere). Over the past two decades, married mothers have experienced a sizable decline in their hours of housework (from about thirty hours to about twenty hours per week); married fathers, however, picked up only part of the slack, increasing their household work from about five hours a week to about ten hours. By 1985, married mothers performed about two-thirds of all housework compared with three-quarters in 1965 (Gershuny and Robinson 1988; Robinson 1988). More recent data on time budgets corroborate the decline in hours that mothers spend on housework and the failure of fathers to compensate fully for mothers' increased market work (Marini and Shelton 1993).

Household tasks continue to differ by gender. Husbands participate most in child care and in yard and home maintenance, assuming about 40 percent of the family workload in these areas (Goldscheider and Waite 1991, chap. 7). Husbands do less than 25 percent of the cooking, cleaning, dishwashing, and laundry and share in just over 25 percent of the grocery shopping and paperwork associated with family finances. In families in which the wife works outside the home, however, husbands perform a greater share of domestic tasks and child care. The higher the wife's contribution to a family's income, the more equitable the division of labor within the home. And couples with egalitarian gender-role attitudes share tasks more often than couples with traditional attitudes (Waite and Goldscheider 1992).

As younger cohorts of women and men with similar labor force and earnings experiences replace cohorts with dissimilar labor force experiences, the gender division of labor in the home may become more equal. Progress toward that goal will be slow, however, since in 1990 married women averaged nine hundred fewer hours of market work a year and earned almost $6 less an hour than married men (see table 6.6 in chapter 6). More promising is the possibility that husbands' participation in housework may increase as a result of the growing diversity in employment schedules among husbands and wives, since variations in work hours are significant determinants of a husband's contribution to traditionally female tasks (Brayfield 1995; Presser 1994). Interestingly, so are women's: those working nonstandard shifts perform *more* housework a week than women who work regular hours. The more flexible an employed woman's job, the more time she spends on housework (Silver and Goldscheider 1994).

These assumptions are based on a rational economic theory of exchange: the more work a woman does for pay, the greater her bargaining power within the marriage and the less nonmarket work she will do (Blau and Ferber 1992). A dissenting theory is that the more wives work outside the home, the *more* traditional the division of labor within the home because women and men will struggle to define appropriate gender roles within the family. This perspective views housework as a "symbolic enactment of gender relations" (South and Spitze 1994). Wives tend to operate on the model that household labor is provided in return for economic support (Walby 1986). Husbands who are out of work or in low-income households do not share the same view, however: these husbands do less housework the more they depend on their wives for income (Brines 1994). Working class or poor husbands may perceive performing household chores as further evidence of their failure to provide for the family. Resisting "women's work" may be one of the few sources of marital power remaining to the unemployed husband, and one of the only ways he can define his masculinity. If economic restructuring continues to affect blue-collar workers disproportionately, higher rates of long-term male joblessness might stall the domestic revolution even further (Brines 1994; Morris 1990; Wheelock 1990).

Husbands are more likely to participate in housework when their wives are highly educated and employed. The effect of education on attitudes toward an appropriate division of labor are influenced by the husband's income, however. As a husband's income rises, his involvement with chores declines. High-income men do more housework only if their wives earn comparable incomes; otherwise they do the least of all married men (Model 1981; Spitze 1988). (At some point, of course, neither partner in a high-income marriage needs to perform major housework if they decide to hire someone else to do it.)

Employed women and men face different dilemmas when juggling home and work responsibilities. Women's family roles tend to intrude on their work roles, whereas men's work roles tend to intrude on their family time. For example, when a child in day care becomes sick, the wife is more likely than the husband to leave work; when an overnight business trip is required, the husband is more likely than the wife to have the job that demands it. Husbands can "take work home" in ways that advance their careers, while taking "home to work" limits women's career development (Pleck 1985). As long as men have fewer family responsibilities and women have many more, the potential exists for women to choose or accept lower occupational status and earnings, which in turn affects their bargaining position within the marriage (Bianchi and Spain 1986, p. 233).

Perceptions of Fairness

Academic researchers seem more troubled by the division of household labor than the women they interview, many of whom think their household arrangement is equitable. The psychological theory of cognitive dissonance suggests that most people perceive their lives to be fair because they need to reconcile expectations with reality (for better or worse) (Festinger 1957). Women are no exception. Most married women are satisfied with the amount of housework they perform, even though most wives do far more housework than their husbands. The majority of husbands and wives believe that housework should be shared equally if both spouses work year round and full time, but these beliefs may not always translate into practice (Huber and Spitze 1983).

Social exchange theory proposes that power and dependency influence how people assess fairness, and that power depends on individual resources (such as income) (Blau 1964). Applying this framework to the family means that the spouse with fewer economic resources, and so fewer alternatives, has less influence on family decision-making (also known as the "principle of least interest," Waller (1938) [1951]). Under this model, wives would have a greater interest in maintaining the marriage than husbands because their earnings are lower, in contemporary society the probability of divorce is high, and wives' investments tend to be in intangible family relationships while husbands' investments tend to produce tangible benefits (England and Kilbourne 1990). A wife's dissatisfaction with the household division of labor, however, can lead to thoughts of divorce (Booth and White 1980; Huber and Spitze 1980).

Perceptions of fairness depend on comparisons of one's status with that of others. A sense of "relative deprivation" is more likely to occur when peers receive different treatment than when actual deprivation occurs (Homans 1961; Merton 1968). Since fewer resources tend to limit one's world, women may compare themselves with other women in similar circumstances and expect less from the marriage (Lennon and Rosenfield 1994). These factors may affect women's assessment of the fairness of housework if their lower wages and greater costs of divorce lead them to think whatever housework their husbands do is fair (Hochschild 1989).

Other explanations for women's perceptions of fairness include the importance of gender ideology. Some women believe they *should* do most of the housework regardless of their employment status. The more conventional an employed wife's view of a woman's role in the family, the more likely she is to perceive an unequal division of household work as fair (Thompson 1991). Another explanation comes from neoclassical economics, which proposes that differential returns to women's and men's market labor affect perceptions of equity (Becker 1981). Husbands who make more money outside the home may be excused from unpaid work within the home. This perspective suggests that the fewer hours women spend in the labor force (compared with their husbands), the more fair they perceive an unequal division of housework to be (Lennon and Rosenfield 1994). It may also be true that women think they deserve little credit for housework (Major 1987), or that women and men value each others' work differently (Thompson 1991).

Empirical research has established support for several of these theories and challenged others. Sanchez (1994) found little evidence of the neoclassical or social exchange models. Her 1988 national data revealed that women's employment hours had no effect on husbands' perceptions of fairness, nor did husbands' work hours affect women's or men's expectations of his contributions. Instead, she found that a sense of equity derived more from a husband's *increased* efforts than a wife's *reduced* efforts. Other research has shown that wives' economic dependence on husbands affects their sense of fairness (Kane and Sanchez 1994; Lennon and Rosenfield 1994).

These theories about the division of household labor and perceptions of its fairness share one drawback with the Butz and Ward (1979) theory about the relationship between women's market work and fertility: they concern married couples only, and women are spending fewer years married. Women's realization that they may do most of the housework regardless of the presence of a husband may contribute to their reluctance to marry (or to remarry). The gender gap in time spent doing housework is widest among married couples, but women spend more time than men in housework regardless of their marital status. This finding has implications for women's well-being because performance of housework is related to decisions about paid work and the pursuit of leisure (South and Spitze 1994).

Adaptations to Employment and Family Obligations

Women juggling home and employment adopt various adaptive strategies, including lower fertility and certain occupational choices. Surprisingly, however, some of the most "feminized" jobs are the least likely to provide the flexibility mothers need.

More than two decades ago, Bumpass and Westoff (1970) asked "Do women limit their fertility in order to have time to pursue their non-family-oriented interests, or do women work if their fertility permits them to do so?" This question has become the demographic equivalent of Freud's classic "What do women want?" After years of research, the answer is still unclear.

Women who work outside the home have fewer children than women who are not employed. In 1992, employed women aged eighteen to thirty-four had an average of 0.9 children compared with an average of 1.7 children for women not in the labor force. Employed women also are more likely to expect to remain childless: 11 percent in 1992 compared with 6 percent of women not in the labor force (see chapter 1, table 1.5).

On one side of the debate are those who argue that the strongest causal relationship is the effect of fertility on labor force participation: the presence and ages of children determine whether and how much a woman will engage in paid work (Sweet 1973). Others argue that the strongest causal direction is from labor force participation to completed fertility: young women who plan to work reduce their fertility in order to achieve labor force goals. Women's plans to work have a substantial impact on the total number of children they expect, while number of children expected has little effect on future labor force plans (Stolzenberg and Waite 1977; Waite and Stolzenberg 1976). Employment may depress fertility by competing for a woman's time. Women who work after marriage tend to delay the birth of the first child and may either delay the second birth or accelerate it in an effort to compress time spent out of the labor force (Blau and Robins 1988).

Models that allow for reciprocity between fertility and employment have not fully resolved the controversy because fertility can affect work patterns in the short run, whereas employment can have long-term effects on fertility (Cramer 1980). Whether fertility is intended or unintended also can affect employment, as do antecedent causes common to both fertility and labor force participation (such as education and age at first marriage). It is also true that both childbearing and employment create "hard choices" that must constantly be renegotiated throughout life (Gerson 1985). The ultimate reason for the negative correlation between fertility and employment—regardless of causation—is that the role of mother often contradicts that of a paid employee (Bianchi and Spain 1986, p. 224). Many women try to resolve this conflict by taking part-time jobs.

Part-time jobs may be compatible with child rearing, but the economic costs are great compared with working full time. A loss of income is not the only penalty: women who work part time also suffer an erosion of their wage rate, a loss of seniority, and often a loss of benefits and job security (Corcoran, Duncan, and Ponza 1984; Holden and Hansen 1987). Although part-time work may result in short-term economic gains compared with non-working mothers, the long-term consequences of part-time work are negative because the effect on women's wages is nearly equivalent to the effects of time spent out of the labor force entirely (primarily because part-time jobs tend to require the least skill) (Corcoran, Duncan, and Ponza 1984). When the cost of day care is added to long-term wage depression, it is understandable that some women say they cannot afford to work.

In addition to working part time, women may choose certain occupations that accommodate family responsibilities. Mothers therefore tend to self-select into jobs that make employment and parenthood easier to balance (Feiner and Roberts 1990; Hall 1986; Polachek 1981). As discussed in chapter 5, human capital theory argues that women choose jobs that permit easy exit and reentry in order to minimize wage and skills loss. Secretarial and clerical work are traditional examples of this occupational category. Although these jobs may be incompatible with parenthood (because of their typically rigid hours) they are relatively easy to quit and to reenter after a period of unemployment. Thus occupational segregation is perpetuated by women's attempts to combine work and family (Polachek 1976, 1981). Mothers even tend to work in occupations with larger than average proportions of other mothers, and their labor force attachment is stronger in such jobs (Desai and Waite 1991).

These theories sound so logical that many mothers choose part-time work or certain occupations based on the assumption that they will provide the flexibility they need. The problem with these theories, however, is that they seldom hold up in the workplace. Predominantly female jobs are often *less* likely to offer the traits that make parenting easier (Bielby and Bielby 1988; Glass

1990). Both part-time and "women's" work reduce the authority and reward structure that enhance job flexibility. Managers or executives, for example, have more control over their own time than secretaries (Glass and Camarigg 1992). Thus the efforts women make to accommodate work and family may have both greater short-term constraints and long-term economic costs than they anticipate.

Another adaptation that employed women make to family responsibilities is to work closer to home than men. Since a wife is typically the secondary wage earner, her job choices may be more limited than those of her husband. Convenience may therefore become a deciding factor in accepting a job, especially since women are more likely than men to use public transit to get to work (Rutherford and Wekerle 1988). Married and unmarried women alike face a similar spatial segregation of jobs that concentrate women's jobs in one part of the metropolitan area and men's jobs in another (Hanson and Pratt 1995). Thus a rational-choice model for women who are primary wage earners (such as single mothers) would be to live near their place of work (Villeneuve and Rose 1988).

Geographers Hanson and Pratt (1991, p. 250) argue that the division of domestic labor, power relations in the household, and the gendered nature of social life lead women and men to search for jobs in different ways, and that geography is at the center of this search. Women's home-based responsibilities lead many to give priority to proximity; their status as secondary wage earners limits job choices; and their network of information about jobs is more locally (and more female) based than men's networks. All these factors result in shorter commutes for women—and often in the reproduction of occupational segregation.

Child Care Arrangements

Child care arrangements are seldom simple for children of any age. Since three-quarters of all mothers of preschoolers were working in 1990 (including one-half of all mothers with infants), child care for very young children is now more critical than it was in the 1950s (when just over one-tenth of mothers of preschoolers were in the labor force) (Bianchi and Spain 1986, p. 225). What was once an individual concern for a minority of mothers has become a public issue. The United States is beginning to acknowledge the importance of child care at the federal level. The Family Support Act of 1988, for example, was meant to facilitate employment for mothers of young children by improving their wages and reducing child care costs. Yet this legislation falls short of the supportive policies of most European nations (Kamerman 1995).

Child care has also become a controversial political issue. An underlying assumption of current efforts at welfare reform, for example, is that unemployed mothers will enter the labor force if adequate child care is available (Blau and Robins 1988). Surveys since the 1970s have found that mothers (often those who are poor) do not seek employment or work fewer hours than they would like because of a shortage of high-quality, affordable child care (Bloom and Steen 1990; Mason and Kuhlthau 1992; Presser and Baldwin 1980; U.S. Department of Labor 1994). Women who already work are more likely to drop out of the labor force if their child care expenses are high (Maume 1991). Income is important in affecting women's *perceptions* of whether available child care is adequate and whether they report that child care problems have limited their employment. Poor women have fewer resources than affluent ones, both in neighborhood access to facilities and ability to afford them, so they are more likely to perceive child care as problematic and as a constraint on their labor force participation. Thus policies designed to improve child care and reduce its costs to low-income women could increase their labor force participation and potentially reduce public assistance (Mason and Kuhlthau 1992).

Working mothers depend less on in-home child care during the 1990s than they did during the 1960s. Although care in the home is probably most satisfying to women and their children, it can also be more expensive than group care when it is provided by a paid babysitter. Therefore, parents, frequently with the help of relatives, tend to arrange their schedules to minimize child care costs. In 1991, 14 percent of children were cared for by their fathers when wives worked full time, while a significantly higher proportion (29 percent) of children whose mothers worked part time were cared for by their fathers (see table 7.1); children whose mothers work part time are more likely to be cared for at

TABLE 7.1 Child Care Arrangements of Working Mothers, Selected Years

Type of Child Care	Worked Full Time				Worked Part Time			
	1965	1977	1982	1991	1965	1977	1982	1991
Total	100.0	100.0	100.0	100.0	100.0	100.0	100.0	100.0
Care in child's home	47.2	28.6	25.7	29.9	47.0	42.7	39.3	45.5
By father	10.3	10.6	10.3	14.8	22.9	23.1	20.3	28.9
By other relative	18.4	11.4	10.3	9.3	15.6	11.2	12.7	12.1
By nonrelative	18.5	6.6	5.1	5.9	8.6	8.4	6.3	4.5
Care in another home	37.3	47.4	43.8	35.0	17.0	28.8	34.0	24.2
By relative	17.6	20.8	19.7	14.4	9.1	13.2	15.6	13.3
By nonrelative	19.6	26.6	24.1	20.6	7.9	15.6	18.4	14.9
Group care center	8.2	14.6	18.8	27.8	2.7	9.1	7.5	14.9
Child cares for self	0.3	0.3	—	—	0.9	0.5	—	—
Mother cares for child while working	6.7	8.2	6.2	5.2	32.3	18.5	14.4	14.6
All other arrangements	0.4	0.8	0.3	2.1	—	0.4	0.1	0.8
Don't know/no answer	—	—	5.3	—	—	—	4.7	—

Source: Lueck, Orr, and O'Connell (1982), table A; O'Connell and Rogers (1982), table A; U.S. Bureau of the Census (1994c), table 1.

Note: Data for children under age 6 of ever married women, 1958 and 1965; data for youngest two children under age 5 of ever married women in 1977; data for youngest child under age 5 of all women in 1982.

home (nearly one-half in 1991). This arrangement is consistent with findings that variable employment schedules facilitate husband's contributions to traditionally female tasks, since women who work part time may be working different hours than their husbands (Brayfield 1995; Presser 1994). Fathers also tend to play an important role in multiple child care arrangements, especially for preschoolers (Folk and Yi 1994).

The proportion of children being cared for in the home by relatives and nonrelatives has declined over time. Group care has taken up the slack, as has care provided in another home. Care in another home is more likely to be provided by a nonrelative than a relative. Growth of child care in group centers has been most explosive for children with full-time working mothers: it grew from 8 percent of all accommodations in 1965 to 28 percent in 1991. Children of part-time working mothers are least likely to be cared for in group centers, but that proportion also grew between 1965 and 1991 (from 3 to 15 percent). As women age, they also tend to rely more on nonrelatives for child care (Blau and Robins 1991).

The increased proportion of employed mothers has transformed the workplace as well as family life. Some employers provide child care or flexible work hours in response to the needs of parents. Some companies allow parents (usually the mother) *paid* leave for the birth or adoption of a child, while others have expanded the definition of paid sick leave to include children's or dependent's illness. Common in white-collar offices is the 3:00 p.m. "children's hour," when children call their mothers to let them know they have arrived home safely from school.

An important issue that researchers are just beginning to address is that of women's responsibilities for care of their elderly parents. The "sandwich generation" of women who delayed childbearing may face the problems of aging parents at the same time they are dealing with the emotional and economic demands of young children. Lower fertility among daughters of the baby boom also means there are fewer siblings with whom to share the costs and time commitments of parental care. Since men do few of the traditional chores in a household, including child care, sons of the elderly may be more likely to make financial contributions to their parents' well-being while daughters are expected to take responsibility for day-to-day care (Spitze 1988).

One line of research suggests that parental care creates demands on women similar to child care in that it reduces the labor force participation of women who live with a disabled parent (Ettner 1995). Other evidence indicates that multigenerational caregiving has little effect on women's lives. Research on the dual burden of caring for one's children and one's parent(s) has yet to show an impact on the quality of women's marriages, their sense of psychological well-being, family financial resources, use of leisure time, or perceived fairness of household division of labor. The absence of stress may be explained by a selectivity effect if only those women with the strongest marriages and caregiving ethic take on such multigenerational responsibilities (Loomis and Booth 1995; Spitze and Logan 1990).

Changing Attitudes About Gender Roles

The success with which women strike a balance between motherhood and employment can be facilitated or hindered by public attitudes toward women's proper roles. Women's behavior may be influenced by public opinion, but public opinion, in turn, is shaped by people's actual behavior. It would be surprising if attitudes toward appropriate gender roles had remained the same since the 1970s in light of the demographic changes documented in this book. The most significant attitudinal change has been Americans' greater acceptance of women's participation in the public sphere, even by those with traditionally conservative religious beliefs (Iannoccone and Mile 1990; Peck, Lowe, and Williams 1991).

Receptivity to women's election to political office, for example, has changed dramatically. The proportion of Americans who say they would vote for a woman for president has increased steadily over time and reached about 90 percent in 1993, while the proportion believing that women should "take care of the home and leave running the country up to men" has declined (see figure 7.1).

Although Americans have not yet had the opportunity to vote for a woman for president, each year they elect more women to Congress. Female membership of Congress increased from 4 to 10

Figure 7.1 Responses to Questions About Women's Employment

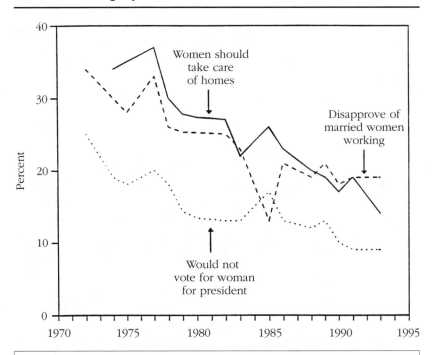

Questions:
(Women should take care of homes): Do you agree or disagree with this statement? Women should take care of running their homes and leave running the country up to men. (Figure shows percent who agree).
(Disapprove of married women working): Do you approve or disapprove of a married woman earning money in business or industry if she has a husband capable of supporting her? (Figure shows percent disapproving).
(Vote for woman for president): If your political party nominated a woman for President, would you vote for her if she were qualified for the job? (Figure shows percent saying no).

Source: National Opinion Research Center (1993), items 198–200; Farley (1996).

percent between 1975 and 1995 (Center for the American Woman in Politics 1995). While this falls far short of a feminist transformation of the institution, it represents new political support for women in nontraditional roles. Geraldine Ferraro's candidacy for vice president in the 1984 election set the stage symbolically for women to run for president, and Sandra Day O'Connor's appointment to the Supreme Court was pathbreaking. Political acceptance of women has translated most clearly into victories for women at the individual state level. In 1995, women held 26 percent of all statewide elective executive offices (Center for the American Woman in Politics 1995).

Most women's concerns, however, are more mundane than getting elected to Congress; they struggle with the decision of how much to work outside the home. Figure 7.1 demonstrates the gradual acceptance (if not endorsement) of married women's employment. The proportion of Americans approving of working wives peaked in 1985 (at about 85 percent) and has declined slightly since then, perhaps in response to fewer economic opportunities for men.

People now recognize and support a multiplicity of roles for women. Public opinion polls have shown a steady decline in negative reactions to working mothers: by 1993, almost two-thirds of those surveyed thought working mothers could establish a warm relationship with their children, an increase from about one-half two decades ago. Americans still hold reservations, however, about the mothers of preschoolers working. Disapproval has declined from almost 70 percent two decades ago but still remained at about 50 percent in 1993. Estimates of the importance of a woman's career have improved, with a comparable decline in the belief that the husband should be the one to achieve outside the home (see figure 7.2).

There is, of course, a reciprocal relationship between attitudes and behavior. Public opinion was negative when few women worked outside the home. As women entered the job market, however, attitudes changed to meet new realities. It is often easier to adapt attitudes to changing necessities than to live with the conflict created by divergent behavior and beliefs (Bianchi and Spain 1986, p. 238).

Racial and Ethnic Comparisons

The roles of motherhood, marriage, and employment differed significantly by race and ethnicity in 1990. White women were the most likely to be married, black women the least likely, and Hispanic women's marriage rates fell between those two groups. All

FIGURE **7.2 Responses to Questions About Women Combining Home and Work**

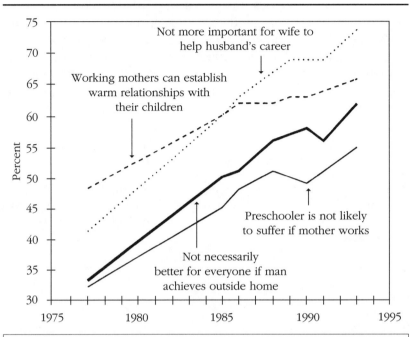

Questions:
(More important for wife to help husband's career): It is more important for a wife to help her husband's career than to have one herself. (Figure shows percent disagreeing.)
(Working mothers can establish warm relationships): A working mother can establish just as warm and secure a relationship with her children as a mother who does not work. (Figure shows percent agreeing.)
(Preschoolers suffer if mother works): A preschool child is likely to suffer if his or her mother works. (Figure shows percent disagreeing.)
(Better for everyone if man achieves outside home): It is much better for everyone involved if the man is the achiever outside the home and the woman takes care of the home and family. (Figure shows percent disagreeing.)

Source: National Opinion Research Center (1993), item 252; Farley (1996).

three groups shared a decline in the prevalence of marriage since 1980. Mothers' labor force participation rates rose for all groups during the 1980s, with white mothers being most likely to work outside the home in 1990 and Hispanic mothers the least likely (McLanahan and Casper 1995, p. 13). Married mothers *not* working outside the home were a distinct minority in 1990 among all racial and ethnic groups (see table 7.2).

"Traditional" families consisting of a homemaker wife who stays home with her children have declined for all women since 1980. White women experienced the largest decline in this type of household between 1980 and 1990 (a drop of nine percentage points). Hispanic women were most likely to be living in such an arrangement in 1990 (16 percent) and black women the

TABLE 7.2 **Women's Employment and Family Status by Race and Ethnicity: 1980 and 1990**

	Percent Distribution in 1980	Percent Distribution in 1990	Percentage Point Change
White women	100	100	
Traditional family			
Married, child, homemaker	21	12	−9
Married, no child, homemaker	8	6	−2
Nontraditional family			
Married, child, employed	21	26	+5
Married, no child, employed	16	20	+4
Single, child, employed	5	5	0
Single, child, homemaker	2	2	0
Nonfamily			
Single, no child, employed	21	24	+3
Single, no child, not employed	6	5	−1
Black women	100	100	
Traditional family			
Married, child, homemaker	9	5	−4
Married, no child, homemaker	4	3	−1
Nontraditional family			
Married, child, employed	17	17	0
Married, no child, employed	8	9	+1

least likely (5 percent). The growth of employed single mothers was greatest for black women (three percentage points) and remained almost stable for Hispanic women; there was no growth among white women who were single employed mothers. The black community may be more supportive of employed mothers than the white community, although black women may also have more economic incentives to work than white women (Jones 1985).

TABLE **7.2** *(continued)*

	Percent Distribution in 1980	Percent Distribution in 1990	Percentage Point Change
Single, child, employed	14	17	+3
Single, child, homemaker	12	11	−1
Nonfamily			
Single, no child, employed	21	25	+4
Single, no child, not employed	15	13	−2
Hispanic women	*100*	*100*	
Traditional family			
Married, child, homemaker	22	16	−6
Married, no child, homemaker	6	6	0
Nontraditional family			
Married, child, employed	22	22	0
Married, no child, employed	10	11	+1
Single, child, employed	7	8	+1
Single, child, homemaker	6	6	0
Nonfamily			
Single, no child, employed	17	21	+4
Single, no child, not employed	10	10	0

Source: McLanahan and Casper (1995), table 1.4.
Notes: Single defined as never married, separated, divorced, widowed, or cohabiting. Child defined as women living with a natural, adopted, or stepchild under age 18. Employed defined as usually worked 20 hours or more a week outside of the home last year.

Regardless of family structure, the racial and ethnic group with the largest number of workers per family in 1990 was Asians. Nearly 20 percent of Asian families had three or more workers in 1990 and just 8 percent contained no workers. Hispanic families ranked next highest in total number of family workers. While whites, blacks, and American Indians were about equally likely to have three or more workers in the family (at 12 to 13 percent); black families were the most likely to report no workers (17 percent) (see table 7.3).

The higher the number of workers, the greater is the potential for adequate family income. Among black families, for example, the presence of other adults enables mothers to return to the labor force quickly (Yoon and Waite 1994). The poor job market for black men and their greater willingness to participate in child care than white husbands suggest that black husbands, when they are present in the household, may compensate for a lack of paid employment with greater contributions to unpaid household work (Hossain and Roopnarine 1993; Taylor and others 1991; Willie 1985).

The interaction between parental employment and family structure has important implications for children's well-being. Policy debates on children in poverty identify the increase in single

TABLE 7.3 **Number of Workers in Family by Race and Ethnicity: 1990**

Workers in Family	Racial or Ethnic Group				
	White	Black	American Indian	Asian	Hispanic
Families (in thousands)	51,337	6,927	464	1,578	4,776
No workers (percent)	12.9	16.6	14.5	8.3	11.2
One worker (percent)	27.1	33.2	33.2	26.2	31.2
Two workers (percent)	47.3	36.9	40.5	45.7	40.1
Three or more workers (percent)	12.8	13.3	11.9	19.8	17.5

Source: Harrison and Bennett (1995), table 4A.1.

mothers and differential employment opportunities as corner-stones to understanding children's poverty (Bianchi 1993; Have-man and Wolfe 1993). The *combination* of single motherhood and poor employment patterns that characterize minorities exacerbates racial and ethnic differences in childhood poverty (Hernandez 1993; Lichter and Eggebeen 1994; Hogan and Lichter 1995).

Poverty rates are highest for black and American Indian children regardless of family structure, while parental work structures are more important among Hispanics than among blacks or whites in determining the incidence of poverty among children. In other words, the low rates of labor force participation among Hispanic women (either due to discrimination or educational or language problems) explain more of the poverty rates among Mexican American and Puerto Rican children than among black or white children (Lichter and Landale 1995). Poverty among minority (and white) children would be virtually eliminated if all children lived in two-parent families in which both parents worked. Changes in family structure alone or in employment patterns alone would not be sufficient to raise children out of poverty, but changes in both could significantly reduce childhood poverty (Hogan and Lichter 1995, p. 114).

International Comparisons

The ways in which women balance employment and family vary by country, both because women's work experiences are different among industrialized nations and because government and private employers' policies differ. The actual amount of time women spend in paid and unpaid work varies considerably among industrialized countries, although the relationship between women' s and men's work is similar: men spend more time on market work and women spend more time on housework. In most countries for which information is available, hours spent on housework are increasing somewhat for men and decreasing for women, whereas just the opposite is true for market work. Men are reducing their hours of paid work while women are increasing theirs (Blau and Ferber 1992, pp. 319–20).

International comparisons of time use demonstrate that men spend about twice as many hours a week as women on paid work; the difference is smallest in Denmark, Finland, Norway, and

Sweden. Men spend the most hours on housework in Sweden (eighteen a week) followed closely by the United States at seventeen hours. Neither women nor men report spending much time on child care, but women's hours are typically double those of men's. Women in the former Soviet Union report the longest work weeks (sixty-nine hours total) and the least free time (ninety-nine hours), while British women have the shortest work weeks (forty-four hours). American women average fifty-six hours of total work per week. Russian, Swedish, and American women work the greatest number of hours for pay: thirty-eight, twenty-seven, and twenty-four hours a week, respectively (see table 7.4).

Expanded labor force participation by mothers (married and unmarried) has characterized most industrialized countries over the past two decades. In the late 1980s, the proportion of married mothers in the labor force ranged from a low of 44 percent in Italy to a high of 89 percent in Sweden; 66 percent of married mothers in the United States worked in 1990. The pattern was identical for single mothers, with a range from 45 percent for Italians to 89 percent for Swedes, with 66 percent for American single mothers (Sorrentino 1990, p. 53).

Married mothers with preschoolers are least likely to be in the labor force in the United Kingdom and Germany (37 to 40 percent), while Danish and Swedish married mothers of preschoolers are most likely to work (84 and 86 percent, respectively). Just over one-half of American married mothers of preschoolers worked for pay in the late 1980s. Single mothers with preschoolers are least likely to be in the labor force in the United Kingdom (23 percent) and most likely to be employed in Denmark and Sweden (81 percent). In the United States, 45 percent of unmarried mothers of preschoolers were employed in the 1980s (see table 7.5).

The tendency for mothers to be employed, and their use of child care, can be facilitated or hindered by public policy. U.S. mothers tend to have labor force participation rates and child care usage rates that are intermediate between Scandinavian countries and many continental European countries (Kamerman 1995). The Scandinavian countries provide universal free or low-cost preschool to children at age two or three. All the countries except the United States provide universal cash benefits (family allowances) based on the number and ages of children, so that mothers in many countries may choose not to work outside the

TABLE 7.4 Weekly Hours in Paid and Unpaid Work for Selected Industrialized Countries

Country	Hours Worked						Total Unpaid				Free Time	
	Total		Paid		Unpaid		Housework		Child Care			
	Women	Men	Women	Men	Women	Men	Women	Men	Women	Men	Women	Men
Australia	49	49	15	31	34	18	28	16	6	2	116	116
Austria	50	46	16	33	34	13	31	12	4	1	113	116
Canada	48	47	19	32	29	16	25	14	4	2	117	116
Denmark	44	46	22	35	22	11	21	10	2	1	120	118
Federal Republic of Germany	45	42	15	30	30	12	27	11	3	1	120	122
Finland	48	44	23	32	24	13	21	11	4	1	115	119
Italy	46	36	11	28	33	8	35	8	2	1	115	124
Japan	47	44	20	41	27	3	24	3	3	1	118	120
Netherlands	45	44	10	27	34	18	31	16	4	1	118	118
Norway	50	49	19	31	31	18	25	16	5	2	114	116
Sweden	60	61	27	41	33	20	28	18	5	2	105	105
United Kingdom	44	38	14	27	30	11	26	10	4	1	124	130
United States	56	60	24	41	32	18	30	17	2	1	112	109
USSR (former)	69	65	38	49	30	16	26	15	4	2	99	103

Source: United Nations (1995), table 8. Data are for the 1980s and 1990s.

Note: Free time includes sleep. Unpaid work is the sum of housework and child care hours.

TABLE 7.5 Labor Force Participation of Women Under Age 60 by Presence of Children in Eight Countries

Country	All Women	All Mothers with Children		Single Mothers with Children	
		Under 18 Years	Under 3 Years	Under 18 Years	Under 3 Years
Canada	66.8	67.0	58.4	63.6	41.3
Denmark	79.2	86.1	83.9	85.9	80.9
France	60.1	65.8	60.1	85.2	69.6
Germany	55.8	48.4	39.7	69.7	50.4
Italy	43.3	43.9	45.0	67.2	68.0
Sweden	80.0	89.4	85.8	—	81.0
United Kingdom	64.3	58.7	36.9	51.9	23.4
United States	68.5	65.0	52.5	65.3	45.1

Source: Sorrentino (1990), p. 53.

Note: Women ages 60 to 64 are included in Canada and Sweden. The bottom of the age range is 16 for the United States and Sweden, 15 for Canada, and 14 for all other countries. For participation rates of women with children, no upper limit is applied for the United States or Canada. These differences do not distort the comparisons because very few women under 16 have children, while few women over 60 live with their minor children. Figures include divorced, separated, never married, and widowed women.

Data for the United States are for March 1988; Canada and Sweden—annual averages for 1988; data for all other countries are for spring 1986.

Children under 16 years for Canada and Sweden.

home. Norwegian family policy specifies that unmarried mothers should have the right to choose between staying at home and taking a job, ensuring that mothers with no other income will receive tax-free cash benefits equaling one-half the median income of a two-parent family. Eight industrialized nations have established special benefits for children in divorced families so that a child is guaranteed custodial support. Most industrialized countries (again with the exception of the United States) also provide national health care. Many countries provide paid parental leave that can extend up to three years from the date of birth. In sum, European countries have developed social policies to alleviate the conflicts created for families when the mother is single or employed. The United States differs from other industrialized countries in its failure to mandate direct income transfers to all families with children. Nor does it publicly provide child care nor have parental leave policies as supportive of families as in Europe (Kamerman 1995).

Summary

Americans have come to accept a greater variety of roles for women over the past two decades. This liberalization has both responded to changes in women's employment patterns and has facilitated the entry of women into the labor force. The primary adjustment that women have had to make (compared with earlier cohorts) is in the balancing of their paid and unpaid work, including child care.

Women still do the majority of housework, regardless of their employment status. Husbands now do more than in the past, but feminists consider men's lack of responsiveness to domestic responsibilities to represent a "stalled revolution" in sex role expectations (Hochschild 1989). Many women, however, feel that the household division of labor is fair.

Women adopt various strategies to successfully combine family and employment obligations. One is to postpone childbearing and to have smaller families. Another adaptation is women's choices of part-time or gender-segregated jobs that are supposedly easier to enter, leave, and reenter. Ironically, however, the very jobs that women seek in order to provide flexibility are the ones that often offer the least autonomy.

Working mothers rely increasingly on child-care arrangements outside the home. The lack of good-quality, affordable child care, however, is often cited by women as a reason for not working. The provision of child care has become an important political issue in the debate over welfare reform. A critical question is whether poor women will enter the labor force if affordable child care is provided. A related issue for women is *parental* care. Like the presence of a child, responsibility for a dependent parent reduces labor force participation for women, although it does not appear to affect women's sense of well-being. As the population ages and as women postpone childbearing, more and more women may face the dual challenges of caring for growing children and aging parents simultaneously.

Racial and ethnic differences in the likelihood that mothers are married and participating in the labor force result in different levels of well-being for children. Hispanic mothers are most likely to be married but least likely to be employed, which creates high levels of poverty for Hispanic children. Black women are least likely to be married (although a high proportion work), which contributes to high poverty rates for black children. Both family structure and employment patterns must be addressed if childhood poverty is to be alleviated.

The United States is similar to other industrialized nations in the number of hours that women spend in paid and unpaid labor, and in the division of labor within the home. Mothers in the United States have labor force participation rates, and child care usage rates, intermediate between the highest and lowest rates for industrialized nations. The United States is one of the few industrialized countries, however, that has failed to produce federal policies (like child care and parental leave) supportive of women's family and work roles. Given the lack of infrastructure available to American women compared with their counterparts internationally, it is perhaps surprising how many women succeed as well as they do in combining work and families.

Conclusion

THE THEME OF THIS BOOK HAS BEEN THE BALANCING ACT WOMEN STRIKE in negotiating their roles as mothers, wives, and breadwinners. Women have always held multiple roles, but the timing of those responsibilities has changed so that they are now simultaneous rather than sequential. Mothers of the baby boom got married, had children, and either stayed at home or entered the labor force after their children were grown. Women today may or may not be married when they have children, and even young mothers are more likely than not to be in the labor force.

With the exception of the baby boom, fertility has declined throughout this century, although the United States has recently returned to replacement-level fertility with an average of 2.1 births per woman. The significant fertility story of the 1980s, however, is nonmarital fertility: it has increased and now accounts for almost one-third of all births. Teenage fertility has also risen, although the majority of births to unwed mothers are to women in their twenties and thirties. In addition, more women are having children later in life, as higher birth rates for women in their thirties illustrate. Birth expectations have remained stable at about 2.2 children per woman. Abortion rates have declined, possibly due to the combined effects of more effective contraceptive use, reduced federal funding, and anti-abortion activists' harassment of doctors performing (and patients receiving) abortions. The most typical form of contraception for married couples is surgical sterility (tubal ligation or vasectomy) and for unmarried women it is the birth control pill.

The majority of women still marry, but they do so at later ages and for shorter periods of time than in the past. Divorce rates have dropped slightly after decades of increase, although by international standards they are still high. The growth of families headed by women continues to be fueled by these high divorce rates, by delayed marriage, and by rising rates of nonmarital fertility. Remarriage rates are also somewhat lower than in the past and reflect the rising popularity of cohabitation after divorce. Older women, while slightly less likely to be widowed than in 1960, are still three times as likely to be widowed as elderly men.

Younger women are now as likely as young men to attain a college degree. The probability that a woman who graduates from high school will attend college is now equal to the probability for male high school graduates, and women have outnumbered men on college campuses for several years. After two decades of decline in the gender segregation of college majors, though, there appears to be a return to gender-stereotyped majors, and occupational and earnings returns to education are still lower for women than for men.

Women's labor force participation rates have continued to rise. Fifty-nine percent of all women are now in the labor force, and the workplace is almost one-half female. Young mothers have accounted for a significant part of the increase in labor force participation. Continuous work experience and higher participation rates distinguish baby boom women from earlier generations. Over 50 percent of women with an infant are in the labor force, and they are returning to work sooner after the birth of a child than their own mothers did. Women still tend to be segregated in clerical jobs, but occupational segregation has declined as more women earn professional degrees that propel them into law, medicine, and business.

The convergence of women's and men's earnings among full-time, year-round workers in the 1980s constitutes the most significant change in the employment experiences of women in the past four decades. After years during which women earned 59 cents for every dollar earned by men, the ratio of women's to men's earnings is now 71 cents. Two factors account for the narrowed wage gap: first, the increase in work experience and resulting rise in women's earnings, particularly among those with a college degree; and, second, the decline in men's earnings, especially among those with a high school degree or less. Ten years ago, a woman with a college degree did not earn as much as a man with a high school degree. That milestone has been passed—a college-educated woman now earns slightly more than a man with a high school diploma—but a woman with a college degree still earns less than a man with a college degree.

Wives are contributing increasing amounts toward family income and are enhancing the standard of living for married couples. Women who maintain households alone, however, are at high risk of living in poverty. The growth of mother-child families slowed in the 1980s but came disproportionately from the least educated and poorest single mothers who had never married. The result has been a widening gap between families with two earners and those with only one or no wage earner.

Greater public acceptance of women's changing roles has replaced the resistance that they once faced when considering public life. The majority of Americans now approve of women running for public office and working outside the home. The proportion of Congress that is female has risen from 4 to 10 percent during the past two decades, and in 1995 one-quarter of all state elective offices were held by women. Overall, though, men and women seem more receptive to the *addition* of roles for women than to the equal division of domestic responsibilities: employed wives still perform the majority of household chores, including caring for children. In response to these growing demands, mothers have increasingly relied on child care outside the home.

Women have made numerous adaptations to the necessity of combining family and employment. Those with doubts about marriage (current or anticipated) may stay in school longer and enter the labor force as an economic hedge in recognition of the high divorce rate. In turn, greater economic independence makes women less likely to enter into or remain in unsatisfactory marriages. Employment can offer women intellectual stimulation but also places additional demands on their time that may make a traditional marriage less attractive. The relatively small proportion of women who remain childless throughout life (compared with the relatively large proportion who delay marriage, who divorce, or who postpone remarriage) suggests that women are more willing to give up the role of wife than of mother. Husbands may have become more dispensable than children in women's efforts to balance work and family.

Demographic profiles for women differ by race and ethnicity. Racial differences in fertility and marital status are particularly pronounced, for example. More than two-thirds of all births to black women and almost one-quarter of all births to white women occur out of wedlock. More than one-half of adult white women were currently married in 1990 compared with just over one-quarter of adult black women and about one-half of Hispanic women. In 1990, nearly one-half of black families were maintained by a woman compared with 14 percent of white families and 22 percent of Hispanic families; only 10 percent of Asian families were headed by women.

Asian women have the highest college completion rates and Hispanic women the lowest. Asian and black women are the most likely to be in the labor force, with Hispanic and American Indian women the least likely. In line with their educational and labor force status, Asian women who worked full time and year round in 1990 had the highest median annual income and Hispanic women had the lowest. One income is seldom enough to ensure financial well-being, however. In 1990, more than one-third of white and Asian mother-child families and over one-half of black, Hispanic, and American Indian mother-child families lived in poverty.

Trends for women in the United States are similar to those for women in other industrialized nations. Fertility continues to decline, although American out-of-wedlock birth rates are exceeded only by those in Scandinavian countries in which cohabitation is an alternative to marriage for a significant proportion of women. American divorce rates are the highest by international standards despite their recent decline. The proportion of college students who are female among European countries and the United States is 50 percent or more. Labor force participation rates for American women are higher than for Italian, French, or German women, but lower than for Swedish women. Australian women have the highest earnings relative to men (a ratio of .91), followed by Sweden (.84) and Denmark (.83), compared with the U.S. ratio of .71.

✳ ✳ ✳

WILL THE ROLES OF BREADWINNER AND MOTHER GAIN GREATER ASCENDANCY over that of wife? Perhaps, if even more dramatic improvements occur in the ratio of women's to men's earnings. Perhaps not, if men begin to redress the imbalance in the care and support of children. Time is finite: in married women's rush to hold paid jobs, propelled by their own expanding opportunities but also by declining male wages and family economic need, they have greatly increased the demands on their time, often with relatively little adjustment on the part of their husbands. Each younger generation has questioned a bit more the "fairness" of an unequal division of labor in the home, but change is gradual. It originates more from the replacement of generations than from dramatic shifts in the behavior of adults during their lifetime.

Historian Gerda Lerner (1993) argues that women's development of a feminist consciousness depends on their ability to live in economic independence, to control their fertility, and to have access to equal education. We provide the evidence to show that women have improved their financial standing and now live increasingly outside marriage (although not always in economic security), that they are exercising reproductive choices, and that educational attainment is now equal for younger women and men. We also find that not all women have risen with the economic and social tide. Many single mothers, in particular, live in severe austerity with their children. That issue, among others, continues to nip the full bloom of a feminist consciousness.

Women (more so than men) will probably continue to put the needs of family ahead of their own jobs. Until wives contribute as much to total family income as husbands, it is unlikely that men will devote as much time to the family as women do. Because of the challenges of combining work and family roles (and the low pay associated with many women's jobs), women will more often work part time or part year and will continue to earn less than men for the foreseeable future.

But seemingly rational labor market adjustments made at an early stage of family life can have negative consequences in the long run. If divorce occurs, which is likely for one-half of all wives, women will be at a disadvantage; women with only modest educations and earnings potential will be especially disadvantaged. In a country in which care and support of children falls disproportionately to women, a traditional division of labor no longer makes sense at any stage of a woman's life.

Women's personal decisions to complete college, delay marriage, enter professional careers, and delay childbearing during the 1980s occurred in the context of federal and local efforts to encourage gender (and racial) integration of education and the workplace. Members of the baby boom generation benefited most greatly from social changes like legalized contraception and abortion, the Equal Pay Act of 1963, the Civil Rights Act of 1964, Title IX in 1972, and affirmative action goals in college admissions and in hiring practices.

Yet affirmative action is politically vulnerable in the 1990s. During the year in which this book was written, the Supreme Court overturned a federal affirmative action preference for hiring minorities in the construction industry, and the governor of California issued an executive order ending three decades of racial and gender preferences in hiring at state agencies; the Board of Regents of the University of California also abolished affirmative action in its admissions procedures. The strong economy of the 1960s that fostered development of such programs stagnated in the 1970s and 1980s, taking with it the sense that social policy should address gender and racial inequalities. If this political climate (and its economic foundations) persist, women's gains in the labor force and in reducing the wage gap with men may be slowed.

Having considered this somewhat pessimistic scenario, however, we also acknowledge that public attitudes toward women's roles and the necessity for women to work have created significant changes from which society cannot easily retreat. Women juggle a variety of roles out of preference *and* necessity. They will become more successful at it the closer society gets to defining the balancing act as a "family" rather than a "women's" issue. Until that time, women will continue to pay a higher price than men for negotiating the transitions necessary to combine family and employment. But there is no sign that the majority of women (or men) desire or can afford to have women abandon either motherhood or paid work.

What might the balancing act for women look like in the twenty-first century? It seems unrealistic to expect a repeat of the 1980s, but gender differences in earnings should continue to narrow slowly. Trends in educational attainment portend continued opening of occupational opportunities for women. The trend toward economic equality might accelerate if there were an exceptionally fast movement toward gender equality on the domestic front. Or the trend toward economic equality might decelerate if there is rapid retrenchment from ensuring opportunity for women or if economic growth is slower or less beneficial to women in the future.

But if the past is any indication, change comes slowly, and permanent transformation results from a process of cohort replacement. Mothers see differences between their own experiences and those of their children: their daughters juggle home and work in ways that seem almost incomprehensible, and their sons and sons-in-law complete household chores their fathers never did. They see great shifts in gender roles, even as significant differences continue.

Meanwhile, their daughters, especially those now in school or who have recently entered the work force, are impatient with the pace of change. Their earnings remain unequal to men's and will likely continue that way throughout their labor force career. The division of labor in their homes is also unequal, and men's care and responsibility toward children and housework are responding only slowly. But failing to recognize that change is occurring is to miss the revolution that has already transformed the economic activity of women, one that will echo for years to come in the domestic roles of men *and* women.

Measures of Fertility

THE MOST EASILY INTERPRETED MEASURE OF FERTILITY IS THE TOTAL fertility rate (TFR), or the average number of children born per woman during her lifetime. For a given year, the TFR indicates the number of births a group of one thousand women would have by the end of their childbearing years if all the women survived and experienced the age-specific birth rates for that year. Thus, the TFR can be thought of as the sum of age-specific birth rates for women of childbearing age. (We express the TFR as a rate "per woman" rather than "per one thousand women" to produce an easier interpretation.) Figure A1 illustrates changes in the TFR over time for blacks and whites.

The figure helps place the baby boom in demographic perspective. Women bore children at a rate of fewer than three births each during most of the 1940s, and at a rate of two or fewer children after 1970. Between 1950 and the mid-1960s, however, women had an average of 3.4 to 3.6 births each. The baby boom was followed by a "baby bust" (a TFR that eventually dipped to 1.7) that persisted for more than a decade. The TFR in 1992 had risen to 2.06, very close to the 2.1 needed for natural replacement of the population (Ventura and others 1994, table 4).

The age-specific fertility rate (ASFR) is used to determine the ages at which most childbearing occurs. As the name indicates, the ASFR standardizes fertility data by age of the woman. It is calculated by dividing the number of live births per year (classified by mother's age) by the total number of women in that age category at the midpoint of the year. Because a woman's prime child-

200

FIGURE A1 Total Fertility of White and Black Women

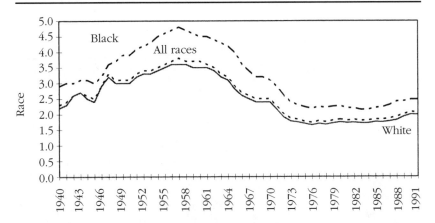

Source: U.S. Bureau of the Census (1975), series B11-B119; National Center for Health Statistics (1993), table 4.
Note: Data for blacks include blacks and other races; birth rates are live births per woman; data for fertility rates of whites and blacks in 1971–88 are according to race of child.

bearing period occurs in her twenties, the ASFR for young women will be higher than the overall birth rate, and the ASFR for older women will be considerably lower. Figure A2 shows the peaks and troughs of childbearing for American women between 1940 and 1992.

The flattening of this curve between 1940 and 1992 dramatically illustrates the lower fertility and delayed timing of childbearing among baby boom and baby bust women. The 1990s are the first era in which fertility to women in their mid-to-late twenties exceeded that for women in their early twenties. The rate of decline in fertility for women in their early thirties also was less steep than in 1980 as more baby boom daughters delayed childbearing than their older sisters in the World War II cohort or their mothers who produced the baby boom.

Another measure that reflects a woman's individual reproductive history is the *number of children ever born.* This measure is the most accurate only for women who have completed their childbearing years, yet it is often used for comparative purposes among younger women. The measure does *not* represent true completed fertility for women still of reproductive age, and com-

FIGURE A2 Age-Specific Fertility

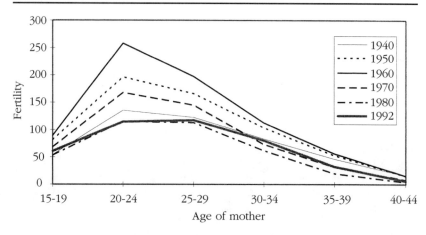

Source: U.S. Bureau of the Census (1975), series B11-19; National Center for Health Statistics (1982), table 3; Ventura, Martin, and Taffel (1994), table 4.
Note: Fertility rates are live births per one thousand women in a specified age group.

parisons can be distorted by changes in the timing of births. Problems with data comparability between the decennial census and the Current Population Survey restrict trend analysis to women aged thirty to thirty-four. The number of children ever born is calculated as a rate per one thousand women but is interpreted as a rate per woman in table A1.

TABLE A1 Children Born to Women Aged 30 to 34 for Selected Years

Year	All Women	Currently Married Women
1967	—	3.05
1976	2.27	2.36
1980	1.90	2.02
1985	1.67	1.83
1990	1.70	1.85
1992	1.68	1.82

Source: Bachu (1993), table 10.

Women aged thirty to thirty-four in 1967 were born between 1933 and 1937, and because they reached childbearing age in the 1950s they contributed substantially to the baby boom. Thus their family size by age thirty to thirty-four is higher than for later cohorts. Women in their early thirties in 1990 reached childbearing age during the 1970s, an era in which contraception and legal abortion were readily available to women. The number of children born to these late baby boom women by their early thirties is historically low, partly due to the availability of educational and occupational opportunities unheard of by earlier generations. Given the delay in marriage and childbearing, women aged thirty to thirty-four in 1990 may not have finished their childbearing yet, so this figure should be considered a preliminary estimate of completed family size.

Chapter Notes

Chapter 1

1. Although fecundity (the ability to reproduce) declines with age, the incidence of biological infertility is relatively low among women under forty-five (Bongaarts and Potter 1983; Menken 1985). Thus the majority of childless women are "child free" by choice or because they postponed fertility decisions until past their reproductive years.

Chapter 2

1. Even the Roman Catholic Church has had to come to terms with cohabitation. In June 1995, the Reverend Brian Jordan of St. Camillus Catholic Church in Silver Spring, Maryland held a joint wedding ceremony for six Latino couples (most of whom had children) who had been living together or who had been married in civil ceremonies. Jordan described the collective event as "an inexpensive way to celebrate and promote the sacrament of marriage" (Constable 1995).

Chapter 3

1. A new measure of educational attainment was introduced in the 1990 census. Before 1990, educational attainment was measured as a single number: highest grade of school completed. But the growing number of part-time students and those who take accelerated or prolonged degree programs made this designation increasingly inappropriate. The 1990 census therefore asked respondents specifically

about the degree completed (high school, college, or postgraduate). Detailed categories were provided at the advanced degree level and broader categories for the elementary and high school level. These changes were made in response to the changing educational composition of the population and have little effect on data comparability among census years (Mare 1995, p. 159).

Chapter 4

1. In addition to domestic work and market work, women often perform a third type of "invisible work," the daily voluntary activities that contribute to the maintenance of community. Such services as delivering meals to the elderly, driving a neighbor to the store, or participating in school fundraisers do not count as either domestic or market work. Milroy and Wismer (1994, p. 82) argue that "if domestic work is building homes, families, and households, and traded work is building companies and economies, then community work is building communities and should properly be identified as a separate nucleus of productive effort." Although a thorough discussion of voluntarism is beyond the scope of this book, we recognize that women typically have taken on voluntary activities in addition to other types of paid and unpaid labor. Whether they can continue to do so as their labor force participation rates rise will be an interesting issue for the twenty-first century.

2. The coding of occupations changed between 1970 and 1980; in the table, data for 1970 have been converted to comparable 1980 codes.

3. In the 1950s, the index of dissimilarity actually increased slightly and then declined by two or three percentage points during the 1960s (Blau and Hendrichs 1979; Gross 1968). As the early baby boom cohort entered the labor force during the 1970s, the decline in occupational concentration accelerated (Bianchi and Rytina 1968; Jacobs 1989). Although the decline was not as great in the 1980s when the later baby boom cohort was moving into the labor force, the change was still twice that of the 1960s.

4. The authors are grateful to Prithwis Das Gupta for providing these calculations. The decomposition method is detailed in Das Gupta (1993).

Chapter 5

1. Acs and Danziger (1990); Blackburn, Bloom, and Freeman (1991);
    Bound and Holzer (1991); Bound and Johnson (1992); Ryscavage
    and Henle (1990).

2. As discussed by Mare (1995), the question about educational attain-
    ment changed between the 1980 and 1990 censuses. In 1980,
    respondents indicated the years of school they had completed; in
    1990, they reported on the degrees they had earned. In order to
    ensure that the comparison of earnings by education was not
    affected by a change in the educational item, March 1980 and 1990
    CPS data are reported in table 5.5 (and table 5.6).

3. If decennial census data rather than CPS data are used to make this
    comparison, the ratio declines by a smaller amount, from 68 to 66
    percent.

4. The status attainment tradition within sociology identifies similar fac-
    tors that might be considered important to earnings attainment and,
    by extension, to gender earnings differentials.

5. The notion that women's work has been systematically undervalued
    remains a cornerstone of feminist writing, nonetheless. Kilbourne
    and others (1994), for example, argue that neoclassical economic
    theory would predict that skill of any kind should increase not
    reduce wages: skill should always command a wage premium. But
    their research indicates that the more a person's occupation requires
    nurturant skill, the lower the pay for men and women, especially
    women. This "devaluation" of nurturant skill explains 3 to 5 percent
    of the wage gap.
       On another note, Beutel and Marini (1995) report amazingly con-
    sistent gender differences in the values of young persons over the
    1970s and 1980s: young women are much more likely to express
    concern and feel responsibility for the well-being of others, less
    likely to accept materialism and competition, and more likely to rate
    "finding meaning in life" as extremely important. Whether these
    persistent gender differences cause women and men to value the
    nonmonetary rewards of work differently remains an open ques-
    tion.

6. One subgroup of Hispanic women—Puerto Rican women—seems to have fared particularly badly in recent decades (Tienda, Donato, and Cordero-Guzman 1992). In 1960, Puerto Rican women's labor force participation was similar to that of other Hispanics, but by the mid-1980s their participation rates had fallen far behind those of all other racial and ethnic groups. The differential was particularly great among those with less than a high school education. Since Hispanics may be of any race, Puerto Rican women may suffer the dual effects of racial and gender discrimination.

Chapter 6

1. Average household, family, and per capita income of women and men, as calculated from the 1960–90 decennial censuses, refers to pretax, posttransfer money income received in the year prior to the census and all amounts have been adjusted to 1989 dollars (see table 6.1). Household income is the sum of money income of all persons who live together: the measure assigns the total household income to each individual in the household and averages this amount across all males and females aged sixteen and over.

The assignment of household income to all individuals who reside together assumes that these individuals pool income. This assumption may be particularly suspect for persons sharing a residence who are not related and, hence, a family income measure is also shown. If an individual is related to the householder by blood, marriage, or adoption–the census definition of family ties–he or she is assigned the sum of income of all family members; otherwise, the person's individual income is assigned. Table 6.1 demonstrates that trends in household and family income are similar.

Finally, because household and family income measures make no adjustment for the number of individuals who must share a given pool of income, a per capita measure is also shown. Household income is divided by the number of people in the household, and this amount is assigned to each individual. Per capita income is a frequently used per person measure of income, but makes no adjustment for economies of scale realized by larger households. Other per person measures are often used, such as the ratio of income to the poverty threshold or an income per adult equivalent measure in which children and adults (after the first in the household) are assigned some fraction of one in adjusting income for household size. In general, there is no universally agreed upon household size adjustment. We use the per capita measure because it is easily constructed from census data, and trends are similar to those using other measures.

2. Because in the gender comparisons of household, family, and per capita income the income of the household in which a man or woman resides is assigned to all individuals in the household, husbands and wives have equal household, family, and per capita income. Hence, if all adult men and women were married, none of the income measures would differ by gender.

3. Data are not shown. The authors make the calculations from the 1980 and 1990 census Public Use Microdata Samples.

4. Dependency between husband and wife is defined as the difference between the proportion of joint earnings provided by the husband minus the proportion of joint earnings provided by the wife. See Sorenson and McLanahan (1987) and Casper, Peltola, and Bianchi (1995) for further discussion.

References

Acs, Gregory, and Sheldon Danziger. 1990. "Educational Attainment, Industrial Structure, and Male Earnings, 1973–87." Population Studies Center Research Report 90-189. Ann Arbor, Mich.: University of Michigan.

Aquilino, William S. 1994. "Later Life Parental Divorce and Widowhood: Impact on Young Adults' Assessment of Parent-Child Relations." *Journal of Marriage and the Family* 56(4): 908–22.

Asbell, Bernard. 1995. *The Pill: A Biography of the Drug that Changed the World*. New York: Random House.

Astin, Alexander. 1985. *Achieving Educational Excellence*. San Francisco: Jossey Bass.

Avery, Roger, Frances Goldscheider, and Alden Speare. 1992. "Feathered Nest/Gilded Cage: Parental Income and Leaving Home in the Transition to Adulthood." *Demography* 29(3): 375–88.

Axinn, William G., and Arland Thornton. 1992. "The Relationship Between Cohabitation and Divorce: Selectivity or Causal Influence?" *Demography* 29(3): 357–74.

Bachu, Amara. 1993. "Fertility of American Women: June 1992." U.S. Bureau of the Census, *Current Population Reports*, P20–470. Washington: U.S. Government Printing Office.

Baker, David P., and Deborah Perkins Jones. 1993. "Creating Gender Equality: Cross-National Gender Stratification and Mathematical Performance." *Sociology of Education* 66 (April): 91–103.

Bancroft, Gertrude. 1958. *The American Labor Force: Its Growth and Changing Composition*. New York: John Wiley & Sons.

Becker, Gary. 1975. *Human Capital: A Theoretical and Empirical Analysis*. Second edition. Chicago: University of Chicago Press.

———. 1981. *A Treatise on the Family*. Cambridge, Mass.: Harvard University Press.

Bergmann, Barbara. 1986. *The Economic Emergence of Women*. New York: Basic Books.

209

Beutel, Ann M., and Margaret Mooney Marini. 1995. "Gender and Values." *American Sociological Review* 60 (June): 436–48.

Bianchi, Suzanne M. 1993. "Children of Poverty: Why Are They Poor?" In *Child Poverty and Public Policy*, edited by Judith A. Chafel. Washington: Urban Institute Press.

———. 1994. "The Changing Demographic and Socioeconomic Characteristics of Single Parent Families." *Marriage and Family Review* 20(1/2): 71–97.

———. 1995. "Changing Economic Roles of Women and Men." In *State of the Union*, edited by Reynolds Farley. New York: Russell Sage Foundation.

Bianchi, Suzanne M., and Nancy Rytina. 1986. "The Decline in Occupational Sex Segregation During the 1970s: Census and CPS Comparisons." *Demography* 23(1): 79–86.

Bianchi, Suzanne M., and Daphne Spain. 1986. *American Women in Transition*. New York: Russell Sage Foundation.

Bielby, Denise D., and William T. Bielby. 1988. "She Works Hard for the Money: Household Responsibilities and the Allocation of Work Effort." *American Journal of Sociology* 93: 1031–59.

Bielby, William T., and James N. Baron. 1984. "A Woman's Place Is with Other Women: Sex Segregation Within Organizations." In *Sex Segregation in the Workplace: Trends, Explanations, Remedies*, edited by Barbara F. Reskin. Washington: National Academy Press.

Blackburn, McKinley L., David E. Bloom, and Richard B. Freeman. 1991. "Changes in Earnings Differentials in the 1980s: Concordance, Convergence, Causes, and Consequences." NBER Working Paper 3901. Cambridge, Mass.: National Bureau of Economic Research.

Blair, Sampson Lee, and Michael P. Johnson. 1992. "Wives' Perceptions of the Fairness of the Division of Household Labor: The Intersection of Housework and Ideology." *Journal of Marriage and the Family* 54: 570–81.

Blair, Sampson Lee, and Daniel T. Lichter. 1991. "Measuring the Division of Household Labor: Gender Segregation of Housework Among American Couples." *Journal of Family Issues* 12: 91–113.

Blake, Judith. 1974. "Can We Believe Recent Data on Birth Expectations in the United States?" *Demography* 11(1): 25–44.

Blau, David M., and Phillip K. Robins. 1988. "Child Care Costs and Family Labor Supply." *Review of Economics and Statistics* 70: 374–438.

———. 1991. "Child Care Demand and Labor Supply of Young Mothers over Time" *Demography* 28(3): 333–60.

Blau, Francine D., and Andrea H. Beller. 1992. "Black-White Earnings over the 1970s and 1980s: Gender Differences in Trends." *Review of Economics and Statistics* 74(2): 276–86.

Blau, Francine D., and Marianne A. Ferber. 1992. *The Economics of Women, Men, and Work.* Second edition. Englewood Cliffs, N.J.: Prentice-Hall.

Blau, Francine D., and W. E. Hendrichs. 1979. "Occupational Segregation by Sex: Trends and Prospects." *Journal of Human Resources* 14: 197–210.

Blau, Francine D., and Lawrence M. Kahn. 1992. "The Gender Earnings Gap: Some International Evidence." NBER Working Paper 4224. Cambridge, Mass.: National Bureau of Economic Research.

Blau, Peter M. 1964. *Exchange and Power in Social Life.* New York: John Wiley & Sons.

Bloom, David E., and Todd P. Steen. 1990. "The Labor Force Implications of the Expanding Child Care Industry." *Population Research and Policy Review* 9: 25–44.

Blossfeld, Hans-Peter, and Johannes Huinink. 1991. "Human Capital Investments or Norms of Role Transition? How Women's Schooling and Career Affect the Process of Family Formation." *American Journal of Sociology* 97(1): 143–68.

Bongaarts, John, and Robert G. Potter. 1983. *Fertility, Biology, and Behavior.* New York: Academic Press.

Booth, Alan, and Lynn White. 1980. "Thinking About Divorce." *Journal of Marriage and the Family* 42: 605–16.

Borjas, George, Jr., Richard B. Freeman, and Lawrence F. Katz. 1992. "On the Labor Market Effects of Immigration and Trade." In *The Economic Effects of Immigration in Source and Receiving Countries,* edited by George Borjas Jr. and Richard B. Freeman. Chicago: University of Chicago Press.

Bound, John, and Harry J. Holzer. 1991. "Industrial Shifts, Skill Levels, and the Labor Market for White and Black Males." Population Studies Center Research Report 91-211. Ann Arbor, Mich.: University of Michigan.

Bound, John, and George Johnson. 1992. "Changes in the Structure of Wages During the 1980s: An Evaluation of Alternative Explanations." *American Economic Review* 82(3): 371–92.

Brayfield, April. 1995. "Juggling Jobs and Kids: The Impact of Employment Schedules on Fathers' Caring for Children." *Journal of Marriage and the Family* 57(May): 321–32.

Brines, Julie. 1994. "Economic Dependency, Gender, and the Division of Labor at Home." *American Journal of Sociology* 100(3): 652–88.

Browne, Irene. 1995. "The Baby Boom and Trends in Poverty, 1967–1987." *Social Forces* 73(March): 1071–95.

Bumpass, Larry L. 1990. "What's Happening to the Family? Interactions Between Demographic and Institutional Change." *Demography* 27(4): 483–98.

Bumpass, Larry L., and R. Kelly Raley. 1995. "Redefining Single-Parent Families: Cohabitation and Changing Family Reality." *Demography* 32(1): 97–110.

Bumpass, Larry L., and James A. Sweet. 1989. "National Estimates of Cohabitation." *Demography* 26(4): 615–25.

Bumpass, Larry L., R. Kelly Raley, and James A. Sweet. 1995. "The Changing Character of Stepfamilies: Implications of Cohabitation and Nonmarital Childbearing." *Demography* 32(3): 425–36.

Bumpass, Larry L., James A. Sweet, and Andrew Cherlin. 1991. "The Role of Cohabitation in Declining Rates of Marriage." *Journal of Marriage and the Family* 53(4): 913–27.

Burkhauser, Richard, and others. 1990. "Economic Burdens of Marital Disruptions: A Comparison of the United States and the Federal Republic of Germany." *Review of Income and Wealth* 36(December): 319–33.

Burr, Jefferey A., and Jan E. Mutchler. 1992. "The Living Arrangements of Unmarried Elderly Hispanic Females." *Demography* 29(1): 93–112.

Burton, Linda M. 1990. "Teenage Childbearing as an Alternative Life-Course Strategy in Multigeneration Black Families." *Human Nature* 1(2): 123–43.

Butz, William, and Michael Ward. 1979. "The Emergence of Counter-cyclical U.S. Fertility." *American Economic Review* 69(June): 318–27.

Cain, Glen G., and Douglas Wissoker. 1990. "A Re-Analysis of Marital Stability in the Seattle-Denver Income Maintenance Experiment." *American Journal of Sociology* 95(5):1235–69.

Casper, Lynne, Pia Peltola, and Suzanne M. Bianchi. 1995. "A Cross-National Look at Women's Economic Dependency." Paper presented at the annual meeting of the American Sociological Association, Washington, D.C. (August).

Casper, Lynne, Sara McLanahan, and Irwin Garfinkel. 1994. "The Gender-Poverty Gap: What Can We Learn from Other Countries." *American Sociological Review* 59(4): 594–605.

Catsambis, Sophia. 1994. "The Path to Math: Gender and Racial-Ethnic Differences in Mathematics Participation from Middle School to High School." *Sociology of Education* 67(July): 199–215.

Center for the American Woman in Politics. 1995. "Women in Elective Office 1995". New Brunswick, N.J.: Eagleton Institute of Politics, Rutgers University.

Charles, Maria. 1992. "Cross-National Variation in Occupational Sex Segregation." *American Sociological Review* 57: 483–502.

Cherlin, Andrew. 1978. "Remarriage as an Incomplete Institution." *American Journal of Sociology* 84(November): 634–50.

———. 1992. *Marriage, Divorce, Remarriage.* Cambridge, Mass.: Harvard University Press.

———, and Frank F. Furstenberg. 1986. *The New American Grandparent: A Place in the Family, A Life Apart.* New York: Basic Books.

Chiswick, Barry R,. and Teresa A. Sullivan. 1995. "The New Immigrants." In *State of the Union,* edited by Reynolds Farley. New York: Russell Sage Foundation.

Clark, S. C. 1995a. "Advance Report of Final Divorce Statistics, 1989 and 1990." *Monthly Vital Statistics Report,* vol. 43(8)(supplement). Hyattsville, Md.: National Center for Health Statistics.

———. 1995b. "Advance Report of Final Marriage Statistics, 1989 and 1990." *Monthly Vital Statistics Report,* vol. 43(12)(supplement). Hyattsville, Md.: National Center for Health Statistics.

Constable, Pamela. 1995. "At Md. Church, Holy Matrimony Times Six." *The Washington Post* June 26, 1995, p. B1, 3.

Cooney, Teresa M. 1994. "Young Adults' Relations with Parents: The Influence of Recent Parental Divorce." *Journal of Marriage and the Family* 56(1): 45–56.

Corcoran, Mary, and Greg J. Duncan. 1979. "Work History, Labor Force Attachment, and Earnings Differences Between the Races and Sexes." *Journal of Human Resources* 14(Winter): 3–20.

———, and Michael Ponza. 1984. "Work Experience, Job Segregation, and Wages." In *Sex Segregation in the Workplace: Trends, Explanations, Remedies,* edited by Barbara Reskin. Washington: National Academy of Sciences.

Cotter, David A., and others. 1995. "Occupational Gender Segregation and the Earnings Gap: Changes in the 1980s." *Social Science Research* 24: 439–54.

Cowan, Ruth Schwartz. 1983. *More Work for Mother: The Ironies of Household Technology from the Open Hearth to the Microwave.* New York: Basic Books.

Cramer, James C. 1980. "Fertility and Female Employment." *American Sociological Review* 45(April): 167–90.

Danziger, Sheldon, and Jonathan Stern. 1990. "The Causes and Consequences of Child Poverty in the United States." *Innocenti* Occasional Paper 10. Florence, Italy: UNICEF International Child Development Centre.

Das Gupta, Prithwis. 1993. "Standardization and Decomposition of Rates: A User's Manual." *Current Population Reports,* Special Studies, series P23, no. 186. Washington: U.S. Bureau of the Census, U.S. Government Printing Office.

Davis, Steven J., and John Haltiwanger. 1991. "Wage Dispersion Between and Within U.S. Manufacturing Plants, 1963–86." *Brookings Papers on Economic Activity: Microeconomics* 1991: 115–80.

Degler, Carl N. 1980. *At Odds: Women and the Family in America from the Revolution to the Present.* New York: Oxford University Press.

DeMaris, A., and V. Rao. 1992. "Premarital Cohabitation and Subsequent Marital Stability in the United States: A Reassessment." *Journal of Marriage and the Family* 54: 178–90.

Desai, Sonalde, and Linda Waite. 1991. "Women's Employment During Pregnancy and After the First Birth: Occupational Characteristics and Work Commitment." *American Sociological Review* 56: 551–66.

Duncan, Greg, and Saul Hoffman. 1985. "A Reconsideration of the Economic Consequences of Marital Dissolution." *Demography* 22(4): 485–98.

———. 1988. "What Are the Economic Consequences of Divorce?" *Demography* 25(4): 641–44.

Easterlin, Richard. 1987. *Birth and Fortune: The Impact of Numbers on Personal Welfare.* Chicago: University of Chicago Press.

Eggebeen, David J., and Daniel T. Lichter. 1991. "Race, Family Structure, and Changing Poverty Among American Children." *American Sociological Review* 56: 801–17.

England, Paula. 1982. "The Failure of Human Capital Theory to Explain Occupational Sex Segregation." *Journal of Human Resources* 17: 358–70.

———. 1992. *Comparable Worth: Theories and Evidence.* New York: Aldine de Gruyter.

———, and Irene Browne. 1992. "Trends in Women's Status." *Sociological Perspectives* 35(1):17–51.

———, and Barbara Stanek Kilbourne. 1990. "Markets, Marriages, and Other Mates: The Problem of Power." In *Beyond the Market Place: Rethinking Economy and Society,* edited by Roger Friedland and A. F. Robertson. New York: Aldine de Gruyter.

Entwisle, Doris R., and Karl L. Alexander. 1995. "A Parent's Economic Shadow: Family Structure Versus Family Resources as Influences on Early School Achievement." *Journal of Marriage and the Family* 57(May): 399–409.

———, and Linda Steffel Olson. 1994. "The Gender Gap in Math: Its Possible Origins in Neighborhood Effects." *American Sociological Review* 59(6): 822–38.

Epsing-Andersen, Gosta. 1990. *The Three Worlds of Welfare Capitalism.* Princeton, N.J.: Princeton University Press.

Ettner, Susan L. 1995. "The Impact of 'Parent Care' on Female Labor Supply Decisions." *Demography* 32(1): 63–80.

Faludi, Susan. 1991. *Backlash: The Undeclared War Against American Women*. New York: Crown Publishers.

Families and Work Institute. 1995. *Women: The New Providers*. Benton Harbor, Mich.: Whirlpool Foundation.

Farley, Reynolds. 1996 (forthcoming). *The New American Reality*. New York: Russell Sage Foundation.

Featherman, David L., and Robert M. Hauser. 1976. "Sexual Inequalities and Socioeconomic Achievement in the U.S., 1962–1973." *American Sociological Review* 41(June): 462–83.

Feiner, Susan, and Bruce Roberts. 1990. "Hidden by the Invisible Hand: Neoclassical Economic Theory and the Textbook Treatment of Race and Gender." *Gender and Society* 4: 159–81.

Festinger, Leon. 1957. *A Theory of Cognitive Dissonance*. Evanston, Ill.: Row, Peterson.

Folk, Karen Fox, and Yunae Yi. 1994. "Piecing Together Child Care with Multiple Arrangements: Crazy Quilt Pattern or Preferred Pattern for Employed Parents of Preschool Children?" *Journal of Marriage and the Family* 56(August): 669–80.

Furstenberg, Frank F., Jr. 1991. "As the Pendulum Swings: Teenage Childbearing and Social Concern." *Family Relations* 40(April): 127–38.

Garfinkel, Irwin, and Sara McLanahan. 1986. *Single Mothers and Their Children*. Washington: Urban Institute Press.

Geronimus, Arline T. 1987. "On Teenage Childbearing in the United States." *Population and Development Review* 13(2): 245–79.

Geronimus, Arline T., and Sanders Korenman. 1992. "The Socioeconomic Consequences of Teen Childbearing Reconsidered." *Quarterly Journal of Economics* 107: 1187–214.

———. 1993. "The Socioeconomic Costs of Teenage Childbearing: Evidence and Interpretation." *Demography* 30(2): 281–90.

Gershuny, Jonathan, and John P. Robinson. 1988. "Historical Changes in the Household Division of Labor." *Demography* 25(4): 537–52.

Gerson, Kathleen. 1985. *Hard Choices: How Women Decide About Work, Career, and Motherhood*. Berkeley, Calif.: University of California Press.

Ghosh, S., Richard A. Easterlin, and Diane J. Macunovich. 1993. "How Badly Have Single Parents Done?: Trends in Economic Status of Single Parents Since 1964." Paper presented at the annual meeting of the Population Association of America, Cincinnati, Ohio (April).

Glass, Jennifer. 1990. "The Impact of Occupational Segregation on Working Conditions." *Social Forces* 90: 779–96.

———, and Valerie Camarigg. 1992. "Gender, Parenthood, and Job-Family Compatibility." *American Journal of Sociology* 98(1): 131–51.

Goldin, Claudia. 1990. *Understanding the Gender Gap: An Economic History of American Women.* New York: Oxford University Press.

———. 1991. "The Role of World War II in the Rise of Women's Employment." *American Economic Review* 81: 741–56.

———. 1992. "The Meaning of College in the Lives of American Women: The Past One Hundred Years." NBER Working Paper 4099. Cambridge, Mass.: National Bureau of Economic Research.

Goldscheider, Frances, and Linda Waite. 1991. *New Families, No Families? The Transformation of the American Home.* Berkeley and Los Angeles: University of California Press.

Goldscheider, Frances, Arland Thornton, and Linda Young-DeMarco. 1993. "A Portrait of the Nest-Leaving Process in Early Adulthood." *Demography* 30(4): 683–99.

Goode, William F. 1963. *World Revolutions and Family Patterns.* New York: Free Press.

Gornick, Janet. 1995. "Women's Work and Women's Wages in Comparative Perspective." Presentation prepared for the Second U.S. LIS Workshop, Washington, D.C. (May).

Green, Patricia. 1993. "High School Seniors Look to the Future, 1972 and 1992." *Statistics in Brief.* NCES No. 93–473. Washington, D.C.: U.S. Department of Education, National Center for Education Statistics.

Greenstein, Theodore N. 1990. "Marital Disruption and the Employment of Married Women." *Journal of Marriage and the Family* 52(August): 657–76.

———. 1995. "Gender Ideology, Marital Disruption, and the Employment of Married Women." *Journal of Marriage and the Family* 57(1): 31–42.

Grief, Geoffrey L. 1995. "Single Fathers with Custody Following Separation and Divorce." *Marriage and Family Review* 20(1/2): 213–31.

Gross, Edward. 1968. "Plus ça Change? The Sexual Structure of Occupations over Time." *Social Problems* 16: 198–208.

Hall, David R., and John Z. Zhao. 1995. "Cohabitation and Divorce in Canada: Testing the Selectivity Hypothesis." *Journal of Marriage and the Family* 57(2): 421–27.

Hall, Jacquelyn D. 1986. "Women's History Goes to Trial: EEOC vs. Sears, Roebuck, and Company." *Signs* 11: 751–79.

Hamburg, B.A. 1986. "Subsets of Adolescent Mothers: Developmental, Biomedical, and Psychosocial Issues." In *School-age Pregnancy and Parenthood,* edited by J. Lancaster and B. Hamburg. New York: Aldine de Gruyter.

Hannan, Michael T., and Nancy Brandon Tuma. 1990. "A Reassessment of the Effect of Income Maintenance on Marital Dissolution in the Seattle-Denver Experiment." *American Journal of Sociology* 95(5): 1270–98.

———, and Lyle P. Groeneveld. 1977. "Income and Marital Events: Evidence from an Income Maintenance Experiment." *American Journal of Sociology* 82: 1186–211.

Hanson, Susan, and Geraldine Pratt. 1991. "Job Search and the Occupational Segregation of Women." *Annals of the Association of American Geographers* 81(2): 229–53.

———. 1995. *Gender, Work, and Space.* London: Routledge.

Harris, Kathleen Mullan. 1993. "Work and Welfare Among Single Mothers in Poverty." In *American Journal of Sociology* 99(September): 317–52.

Harrison, Roderick J., and Claudette Bennett. 1995. "Racial and Ethnic Diversity." In *State of the Union*, vol. 2, edited by Reynolds Farley. New York: Russell Sage Foundation.

Hatchett, Shirley, Joseph Veroff, and Elizabeth Douvan. 1995. "Marital Instability Among Black and White Couples in Early Marriage." In *The Decline in Marriage Among African Americans*, edited by M. Belinda Tucker and Claudia Mitchell-Kernan. New York: Russell Sage Foundation.

Haveman, R., and B. Wolfe. 1993. "Children's Prospects and Children's Policy." *Journal of Economic Perspectives* 7: 153–74.

Hayden, Dolores. 1984. *Redesigning the American Dream.* New York: Norton.

Hayes, C. D., ed. 1987. *Risking the Future: Adolescent Sexuality, Pregnancy, and Childbearing.* Washington: National Academy Press.

Hayghe, Howard V., and Suzanne M. Bianchi. 1994. "Married Mother's Work Patterns: The Job-Family Compromise." *Monthly Labor Review* 117(June): 24–30.

Hernandez, Donald J. 1993. *America's Children: Resources from Family, Government, and the Economy.* New York: Russell Sage Foundation.

Hernandez, Pedro, Andrea Beller, and John W. Graham. 1995. "Changes in the Relationship Between Child Support Payments and Educational Attainment of Offspring, 1977–1988." *Demography* 32(2): 249–60.

Hill, Anne M., and June E. O'Neill. 1992. "Intercohort Change in Women's Labor Market Status." In *Research in Labor Economics*, vol. 1, edited by R. G. Ehrenberg. Greenwich, Conn.: JAI Press.

Hochschild, Arlie, with Anne Machung. 1989. *The Second Shift: Working Parents and the Revolution at Home.* New York: Viking.

Hoem, Jan. 1990. "Social Policy and Recent Fertility Change in Sweden." *Population and Development Review* 16(December): 735–48.

Hoffman, Saul, and Greg J. Duncan. 1988. "What Are the Economic Consequences of Divorce?" *Demography* 25(4): 641–45.

Hoffman, Saul D., E. Michael Foster, and Frank F. Furstenberg, Jr. 1993. "Reevaluating the Costs of Teenage Childbearing." *Demography* 30(1): 1–13.

Hogan, Dennis P. 1987. "Demographic Trends in Human Fertility, and Parenting Across the Life Span." In *Parenting Across the Life Span,* edited by J. B Lancaster and others. New York: Aldine de Gruyter.

Hogan, Dennis P., and Daniel T. Lichter. 1995. "Children and Youth: Living Arrangements and Welfare." In *State of the Union,* vol. 2, edited by Reynolds Farley. New York: Russell Sage Foundation.

Hogan, Dennis P., Ling-xin Hao, and William L. Parish. 1990. "Race, Kin Networks, and Assistance to Mother-Headed Families." *Social Forces* 68(3): 797–812.

Holden, Karen, and W. Lee Hanson. 1987. "Part-Time Work, Full-Time Work, and Occupational Segregation." In *Gender in the Workplace,* edited by C. Brown and J. Pechman. Washington: Brookings Institution.

Holden, Karen C., and Pamela J. Smock. 1991. "The Economic Costs of Marital Dissolution: Why Do Women Bear a Disproportionate Cost?" *Annual Review of Sociology* 17: 51–78.

Homans, George C. 1961. *Social Behavior: Its Elementary Forms.* New York: Harcourt, Brace.

Honey, Maureen. 1984. *Creating Rosie the Riveter: Class, Gender, and Propaganda During World War II.* Amherst, Mass.: University of Massachusetts Press.

Hossain, A., and J. L. Roopnarine. 1993. "Division of Household Labor and Child Care in Dual-Earner African American Families with Infants." *Sex Roles* 29: 571–83.

Huber, Joan, and Glenna Sptize. 1980. "Considering Divorce." *American Journal of Sociology* 86: 75–89.

———. 1983. *Sex Stratification.* New York: Academic Press.

Hughes, James W. 1994. "Economic Shifts and the Changing Home Ownership Trajectory." Paper presented to the Office of Housing Research, Fannie Mae, Conference on Understanding Household Savings for Homeownership. Washington, D.C. (November).

Hyde, Janet S., Elizabeth Fennema, and Susan J. Lamon. 1990. "Gender Differences in Mathematics Performance: A Meta-Analysis." *Psychological Bulletin* 107: 139–55.

Iams, Howard M. 1993. "Earnings of Couples: A Cohort Analysis." *Social Security Bulletin* 56(3): 22–33.

Iannoccone, Laurence R., and Carrie A. Miles. 1990. "Dealing with Social Change: The Mormon Church's Response to Change in Women's Roles." *Social Forces* 68 (June): 1231–50.

Jacobs, Jerry A. 1989a. "Long-Term Trends in Occupational Segregation by Sex." *American Journal of Sociology* 95(1): 160–73.

———. 1989b. *Revolving Doors: Sex Segregation and Women's Careers.* Stanford, Calif.: Stanford University Press.

———. 1992. "Women's Entry into Management: Trends in Earnings, Authority, and Values Among Salaried Managers." *Administrative Science Quarterly* 37: 282–301.

———. 1995. "Gender and Academic Specialties: Trends Among Recipients of College Degrees in the 1980s." *Sociology of Education* 68(April): 81–98.

Jacobs, Jerry A., and Suet T. Lim. 1995. "Trends in Occupational and Industrial Sex Segregation in 56 Countries, 1960–1980." In *Gender Inequality at Work,* edited by Jerry A. Jacobs. Thousand Oaks, Calif.: Sage Publications.

Jacobs, Jerry A., and Ronnie Steinberg. 1990. "Compensating Differentials and the Male-Female Wage Gap: Evidence from the New York State Pay Equity Study." *Social Forces* 69(2): 439–68.

———. 1995. "Further Evidence on Compensating Differentials and the Gender Gap in Wages." In *Gender Inequality at Work,* edited by Jerry A. Jacobs. Thousand Oaks, Calif.: Sage Publications.

Johnson, William R., and Jonathan Skinner. 1986. "Labor Supply and Marital Separation." *American Economic Review* 76(June): 455–69.

Jones, Elise, and Charles F. Westoff. 1979. "The End of 'Catholic' Fertility." *Demography* 16(2): 209–18.

Jones, Jacqueline. 1985. *Labor of Love, Labor of Sorrow.* New York: Basic Books.

Kalmijn, Matthijs. 1994. "Mother's Occupational Status and Children's Schooling." *American Sociological Review* 59(April): 257–75.

Kamerman, Sheila B. 1995. "Gender Role and Family Structure Changes in the Advanced Industrialized West: Implications for Social Policy." In *Poverty, Inequality, and the Future of Social Policy,* edited by Katherine McFate, Roger Lawson, and William Julius Wilson. New York: Russell Sage Foundation.

Kamerman, Sheila B., and Alfred J. Kahn. 1988. "Social Policy and Children in the United States and Europe." In *The Vulnerable,* edited by John L. Palmer, Timothy Smeeding, and Barbara B. Torrey. Washington: Urban Institute Press.

———. 1991. *Child Care, Parental Leave, and the Under 3s: Policy Innovation in Europe.* Westport, Conn: Auburn House-Greenwood Group.

Kane, Emily W., and Laura Sanchez. 1994. "Family Status and Criticism of Gender Inequality at Home and at Work." *Social Forces* 72(4): 1079–102.

Kasarda, John D. 1995. "Industrial Restructuring and the Changing Location of Jobs." In *State of the Union,* vol. 1, edited by Reynolds Farley. New York: Russell Sage Foundation.

Katz, Lawrence F., and Kevin M. Murphy. 1992. "Changes in Relative Wages, 1963–87: Supply and Demand Factors." *Quarterly Journal of Economics* 107: 35–78.

Kiecolt, K. Jill, and Mark A. Fossett. 1995. "Mate Availability and Marriage Among African Americans: Aggregate and Individual-Level Analyses." In *The Decline in Marriage Among African Americans,* edited by M. Belinda Tucker and Claudia Mitchell-Kernan. New York: Russell Sage Foundation.

Kilbourne, Barbara Stanek, and others. 1994. "Returns to Skill, Compensating Differentials, and Gender Bias: Effects of Occupational Characteristics on the Wages of White Women and Men." *American Journal of Sociology* 100(November): 689–719.

Kraft, Joan Marie, and James E. Coverdill. 1994. "Employment and the Use of Birth Control by Sexually Active Single Hispanic, Black, and White Women." *Demography* 31(4): 593–602.

Kramorow, Ellen. 1995. "The Elderly Who Live Alone in the United States: Historical Perspectives on Household Change." *Demography* 32(3): 335–52.

Krueger, A. 1991. "How Computers Have Changed Wage Structure." Unpublished paper. Princeton, N.J.: Princeton University.

Landale, Nancy S. 1994. "Migration and the Latino Family: The Union Formation Behavior of Puerto Rican Woman." *Demography* 31(1): 133–57.

Lee, Valerie E., and Kenneth A. Frank. 1990. "Students' Characteristics That Facilitate the Transfer from Two-Year to Four-Year Colleges." *Sociology of Education* 63(July): 178–93.

Lennon, Mary Clare, and Sarah Rosenfield. 1994. "Relative Fairness and the Division of Housework: The Importance of Options." *American Journal of Sociology* 100(2): 506–31.

Lerner, Gerda. 1993. *The Creation of Feminist Consciousness: From the Middle Ages to Eighteen-seventy.* New York: Oxford University Press.

Lester, Gordon. 1991. "Child Support and Alimony: 1989." *Current Population Reports,* series P60, no. 173. Washington: U.S. Bureau of the Census, U.S. Government Printing Office.

Levy, Frank. 1995. "Incomes and Income Inequality." In *State of the Union: America in the 1990s. Volume 1. Economic Trends.* Edited by Reynolds Farley. New York: Russell Sage Foundation.

Levy, Frank, and Richard J. Murnane. 1992. "U.S. Earnings Levels and Earnings Inequality: A Review of Recent Trends and Proposed Explanations." *Journal of Economic Literature* 30: 1333–81.

Lichter, Daniel T., and Janice A. Costanzo. 1987. "How Do Demographic Changes Affect Labor Force Participation of Women?" *Monthly Labor Review* 110(11): 23–25.

Lichter, Daniel T. and David J. Eggebeen. 1994. "The Effect of Parental Work Patterns on Child Poverty." *Journal of Marriage and the Family* 56: 633–45.

Lichter, Daniel T., and Nancy S. Landale. 1995. "Parental Work, Family Structure, and Poverty Among Latino Children." *Journal of Marriage and the Family* 57(May): 346–54.

Lichter, Daniel T., Felicia B. LeCleve, and Diane K. McLaughlin. 1991. "Local Marriage Markets and the Marital Behavior of Black and White Women." *American Journal of Sociology* 96(4): 843–67.

Lichter, Daniel T., and others. 1992. "Race and the Retreat from Marriage: A Shortage of Marriageable Men?" *American Sociological Review* 57(December): 781–99.

Lillard, Lee A., Michael J. Brien, and Linda J. Waite. 1995. "Pre-marital Cohabitation and Subsequent Marital Dissolution: A Matter of Self-selection?" *Demography* 32(3): 437–58.

Loomis, Laura Spencer, and Alan Booth. 1995. "Multigenerational Caregiving and Well-Being: The Myth of the Beleaguered Sandwich Generation." *Journal of Family Issues* 16(March): 131–48.

Loomis, Laura Spencer, and Nancy S. Landale. 1994. "Nonmarital Cohabitation and Childbearing Among Black and White American Women." *Journal of Marriage and the Family* 56(4): 949–62.

Luker, Kristen. 1990. "The Social Construction of Teenage Pregnancy." Paper presented at the annual meeting of the American Sociological Association, Washington, D.C. (March).

Lye, Diane L., and others. 1995. "Childhood Living Arrangements and Adult Children's Relations with Their Parents." *Demography* 32(2): 261–80.

Macunovich, Diane J., and others. 1995. "Echoes of the Baby Boom and Bust: Recent and Prospective Changes in Living Alone Among Elderly Widows in the United States." *Demography* 32(1): 17–28.

Major, Brenda. 1987. "Gender, Justice, and the Psychology of Entitlement." In *Sex and Gender*, vol. 7 of *Review of Personality and Social Psychology*, edited by Phillip Shaver and Clyde Hendrick. Thousand Oaks, Calif.: Sage Publications.

Manning, Wendy D. 1995. "Cohabitation, Marriage, and Entry into Motherhood." *Journal of Marriage and the Family* 57(February): 191–200.

Mare, Robert D. 1991. "Five Decades of Educational Assortive Mating." *American Sociological Review* 56(February): 15–32.

———. 1995. "Changes in Educational Attainment and School Enrollment." In *State of the Union*, edited by Reynolds Farley. New York: Russell Sage Foundation.

Mason, Karen Oppenheim, and Karen Kuhlthau. 1992. "The Perceived Impact of Child Care Costs on Women's Labor Supply and Fertility." *Demography* 29(4): 523–43.

Mason, Karen Oppenheim, and Yu-Hsia Lu. 1988. "Attitudes Toward Women's Familial Roles: Changes in the United States, 1977–1985." *Gender and Society* 2(1): 39–57.

Maume, David J., Jr. 1991. "Child Care Expenditures and Women's Employment Turnover." *Social Forces* 70(2): 495–508.

McLanahan, Sara, and Lynne Casper. 1995. "Growing Diversity and Inequality in the American Family." In *State of the Union*, vol. 2, edited by Reynolds Farley. New York: Russell Sage Foundation.

McLanahan, Sara, and Gary Sandefur. 1994. *Growing Up with a Single Parent: What Helps, What Hurts.* Cambridge, Mass.: Harvard University Press.

Menken, Jane. 1985. "Age and Fertility: How Late Can You Wait?" *Demography* 22(4): 469–84.

Merton, Robert K. 1968. *Social Theory and Social Structure.* New York: Free Press.

Meyer, Daniel R. 1993. "Child Support and Welfare Dynamics: Evidence from Wisconsin." *Demography* 30(1): 45–62.

Miller, Brent C., and Kristen A. Moore. 1990. "Adolescent Sexual Behavior, Pregnancy, and Parenting: Research Through the 1980s." *Journal of Marriage and the Family* 52(November): 1025–44.

Milroy, Beth Moore, and Susan Wismer. 1994. "Communities, Work, and Public/Private Sphere Models." *Gender, Place, and Culture* 1(1): 71–90.

Mincer, Jacob. 1962. "On-the-Job Training: Costs, Returns and Some Implications." *Journal of Political Economy* 70(October): S50–S79.

———. 1991. "Human Capital, Technology, and the Wage Structure: What Do Time Series Show?" NBER Working Paper 3581. Cambridge, Mass.: National Bureau of Economic Research.

Mincer, Jacob, and Haim Ofek. 1982. "Interrupted Work Careers: Depreciation and Restoration of Human Capital." *Journal of Human Resources* 17(Winter): 3–24.

Mincer, Jacob, and Solomon Polachek. 1974. "Family Investment in Human Capital: Earnings of Women." In *Marriage, Family Human Capital, and Fertility,* edited by Theodore W. Schultz. Chicago: University of Chicago Press.

Model, Suzanne. 1981. "Housework by Husbands: Determinants and Implications" *Journal of Family Issues* 2 (June): 225–237.

Modell, John, Frank F. Furstenberg Jr., and Douglas Strong. 1978. "The Timing of Marriage in the Transition to Adulthood: Continuity and Change, 1860–1975." *American Journal of Sociology* 84(supplement): S120-S150.

Moffitt, Robert. 1992. "Incentive Effects of the U.S. Welfare System: A Review." *Journal of Economic Literature* 30(March): 1–61.

Moffitt, Robert A., and Michael S. Rendall. 1995. "Cohort Trends in the Lifetime Distribution of Female Family Headship in the U.S., 1969–1985." *Demography* 32(3): 407–24.

Monk-Turner, Elizabeth. 1990. "The Occupational Achievements of Community and Four-Year College Entrants." *American Sociological Review* 55(October): 719–25.

Morgan, S. Phillip. 1991. "Late Nineteenth- and Early Twentieth-Century Childlessness." *American Journal of Sociology* 97(3): 779–807.

Morris, Lydia. 1990. *Workings of the Household: A U.S.-U.K. Comparison.* Cambridge: Polity Press.

Mosher, William D., and Gerry E. Hendershot. 1984. "Religious Affiliation and the Fertility of Married Couples." *Journal of Marriage and the Family* 46(August): 671–78.

Mosher, William D., Linda B. Williams, and David P. Johnson. 1992. "Religion and Fertility in the United States: New Patterns." *Demography* 29(2): 199–214.

Moynihan, Daniel P. 1965. *The Negro Family: The Case for National Action.* Washington: U.S. Government Printing Office.

Mueller, Charles W., Sarosh Kuruvilla, and Roderick D. Iverson. 1994. "Swedish Professionals and Gender Inequalities." *Social Forces* 73(December): 555–73.

Murphy, Kevin, and Finis Welch. 1992. "The Role of International Trade in Wage Differentials." In *Workers and Their Wages*, edited by M. Kosters. Washington: AEI Press.

Murray, Charles. 1984. *Losing Ground: American Social Policy, 1950–1980.* New York: Basic Books.

Myers, Dowell. 1985. "Wives' Earnings and Rising Costs of Homeownership." *Social Science Quarterly* 66: 319–29.

Myers, Dowell, and Jennifer R. Wolch. 1995. "The Polarization of Housing Status." In *State of the Union*, vol. 1, edited by Reynolds Farley. New York: Russell Sage Foundation.

National Center for Education Statistics. 1994. *Digest of Education Statistics.* Washington: U.S. Government Printing Office.

National Center for Health Statistics. 1993. "Advance Report of Natality Statistics, 1990." *Monthly Vital Statistics Report*, vol. 41(9)(Supplement). Hyattsville, Md.: Public Health Service.

————. Selected Years. *Vital Statistics of the United States*. Washington: U.S. Government Printing Office.

Nock, Steven L. 1995. "A Comparison of Marriages and Cohabiting Relationships." *Journal of Family Issues* 16(1): 53–76.

O'Connell, Martin. 1991. "Late Expectations: Childbearing Patterns of American Women for the 1990s." *Current Population Reports*, series P23, no. 176. Washington: U.S. Bureau of the Census, U.S. Government Printing Office.

O'Neill, June, and Solomon Polachek. 1993. "Why the Gender Gap in Wages Narrowed in the 1980s." *Journal of Labor Economics* 11(part 1): 205–28.

Oppenheimer, Valerie Kincade. 1970. *The Female Labor Force in the United States*. Westport, Conn.: Greenwood Press.

————. 1988. "A Theory of Marriage Timing." *American Journal of Sociology* 94: 563–91.

————. 1994. "Women's Rising Employment and the Future of the Family in Industrial Societies." *Population and Development Review* 20(June): 293–342.

Organisation for Economic Cooperation and Development. 1992. *OECD in Figures: Statistics on the Member Countries*. Washington: OECD.

Pampel, Fred C. 1993. "Relative Cohort Size and Fertility: The Socio-Political Context of the Easterlin Effect." *American Sociological Review* 58(August): 496–514.

Pavalko, Eliza K., and Glen H. Elder. 1990. "World War II and Divorce: A Life-Course Perspective." *American Journal of Sociology* 95(5): 1213–34.

Peek, Charles W., George D. Lowe, and L. Susan Williams. 1991. "Gender and God's Word: Another Look at Religious Fundamentalism and Sexism." *Social Forces* 69(June): 1205–21.

Persell, Caroline Hodges, Sophia Catsambis, and Peter W. Cookson Jr. 1992. "Differential Asset Conversion: Class and Gendered Pathways to Selective Colleges." *Sociology of Education* 65(July): 208–25.

Peters, H. Elizabeth, and others. 1993. "Enforcing Divorce Settlements: Evidence from Child Support Compliance and Award Modifications." *Demography* 30(4): 719–35.

Peterson, Linda S. 1995. "Contraceptive Use in the United States: 1982–90." *Advance Data from Vital and Health Statistics*, series 16, no. 260. Hyattsville, Md.: National Center for Health Statistics.

Petersen, T., and L. Morgan. 1995. "Separate and Unequal: Occupation-Establishment Segregation and the Gender Wage Gap." *American Journal of Sociology* 101(2): 329–65.

Pleck, Joseph. 1985. *Working Wives/Working Husbands*. Beverly Hills, Calif.: Sage.

Polachek, Solomon W. 1981. "Occupational Self-Selection: A Human Capital Approach to Sex Differences in Occupational Structure." *Review of Economics and Statistics* 63(February): 60–69.

Presser, Harriet B. 1989. "Can We Make Time for Children? The Economy, Work Schedules, and Child Care." *Demography* 26(4): 523–43.

———. 1994. "Employment Schedules Among Dual-Earner Spouses and the Division of Household Labor by Gender." *American Sociological Review* 59(June): 348–64.

Presser, Harriet B., and Wendy Baldwin. 1980. "Child Care as a Constraint on Employment: Prevalence, Correlates, and Bearing on the Work and Fertility Nexus." *American Journal of Sociology* 85: 1202–13.

Qian, Zhenchao, and Samuel H. Preston. 1993. "Changes in American Marriage, 1972 to 1987: Availability and Forces of Attraction by Age and Education." *American Sociological Review* 58(August): 482–95.

Rawlings, Steve W., and Arlene F. Saluter. 1995. "Household and Family Characteristics: March 1994." *Current Population Reports*, series P20, no. 483. Washington: U.S. Bureau of the Census, U.S. Government Printing Office.

Reskin, Barbara F., ed. 1984. *Sex Segregation in the Work Place: Trends, Explanations, Remedies.* Washington: National Academy Press.

———. 1988. "Bringing the Men Back In: Sex Differentiation and the Devaluation of Women's Work." *Gender and Society* 2(March): 58–81.

———. 1990. *Job Queues, Gender Queues: Explaining Women's Inroads into Male Occupations.* Philadelphia: Temple University Press.

Rexroat, Cynthia. 1992. "Changes in the Employment Continuity of Succeeding Cohorts of Young Women." *Work and Occupations* 19: 18–34.

Rindfuss, Ronald R., S. Phillip Morgan, and Gray Swicegood. 1988. *First Births in America: Changing Patterns of Parenthood.* Berkeley and Los Angeles: University of California Press.

Robinson, James Gregory. 1988. "A Cohort Analysis of Trends in the Labor Force Participation of Men and Women in the United States: 1890 to 1985." Doctoral dissertation. Philadelphia: University of Pennsylvania.

Robinson, John P. 1988. "Who's Doing the Housework?" *American Demographics* 10: 24–28.

Romano, Angela. 1995. "Changing Gender Ideology: 1977–1993." Unpublished paper. College Park: University of Maryland.

Roos, Patricia A., and Barbara F. Reskin. 1992. "Occupational Desegregation in the 1970s: Integration and Economic Equity?" *Sociological Perspectives* 35: 69–91.

Ruggles, Steven. 1994. "The Origins of African-American Family Structure." *American Sociological Review* 59(February): 136–51.

Rutherford, Brent M., and Gerda Wekerle. 1988. "Captive Rider, Captive Labor: Spatial Constraints and Women's Employment." *Urban Geography* 9(March-April): 116–37.

Ryscavage, Paul, and Peter Henle. 1990. "Earnings Inequality in the 1980s." *Monthly Labor Review* 113(12): 3–16.

Sampson, Robert J. 1995. "Unemployment and Imbalanced Sex Ratios: Race-specific Consequences for Family Structure and Crime." In *The Decline in Marriage Among African Americans*, edited by M. Belinda Tucker and Claudia Mitchell-Kernan. New York: Russell Sage Foundation.

Sanchez, Laura. 1994. "Gender, Labor Allocations, and the Psychology of Entitlement Within the Home." *Social Forces* 73(2): 533–53.

Sawhill, Isabel V. 1988. "Poverty in the U.S.: Why Is It So Persistent?" *Journal of Economic Literature* 26(September): 1073–119.

Schoen, Robert. 1995. "The Widening Gap Between Black and White Marriage Rates: Context and Implications." In *The Decline in Marriage Among African Americans*, edited by M. Belinda Tucker and Claudia Mitchell-Kernan. New York: Russell Sage Foundation.

Schor, Juliet B. 1992. *The Overworked American: The Unexpected Decline of Leisure*. New York: Basic Books.

Schultz, Theodore W. 1960. "Investment in Human Capital." *American Economic Review* 51(March): 1–17.

Scoon-Rogers, Lydia, and Gordon H. Lester. 1995. "Child Support for Custodial Mothers and Fathers: 1991." *Current Population Reports*, series P60, no. 187. Washington: U.S. Bureau of the Census, U.S. Government Printing Office.

Sewell, William H., Robert M. Hauser, and Wendy C. Wolf. 1980. "Sex, Schooling, and Occupational Status." *American Journal of Sociology* 86(November): 551–83.

Shelton, Beth Anne. 1992. *Women, Men, and Time: Gender Differences in Paid Work, Housework, and Leisure*. Westport, Conn: Greenwood Press.

Silver, Hilary, and Frances Goldscheider. 1994. "Flexible Work and Housework: Work and Family Constraints on Women's Domestic Labor." *Social Forces* 72(4): 1103–119.

Sloane, Douglas M. and Che-Fu Lee. 1983. "Sex of Previous Children and Intentions for Further Births in the United States, 1965–1976." *Demography* 20(3): 353–67.

Smith, Herbert L., and Brian Powell. 1990. "Great Expectations: Variations in Income Expectations Among College Seniors." *Sociology of Education* 63(July): 194–207.

Smith, James P., and Michael Ward. 1989. "Women in the Labor Market and the Family." *Journal of Economic Perspectives* 3(Winter): 9–23.

Smith, James P., and Finis Welch. 1989. "Black Economic Progress After Myrdal." *Journal of Economic Literature* 27(2): 419–564.

Smock, Pamela J. 1993. "The Economic Costs of Marital Disruption for Young Women over the Past Two Decades." *Demography* 30(3): 353–71.

———. 1994. "Gender and the Short-Run Economic Consequences of Marital Disruption." *Social Forces* 73(1): 243–62.

Snipp, C. Matthew. 1989. *American Indians: The First of this Land.* New York: Russell Sage Foundation.

Sorenson, Elaine. 1989. "The Wage Effects of Occupational Sex Composition: A Review and New Findings." In *Comparable Worth: Analyses and Evidence,* edited by M. Anne Hill and Mark Killingsworth. Ithaca, N.Y.: ILR Press.

Sorrentino, Constance. 1990. "The Changing Family in International Perspective." *Monthly Labor Review* 113(3): 41–58.

South, Scott J., and Kim M. Lloyd. 1995. "Spousal Alternatives and Marital Dissolution." *American Sociological Review* 60(February): 21–35.

South, Scott J., and Glenna Spitze. 1994. "Housework in Marital and Nonmarital Households." *American Sociological Review* 59(June): 327–47.

Spain, Daphne. 1992. *Gendered Spaces.* Chapel Hill, N.C.: University of North Carolina Press.

Spitze, Glenna. 1988. "Women's Employment and Family Relations: A Review." *Journal of Marriage and the Family* 50(August): 595–618.

Spitze, Glenna, and John Logan. 1990. "More Evidence on Women (and Men) in the Middle." *Research on Aging* 12: 182–98.

Spitze, Glenna, and Scott J. South. 1985. "Women's Employment, Time Expenditure, and Divorce." *Journal of Family Issues* 6(September): 307–29.

Steelman, Lal Carr, and Brian Powell. 1991. "Sponsoring the Next Generation: Parental Willingness to Pay for Higher Education." *American Journal of Sociology* 96(6): 1505–29.

Stolzenberg, Ross, and Linda Waite. 1977. "Age, Fertility Expectations, and Plans for Employment." *American Sociological Review* 42(October): 769–83.

Sweet, James A. 1990. "Changes in the Life-cycle Composition of the United States Population and the Demand for Housing." In *Housing Demography,* edited by Dowell Myers. Madison, Wis.: University of Wisconsin Press.

Sweet, James A., and Larry Bumpass. 1987. *American Families and Households.* New York: Russell Sage Foundation.

Taylor, R. J., and others. 1991. "Developments in Research on Black Families: A Decade Review." *Journal of Marriage and the Family* 52: 993–1014.

Teachman, Jay D., and Karen Polonko. 1990. "Cohabitation and Marital Stability in the United States." *Social Forces* 69(1): 207–20.

Thompson, Linda. 1991. "Family Work: Women's Sense of Fairness." *Journal of Family Issues* 12: 181–95.

Thornton, Arland. 1991. "Influences of the Marital History of Parents on the Marital and Cohabitational Experiences of Children." *American Journal of Sociology* 96(4): 868–94.

Tienda, Marta, Katharine M. Donato, and Hector Cordero-Guzman. 1992. "Schooling, Color, and the Labor Force Activity of Women." *Social Forces* 71(2): 365–395.

Tomaskovic-Devey, Donald. 1993. "The Gender and Race Composition of Jobs and the Male, Female, White/Black Pay Gaps." *Social Forces* 72: 999–1029.

———. 1995. "Sex Composition and Gendered Earnings Inequality: A Comparison of Job and Occupational Models." In *Gender Inequality at Work*, edited by Jerry A. Jacobs. Thousand Oaks, Calif.: Sage Publications.

Treas, Judith. 1993. "Money in the Bank: Transaction Costs and the Economic Organization of Marriage." *American Sociological Review* 58(October): 723–34.

Treas, Judith, and Ramon Torrecilha. 1995. "The Older Population." In *State of the Union,* vol. 2, edited by Reynolds Farley. New York: Russell Sage Foundation.

Treiman, Donald J., and Heidi I. Hartmann. 1981. *Women, Work, and Wages.* Washington: National Academy Press.

Treiman, Donald J., and Kermit Terrell. 1975. "Sex and the Process of Status Attainment." *American Sociological Review* 40(April): 174–200.

Tucker, M. Belinda, and Claudia Mitchell-Kernan, eds. 1995. *The Decline in Marriage Among African Americans.* New York: Russell Sage Foundation.

U.S. Bureau of the Census. 1953. *Census of Population: 1950.* Vol. 2, part 1. Washington: U.S. Government Printing Office.

———. 1963. *Census of Population: 1960.* Vol. 1, part 1. Washington: U.S. Government Printing Office.

———. 1973. *Census of Population: 1970.* Vol. 1, part 1. Washington: U.S. Government Printing Office.

———. 1975. *Historical Statistics of the United States: Colonial Times to 1970.* Bicentennial edition. Washington: U.S. Government Printing Office.

———. 1981. "Marital Status and Living Arrangements: 1980." *Current Population Reports,* series P20, no. 365. Washington: U.S. Government Printing Office.

————. 1983a. *Census of the Population: 1980.* Vol. 1, chapter D. Washington: U.S. Government Printing Office.

————. 1983b. "Money Income of Households, Families, and Persons in the United States: 1982." *Current Population Reports,* series P60, no. 184. Washington: U.S. Government Printing Office.

————. 1991. "Fertility of American Women: June 1990." *Current Population Reports,* series P20, no. 454. Washington: U.S. Government Printing Office.

————. 1992a. *Census of the Population: 1990.* U.S. summary. Washington: U.S. Government Printing Office.

————. 1992b. "Households, Families, and Children: A 30-Year Perspective." *Current Population Reports,* series P23, no. 181. Washington: U.S. Government Printing Office.

————. 1992c. "Marital Status and Living Arrangements: March 1992." *Current Population Reports,* series P20, no. 468. Washington: U.S. Government Printing Office.

————. 1992d. "School Enrollment–Social and Economic Characteristics of Students: October 1990." *Current Population Reports,* series P20, no. 460. Washington: U.S. Government Printing Office.

————. 1993a. "Money Income of Households, Families, and Persons in the United States: 1992." *Current Population Reports,* series P60, no. 184. Washington: U.S. Government Printing Office.

————. 1993b. "Poverty in the United States: 1992." *Current Population Reports,* series P60, no. 185. Washington: U.S. Government Printing Office.

————. 1993c. "Household and Family Characteristics: March 1992." *Current Population Survey,* series P20, no. 467. Washington: U.S. Government Printing Office.

————. 1994a. "Marital Status and Living Arrangements: March 1993." *Current Population Reports,* series P20, no. 478. Washington: U.S. Government Printing Office.

————. 1994b. "School Enrollment–Social and Economic Characteristics of Students: October 1993." *Current Population Reports,* series P20, no. 479. Washington: U.S. Government Printing Office.

————. 1994c. "Household and Family Characteristics: March 1993." *Current Population Survey,* series P20, no. 477. Washington: U.S. Government Printing Office.

U.S. Department of Labor, Bureau of Labor Statistics. 1978. *Handbook of Labor Statistics.* Washington: U.S. Government Printing Office.

————. 1979. "Women in the Labor Force: Some New Data Series." Report 575. Washington: U.S. Government Printing Office.

————. 1984. *Employment and Earnings* (January issue). Washington: U.S. Government Printing Office.

————. 1988. *Labor Force Statistics Derived from the Current Population Survey, 1948–87.* Bulletin 2307. Washington: U.S. Government Printing Office.

————. 1989. *Handbook of Labor Statistics.* Washington: U.S. Government Printing Office.

————. 1991. *Employment and Earnings* (January issue). Washington: U.S. Government Printing Office.

————. 1993. "Trends in Labor Force Participation of Major Population Groups, 1965–92." Draft chartbook. Washington: U.S. Department of Labor.

————. 1994a. "Comparative Labor Force Statistics: Ten Countries, 1959–1993." Unpublished tabulations. Washington: U.S. Department of Labor.

————. 1994b. *Employment and Earnings* (January issue). Washington: U.S. Government Printing Office.

————. 1994c. "Who's Minding the Kids? Child Care Arrangements: Fall 1991." *Current Population Reports,* series P70, no. 36. Washington: U.S. Government Printing Office.

————. 1995. *Employment and Earnings* (January issue). Washington: U.S. Government Printing Office.

U.S. Department of Labor, Women's Bureau. 1994. "Working Women Count! A Report to the Nation." Washington: U.S. Government Printing Office.

United Nations. 1982. *Demographic Indicators of Countries: Estimates and Projections as Assessed in 1980.* New York: United Nations.

————. 1994. *Statistical Yearbook 1992.* New York: United Nations.

————. 1995. *The World's Women 1995: Trends and Statistics.* New York: United Nations.

Vanek, Joann. 1974. "Time Spent in Housework." *Scientific American* 231: 116–20.

Ventura, S. J. 1995. "Births to Unmarried Mothers: United States, 1980–1992" *Vital Health Staistics,* vol. 21(53). Hyattsville, Md.: National Center for Health Statistics.

Ventura, S. J., and others. 1994. "Advance Report of Final Natality Statistics, 1992." *Monthly Vital Statistics Report,* vol. 43(5). Hyattsville, Md.: National Center for Health Statistics.

Ventura, S. J., and others. 1995a. "Advance Report of Final Natality Statistics, 1993." *Monthly Vital Statistics Report,* vol. 44(3)(supplement). Hyattsville, Md.: National Center for Health Statistics.

Ventura, S. J., and others. 1995b. "Trends in Pregnancies and Pregnancy Rates: Estimates for the United States, 1980–92." *Monthly Vital Statistics*

Report, vol. 43(11(supplement). Hyattsville, Md.: National Center for Health Statistics.

Villeneuve, Paul, and Damaris Rose. 1988. "Gender and the Separation of Employment from Home in Metropolitan Montreal, 1971–1981." *Urban Geography* 9(March-April): 155–79.

Waite, Linda, and Frances K. Goldscheider. 1992. "Work in the Home: The Productive Context of Family Relationships." In *The Changing American Family,* edited by Scott J. South and Stewart E. Tolnay. Boulder, Colo.: Westview Press.

Waite, Linda J., and Lee A. Lillard. 1991. "Children and Marital Disruption." *American Journal of Sociology* 96(4): 930–53.

Waite, Linda, and Ross Stolzenberg. 1976. "Intended Childbearing and Labor Force Participation of Young Women: Insights from Nonrecursive Models." *American Sociological Review* 41(April): 235–52.

Waldauer, Charles. 1984. "The Non-Comparability of the 'Comparable Worth' Doctrine: An Inappropriate Standard for Determining Sex Discrimination in Pay." *Population Research and Policy Review* 3(June): 141–66.

Waller, Willard. 1951 [1938]. *The Family: A Dynamic Interpretation,* revised by Reuben Hill. New York: Henry Holt.

Ward, Michael, and William Butz. 1980. "Completed Fertility and its Timing." *Journal of Political Economy* 88(October): 917–40.

Watson, Joellen. 1977. "Higher Education for Women in the United States: A Historical Perspective." *Educational Studies* 8(Summer): 133–44.

Weinick, Robin. 1995. "Sharing a Home: The Experiences of American Women and Their Parents over the Twentieth Century." *Demography* 32(3): 281–97.

Wellington, Alison. 1993. "Changes in the Male/Female Wage Gap, 1976–85." *Journal of Human Resources* 28: 383–411.

Westoff, Charles F., and Norman B. Ryder. 1977. "The Predictive Validity of Reproductive Intentions." *Demography* 14(4): 431–54.

Wetzel, James. 1995. "Labor Force, Unemployment, and Earnings." In *State of the Union,* vol. 1, edited by Reynolds Farley. New York: Russell Sage Foundation.

Wheelock, Jane. 1990. *Husbands at Home: The Domestic Economy in a Postindustrial Society.* London: Routledge.

Willie, Charles V. 1985. *Black and White Families: A Study in Complementarity.* Bayside, N.Y.: General Hall.

Wilson, Kenneth L., and Janet P. Boldizar. 1990. "Gender Segregation in Higher Education: Effects of Aspirations, Mathematics Achievement, and Income." *Sociology of Education* 63(January): 62–74.

Wilson, William J. 1987. *The Truly Disadvantaged: The Inner City, the Underclass, and Public Policy.* Chicago: University of Chicago Press.

Wojtkiewicz, Roger A., Sara S. McLanahan, and Irwin Garfinkel. 1990. "The Growth of Families Headed by Women: 1950–1980." *Demography* 27(1): 19–30.

Wright, Rosemary, and Jerry A. Jacobs. 1994. "Male Flight from Computer Work: A New Look at Occupational Resegregation and Ghettoization." *American Sociological Review* 59(June): 511–36.

Wu, Zheng. 1995. "The Stability of Cohabitation Relationships: The Role of Children." *Journal of Marriage and the Family* 57(February): 231–36.

Wu, Zheng, and T. R. Balakrishnan. 1994. "Cohabitation After Marital Disruption in Canada." *Journal of Marriage and the Family* 56(3): 723–34.

Yamaguchi, Kazuo, and Linda R. Ferguson. 1995. "The Stopping and Spacing of Childbirths and Their Birth-History Predictors: Rational Choice Theory and Event-History Analysis." *American Sociological Review* 60(April): 272–98.

Yoon, Young-Hee, and Linda Waite. 1994. "Converging Employment Patterns of Black, White, and Hispanic Women: Return to Work after First Birth." *Journal of Marriage and the Family* 56(February): 209–17.

Zhan, Li. 1992. "Family Demographic Change and Labor Force Participation of Black and White Women, 1970–1990." Unpublished paper. State Park, Penn.: Population Research Center, Pennsylvania State University.

Index